CONTENTS

CW00469239

ACKNOWLEDGEMENTS

Many people and organisations have supported us in the production of this publication, and to all of you we offer our grateful thanks.

However, special thanks have to be extended to the following for their invaluable contributions:

The **County Archivist and staff** at the **Northamptonshire Record Office**, for unearthing some fascinating Rance material for us.

Andrea and the team at **Kettering Library**, for tolerating our weekly visits and accomodating our every request in an ever cheery manner.

Sally and the girls at **Rushden Library**, for creating such a happy research environment.

Chantelle, Max & Maddie Dace, for always putting a smile on Daddy's face.

Angela Vernals, for marking our homework.

Maggie Bence, our "mistress of all trades".

Everyone who has purchased **"A Wall Unto Us"**.

And finally .....

We would like to dedicate this book
to the memory of our dear friend and group founder member,

Tony Deviny

1932 – 2008

Steve Bence & Andrew Dace

INTRODUCTION

Whilst researching material for *"A Wall Unto Us – The Raunds Roll of Honour"*, we spent many hours reading the local newspapers, publications and other records held in the nearby archives.

During this search we not only found articles on the men from the town who were killed during the Great War but also many stories of those who survived the war and of domestic events taking place in the town and beyond, sometimes because of, but often despite, the presence of the conflict.

It soon became clear to us that a collation of these accounts could possibly make a complementary publication to our *"Raunds Roll of Honour"*.

From that idea this book was born, the first of two planned volumes that will cover the period from January 1914 to October 1921 (when the town's War Memorial was unveiled).

With a few exceptions, all of the narrative is taken from articles appearing in the Kettering Leader, Northamptonshire Evening Telegraph or Rushden Echo, which are stored on microfilm in the local libraries, or from the Church of England School records, St Mary's* Church Parish Magazines and Wesleyan Methodist Church records held in the Northamptonshire Record Office. And in order to maintain the atmosphere of the period, the words and phrases utilised are as they were written by those journalists and scribes nearly one hundred years ago.

We have also tried to only use photographs that have not appeared, to the best of our knowledge, in any previous publication, so hopefully there are some surprises in store for you. The source of the photographs is individually acknowledged below each picture.

Wherever the name of one of the town's Great War victims is mentioned, his name appears in **bold type**, followed by his corresponding page number from *"A Wall Unto Us"* in brackets **(x)**. Significant events of the Great War appear in ***bold italics***.

The currency quoted throughout is good old pounds, shillings and pence (£sd). For the uninitiated, there were twelve pence (d) in a shilling (s) and twenty shillings in a pound (£). The occasionally used guinea comprised of twenty-one shillings.

And where court cases are reported, the identities of all parties involved have generally been kept anonymous in respect for the feelings of any surviving relatives.

Raunds in 1914

At the beginning of 1914, the town had a population of just under 4,000. In recent decades it had grown to become of considerable importance in the manufacture of boots and shoes, chiefly for the Government, specialising in hand-sewn work, and the industry now provided employment for the majority of its residents of working age. However, agriculture still also sustained a significant workforce.

The town's spiritual leaders were the Rev. Cyril Clowes Aldred, Vicar of St Mary's*; the Rev. Joseph Burrows, Superintendent Minister of the Raunds Wesleyan Methodist Circuit; and Pastor S Gray, guiding the Baptists.

And its civic officers, Urban District Council Chairman: Jesse Shelmerdine; Treasurer: Charles Modlen; Clerk & Collector: William Fellows Corby; Medical Officer of Health: Dr William Mackenzie; Inspector of Nuisances: Thomas Yorke; Parish Clerk: Henry Stubbs; Postmaster: George Walker; Station Master: William H Rodway; Police Sergeant: Henry Ellingham.

Commercially, the principle boot and shoe manufacturers were: Adams Brothers, Park Road & Spencer Street; R Coggins and Sons Ltd, Marshall's Road; John Horrell & Son, Wellington Road; Walter Lawrence, High Street; Neal & Gates, Park Road; C E Nichols, Midland Road; Owen Smith & Company, Grove Street; St. Crispin's Productive Society Ltd, Sackville Street; Tebbutt & Hall Bros, Clare Street; Wellington Boot & Shoe Company Ltd, Wellington Road.

Whilst craftsmen and tradesmen included thirteen butchers, eight bakers, seven grocers, five tailors, five blacksmiths, four hairdressers, three confectioners, three motor & cycle agents, three insurance agents, two fruiterers, two coal merchants, two masons, two fishmongers, two newsagents, a chemist, a milliner, an estate agent, an undertaker, a wheelwright, a printer & stationer, a saddler & stationer, a photographer & picture framer, and a "commission agent"!

And quaintly, the curfew bell was still rung at 8pm daily from Michaelmas (29 September) to Lady Day (25 March), except on Sundays.

*As explained in the superb 1988 book "Raunds, Picturing the Past", by David Hall, Ruth Harding and Cyril Putt, the church at Raunds is actually dedicated to St. Peter. However, during the late Victorian period through to the time of the Great War, the commonly used name was that of St. Mary's, the early 16th-century patronal saint.

We do hope that you enjoy your amble through this first volume of Rance's "Great War Diary".

Steve Bence & Andrew Dace

September 2008

PROLOGUE

Like the rest of the country, the residents of Raunds enjoyed the **Christmas 1913** festivities blissfully unaware that it would be 5 long years before such celebrations would again be held in peacetime.

Over the holiday period, diverse pursuits and entertainments to suit all tastes were available to the townsfolk.

On **Boxing Day**, the Wesleyan Church held their "Annual Sale of Work" in a "nicely decorated schoolroom", the proceedings being presided over by the Rev Joseph Burrows. Mrs George Bass performed the opening ceremony, receiving a vote of thanks from Mr John Adams CC, seconded by Mr W F Corby. She was then presented with a bouquet of white flowers by Miss Louie Broker. Tea was provided, supervised by Miss E Pulpher. Stalls included those from the congregation, young women and girls, in addition to refreshments and competitions.

Mr Charles Cannell from Wellingborough gave a "sleight of hand" performance and two half-hour concerts were held, artistes included Messrs **H Bugby (29), A Burrows (30), W Groom (56),** J W Hall, O D Hall, Miss Edith Adams, Miss Grace Lawrence and Miss Winnie Pentelow.

In all, nearly £80 was raised towards circuit funds.

For the more outdoor types, Boxing Day also offered several football matches. In the Northants League, Raunds Town, sitting 11th in the table, drew 1-1 with the league leaders Bedford Town. Raunds Athletic beat Wellingborough Corinthians 4-1 in the Denford Cup, while in friendly fixtures, Raunds Albion crushed Irthlingborough Wesleyans 7-1 and although Raunds Rovers lost 1-2 to Chelveston Swifts in the morning, they immediately gained their revenge with a 1-0 win in the return afternoon fixture.

On the afternoon of Sunday, **28 December**, a musical service was held in the Temperance Hall with Miss E Pulpher presiding. Elsewhere, at a meeting of "The Brotherhood" in the Wesleyan Church and presided over by Mr James Coles, Pastor S Gray, of the Baptist Chapel, spoke on "The value of hindsight", with instrumental interludes being provided by Messrs **H Bugby (29)** and **W Groom (56).**

The Primitive Methodist Church held an "At Home" on Monday, **29 December**. Tea was followed by "games and amusements". Later, songs and other musical items were performed by Misses Mabel Lawrence, Winnie Pentelow, A Vorley and Gertie Reynolds, Messrs Walter & Fred Harris and Master Willis Rands. Proceeds for chapel funds amounted to £2-12s-0d.

On that same evening a "Long Night Dance" was held in the National Schools in aid of the school's building fund, refreshments were provided and songs were sung by Miss Tomlin.

Tuesday, **30 December** saw the annual tea and social arranged by members and teachers of the Vicarage & Vestry Classes. About 130 sat down to an "excellent spread" and this was followed by a dance, interspersed with songs from the Rev C N Daybell, Mr H Bamford and Mr W Gibbs.

At nearby Thrapston's weekly wholesale market, butter was selling at 1s-6d per pound, eggs at 2s-3d per score, beef at 8s-6d to 9s-0d per stone, mutton at 6s-8d to 7s-0d per stone and pork at 8s-9d to 9s-0d per stone.

Finally, on **New Year's Eve**, the Raunds Primrose League arranged their "Annual Fancy Dress Ball" where the prize winners were: 1st, Mrs W H Spicer, "Egyptian Enchantress", 2nd, Mrs A Camozzi, "18th Century" and 3rd, Mrs A Bamford, "Squaw".

* * * * * * * * * * * * * * * * * * * *

* * * * * * * * * * * * * * * * * * * *

Chapter 1 – January to March 1914

Ringing in the new and Strangward's misdemeanor.

JANUARY – The New Year was "rung in" at the parish church by a team of bell ringers that included Mr Henry Stubbs, sexton of the church, who was taking part in his 50th consecutive annual campanological welcome.

The freezing weather on **New Year's Day** meant that ice skating was possible in the water meadows down by the river and Mr F W Dix, the town's international ice-skating champion, was seen on the ice near Ringstead Station "busily getting fit for the big events that will come along if the frosts last".

The Midland Railway timetable of January 1914, printed in the Rushden Echo, showed that four trains in each direction stopped on most weekdays at Raunds station with additional trains on Mondays and Tuesdays.

In a statement by the town's medical officer, Dr Mackenzie, he advised that a total of 23 people over the age of 70 years had died in Raunds during 1913.

The first Parish Magazine of the year showed that the Vicar was aided by his Curate, the Rev C N Daybell, with Messrs A Camozzi and J Shelmerdine, the churchwardens. The Young Men's Class met on Sundays in the church, the Young Women's Class on Sundays in the Institute and the Sunday School in the schoolrooms, all at 1.30pm.

In his notes, the Vicar wished that "this year be to you all happy and prosperous" (he couldn't have known how it would end!), he then went on to say "Goodbye" to Mr Shelmerdine, who was "retiring after 41 years faithful service as headmaster of the C of E School" and "Welcome" to Mr and Mrs Potter from Earls Barton, the former being the new headmaster.

A feature titled "Raunds Folk Across The Sea" remembered old boys and girls of the church who had left to seek their fortunes abroad, these included **Arthur Burton (31)** and **Herbert Robinson (101)**, both now resident in Victoria, Australia but destined to return to Europe and become names on the Menin Gate in Ypres.

Folk looking for live entertainment only had to travel the 4 miles to Rushden where, at the Palace Theatre, from **5 to 7 January** and for as little as 2d, they could enjoy Henry Herne & Co in the celebrated dramatic episode "The Colleen Bawn", with the stage converted into a lake of real water and ably supported by "Zarinella", burlesque juggling comedian and Renee Grahame, the beau-ideal boy.

And from **8 to 10 January**: "The Crooks", in a novelty comedy creation entitled "Enter-Prizing Burglars", Nellie Hayden, dainty comedienne, speciality & skipping rope dancer and "Zasma", gentleman society gymnast, in a magnificent gymnastic scena entitled "Pastimes on the Lawn".

Meanwhile, their rivals at the Royal Variety Theatre offered: Charles Mildare, a great novelty, "The man with the throat of a bird" in a novel scena entitled "The Missing Bird", assisted by Miss Marie Roze, dancer, Miss Ethel Entwistle, "The Singing Nightingale" and Cox & Fynbo, the great tumbling eccentrics. However, such delicacies were for the slightly more affluent as the minimum seat charge was 3d!

It was also reported that during the previous week the wife of the Raunds postmaster, Mrs Walker, had died at the age of 62 after a "long and painful illness".

The hard frost on Wednesday, **7 January** prevented the Fitzwilliam Hunt, who had met at Raunds Grange, from having a run. It was also during this abortive meet that an accident occurred when Mr H Turnhill, of Grove Street, was thrown from his horse when the animal shied. He was picked up unconscious with nasty scalp wounds but was later said to be progressing favourably.

There was excitement in Marshall's Road when a fire broke out at the Woodbine Working Men's Club completely destroying the bar. The outbreak was discovered by the stewardess when she went down to clean up and raised the alarm, the fire brigade being summoned at once by rocket! Happily, their "promptitude in taking the call" and there being a good pressure of water resulted in the fire being speedily extinguished.

On Thursday, **8 January**, the managers of the Church of England School announced the appointment of Miss Florence Kirk as a probationary teacher. They also questioned the hours of duty of the caretaker and asked for a job specification to be drawn up to settle certain issues under debate.

Saturday, **10 January** saw Raunds Town entertain Rushden Fosse in the Northants League and emerge 1-0 winners with Maddocks scoring the only goal. This win lifted the team up to 10th in the table.

The meeting of the Urban Council on Monday, **12 January** heard the reading of a letter from the local branch of the Union of Shoe Operatives supporting the nomination of Messrs George Underwood and Ralph Lawrence for the management board of the Council School.

A motion "of a rather peculiar nature" was also brought before the council. Mr John Adams called attention to the fact that a different bell was tolled for funerals according to whether the internment was in the churchyard or chapel burial ground. He stated that non-conformists felt very keenly that any such distinction should be made, and he moved a resolution that the Vicar be asked to discontinue the practice forthwith. Several members present stated that they were not aware that any such custom was in existence. The proposition was carried, and it was thought that the Vicar, now that his attention had been drawn to the matter, would doubtless accede to the wishes of the council.

Competing at the International Skating Championships in Davos, Switzerland on Saturday, **17 January**, the town's F W Dix, British Champion, finished 4th in the 5,000 metre race which was won by Mathieson of Norway in a record time. FWD then finished 7th in the 500 metre event.

On that same afternoon, Raunds Town lost 0-1 at Wellingborough Redwell in the Northants League.

At Sunday, **18 January**'s Brotherhood meeting, Pastor S Gray presided as the Rev J Burrows spoke on "The Town Crier". Solos "How willing my paternal love" and "At eventide" were sung by Mr W Gibbs.

"Wireless Telegraphy" arrived in the town on Monday, **19 January** when Mr E T Cottingham of Thrapston gave a lecture on the subject at the Wesley Guild meeting. During the talk the speaker rigged up a wireless apparatus and amazed his audience when messages being sent out from the Eiffel Tower in Paris were picked up.

The Temperance Band arranged a whist drive for Friday, **23 January** in which the winners were: 1st, Mr L Coles, 2nd, Mr B Maddock, 3rd, Mr J Coles.

The following day on the football field saw a local derby in the Northants Senior Cup where Rushden Fosse "struggled" to defeat their old rivals Raunds Town 2-0 in a 2nd round replay.

At the afternoon meeting of the Brotherhood on Sunday, **25 January**, presided over by Mr James Jaques of Rushden, the Rev C J Keeler of Rushden spoke ably on "A Safe Bank & High Interest", Mrs Jaques read the lesson and Miss Edwards of Earls Barton sang "Babylon" and "The Song of Thanksgiving".

The annual tea & concert of the Hospital Committee was held in the Church Rooms where the Raunds Wesleyan Prize Choir performed under the conductorship of Mr W Hall. Songs and duets were given by Misses Louie Smith, Grace Lawrence & May Hazeldine and Messrs T Hazeldine, O D & W Hall.

A motion on the agenda at the annual meeting of the Raunds Distributive Co-Operative Society asked members to sanction the investment of £10 in the "Daily Citizen". The proposal, which gave rise to considerable discussion and a very sharp division of opinion, was eventually defeated by 101 votes to 7!

A fine of 10s-0d was inflicted on a Raunds shoehand at the Thrapston Petty Sessions on Tuesday, **27 January**, having been found guilty of "using obscene language on the public highway to the annoyance of the passengers."

The final day of January saw Raunds Town lose by the only goal to Northants League leaders Wolverton.

FEBRUARY – In his notes in the Parish Magazine, the Vicar announced that it would soon be "Goodbye" to the Curate, Mr Daybell, who would be leaving at Easter for a "larger sphere of work in Leicester".

He then went on to ask for contributions to cover the cost of altering the chandelier in the nave to facilitate cleaning and also to replace the old wooden gates in the churchyard.

Among the baptisms recorded in January was that of Ida Robins, the youngest daughter of **Cornelius Robins (100).**

On Monday, **2 February**, the following were appointed as managers of the new Council Schools: Messrs J Gant, W F Corby, John Adams, J Shelmerdine, J Hodson and G E Smith.

At the Thrapston Petty Sessions on Wednesday, **4 February**, a sentence of two months imprisonment was passed on a Raunds shoehand in default of paying affiliation arrears of £9-12s-0d to a slighted Miss!

At the same hearing, a Ringstead shoehand was remanded in custody for a week having been charged with stealing 9 pairs of boots, value £4-5s-3d, the property of Tebbutt & Hall Bros. Mr J W Hall, manager of the company, identified the boots and said that the prisoner was a former employee of the company. Police Sergeant Riseley, giving evidence of the arrest, quoted the prisoner as saying "I see I am in it now, I am sorry I did it. When I get out of this I will turn over a new leaf."

Saturday, **7 February**'s football fixtures resulted in a 1-0 victory for Raunds Town playing against Market Harborough in the Northants League, while Raunds Albion drew 1-1 with Rothwell Albion in the semi-final of the Denford Cup.

Among the many items on the agenda at Tuesday, **10 February**'s Thrapston Petty Sessions was the case of a retired Raunds huntsman who was committed to the Assizes on a charge of criminally assaulting a 15 year old Raunds girl in the town on 5 November 1913. The Bench were advised that through the illness of the prisoner, currently in St Andrew's Hospital, Northampton, the case had already been adjourned several times. Against unspecified charges to which he pleaded guilty, the Justices also sentenced another Raunds man to 3 months hard labour.

In the Licensing section of the Sessions, the Bench objected to the renewal of the licences for the "Golden Fleece" at Raunds and the "Wagon & Horses" at Hargrave, as they were of the opinion that new licences were not yet required.

At the monthly meeting of the managers of the Church of England Schools on Wednesday, **11 February**, the dates for the Shrove Tuesday, Easter, Ascension Day, Whitsuntide, Summer, Statute Monday and Christmas school holidays in 1914 were agreed. The managers also considered a request from the headmaster for the procurement of three tables and a set of steps "for window cleaning".

On Friday and Saturday, **13 & 14 February**, the "Annual Church Sunday School Concerts" were held in the National Infants School. The event attracted large crowds, especially on the Saturday when the schoolroom was packed. In addition to items from the children, a farce, "Turn Him Out", was given by Messrs C H Medlock, A March, H Hall, G Hall, H Edwards, Mrs W H Spicer and Mrs G Bailey. The teachers had taken vast pains in training the children and were to be congratulated on the splendid results. Those responsible were Miss K Atkins, Miss E George, Miss W Y Clarke, Miss G Bailey, Miss G Carter and Mr T Edge.

Friendly matches took place on the Saturday afternoon for two Raunds football teams. The Raunds Band Boys slumped to a 3-0 defeat away to Irchester Vics but Raunds Athletic fared much better, beating Kettering St Mary's 4-1.

At the first meeting of the managers of the new Council Schools on Monday, **16 February**, it was resolved to recommend to the County Education Committee, to transfer to the new schools for six months, all of the current Wesleyan School teachers. It was also decided to advertise for a caretaker at a fixed salary. *(Plate 7)*

A brief "News Nugget" in the Rushden Echo informed the world that Raunds had the dubious distinction of having one public house for every 274 members of its population!

In the Northants League on Saturday, **21 February**, Raunds Town entertained Desborough, losing by 3 goals to nil. Raunds Fosse completed a miserable day for the town, being beaten in a friendly match against Rushden CLB by 5 goals to 1.

"Choir Sunday" was celebrated the following day at the Wesleyan Church. The Rev J Burrows preached in the morning and some favourite tunes were sung. In the evening the choir gave, in an artistic manner, the introit "Cast me not away", the anthem "At thy feet" and the "Hallelujah" chorus.

The Raunds Conservative Club held their annual dinner on Monday, **23 February**. The retiring directors, Messrs J Shelmerdine, W H Wingell and A Lawrence, were re-elected. Mr & Mrs Cooch (steward & stewardess), were heartily thanked for the excellent way in which they had performed their duties during the year. An intriguingly named "Smoking Concert" then followed.

"A Raunds Educationalist Honoured" was the headline of a report of the gathering held in honour of Mr Jesse Shelmerdine on Tuesday, **24 February**, retiring after 41 years as the respected headmaster of the Church of England schools. The guest speaker, Sir Arthur de Capell Brooke, said "I cannot help thinking of Mr Sheldmerdine as a model teacher. Vast numbers of people, including the thousands of scholars who have passed through his school, will heartily endorse this fine and well deserved tribute. Mr Shelmerdine has now retired and his friends have done well to honour him with an illuminated address, a purse of £64 and an album containing the names of the subscribers." *(Plate 3)*

Forthcoming marriages were the main topic at the latest meeting of the Church of England School managers on Thursday, **26 February**. They were asked to consider a request from Miss Bailey, who planned to marry in early summer, to be retained in her position in the Infants Department. This request was approved by 3 votes to 2 with the Chairman's vote proving decisive.

The matter had been considered critical in light of the fact that both Miss George and Miss Clarke, likewise of the Infants Department, were also soon to be wed. It was therefore decided to seek the ruling of the Local Education Authority on the impending change of circumstance of all three teachers.

At the Sharnbrook Petty Sessions, in which a Stanwick man was charged with stealing a pair of gloves at Yeldon, one of the witnesses, a Raunds man, was also taken to task by the Bench. The man, a butcher by trade, explained: "I met the defendant at 10am in a Raunds street, he asked me if I wanted to buy a pair of gloves for 2s-0d, I gave him 1s-6d. I did not ask where they came from and he did not say. It did not occur to me to ask where he got them from."

PC Knight then explained that the gloves were then sold on to another Raunds man from whom he retrieved them. Inspector Bliss asked the Bench to disallow the expenses of the Raunds butcher who, he considered had, by his conduct, placed difficulties in the way of the police. The Bench concurred, the Chairman informing the butcher that by purchasing the gloves he had but narrowly escaped coming within the grip of the law.

And it was obviously a bad day for Raunds butchers, for another member of that profession from the town was declared bankrupt at a different court session!

* * * * * * * * * * * * * * * * * * * *

* * * * * * * * * * * * * * * * * * * *

MARCH – The Vicar began his notes in the Parish Magazine with the news that Mr W S Bethway, late of Trinity College, Cambridge, hoped soon to take up work at St Mary's as Assistant Curate.

He also advised that the envelopes for Ember Pennies would be sent out in the week before Ember Sunday, 8 March.

He closed with an account of the gathering on Shrove Tuesday evening, 24 February, when a large number of old scholars and friends met to give the late headmaster, Mr Shelmerdine, some "tangible recognition of their esteem and respect". He congratulated Mr Edge for his work producing the "Illuminated Address", one of the gifts presented, and ventured the opinion that "the old scholars and friends are not likely to forget the good work of Mr Shelmerdine."

The magazine also carried a list of donors to the "All Saints Tea". 11 each contributed a tray; 93, half-trays and 27, quarter-trays. The long list included the family names of **Archer, Bailey, Bamford, Bugby, Clarke, Cobley, Coles, George, Gilbert, Hazeldine, Knighton, Pentelow, Smith, Spicer, Stubbs, Vorley, Whitney** and **Wood**, all whom would soon be mourning the loss of relatives in the Great War.

Meanwhile, at the Wesleyan Church, the register of the "Young Men's Class" for 1914 had entries for **Harry Finding (50)** in Mr J Gaunt's class and **Arthur Groom (55)** in Mr George Lee's class. Sadly, both entries would be appended with "died in action" in the not too distant future!

The Brotherhood meeting of Sunday, **1 March**, had Mr C Groom in the chair and heard the Rev R Heaps of Rushden speak on "The gambling evil; Why it is an evil." Miss Streeton of Irthlingborough provided the musical interludes of "There is a green hill" and "Lead, kindly light."

On Monday, **2 March**, the Wesley Guild speaker was Mr L G H Lee who gave an address on "Macbeth". Miss Louie Smith sang two solos accompanied by Mr J W Hall. The Rev J Burrows presided over the meeting.

And at the monthly meeting of the Boot & Shoe Operatives Union, Higham Ferrers, Rushden, Irthlingborough and Raunds District Branch, the members approved a grant of £2-2s-0d to the High Wycombe strikers' fund.

Later that week, the annual meeting of the Raunds Gas Company, chaired by Mr J Gant, JP, reported to its shareholders an increase in the sale of gas of one and a half million cubic feet. A dividend of seven and a half percent was then declared.

In football, the final of the Denford Cup was held on Saturday, **7 March** and Raunds Athletic ran out victors over Raunds Albion by 5 goals to 1.

At Monday, **9 March**'s meeting of the Urban Council, with G E Smith in the chair, the Clerk to the Council read out the response to their application that Raunds should be a separate electoral area for County Council elections. The letter stated that "the difficulty was that the taking of the rural parishes from the Raunds division would necessitate a re-arrangement and other urban parishes being placed in exactly the same position as Raunds now is." It was therefore decided to take no further action.

The medical officer, Dr Mackenzie, reported that there had been 2 deaths and 4 births registered in the town during February, and 1 case of scarlatina and 2 of pulmonary tuberculosis reported. Messrs Denton, James Adams, Bass and Hodson were then appointed overseers for the year.

Two cases involving Raunds men appeared on the agenda of Thrapston Petty Sessions of Tuesday, **10 March**. First, a labourer was summoned "for using obscene language to the annoyance of the passengers on the highway at Raunds at 11pm on February 21". As this was his first offence the defendant was treated leniently by the Bench and fined 5s-0d inclusive of costs.

Later, "Strangward", a farmer, was fined 2s-6d with 6s-0d costs for keeping a dog without a licence, but this would not be the last that we would be hearing of "Strangward"!

In the Northants League on Saturday, **14 March**, Raunds Town travelled to "The Eyrie", home of the Bedford Eagles and very much felt the sharpness of their talons when going down to a 5-0 defeat.

At a well attended meeting of the Brotherhood on Sunday, **15 March**, Mr Frank Edwards, a London City Missioner, spoke on "God's dynamite!" A collection on behalf of the mission realised 13s-6d.

In a welcome move for all Raunds housewives, the bakers of the district this week agreed to reduce the price of bread from 5½d to 5d for a 4lb loaf.

Raunds Women's Liberal Association held their spring meeting on Tuesday, **17 March**, at which Mrs James Jaques of Rushden presided. Mrs Jaques spoke in favour of women's suffrage but disassociated herself entirely from militant tactics. She urged women to work for the vote in a dignified, womanly manner, and to use it for the uplifting of the community.

When nominations for seats on Raunds Urban Council closed on Thursday, **19 March**, the following had confirmed their intention to stand for election:

Liberal: John Adams, Joseph Gant, Charles Groom, A Hazeldine, A W Lawrence, H A Sanders and G E Smith; *Conservative*: W Agutter, W Asberry, A W Bailey, A Camozzi, W Denton, Amos Lawrence, J W Pentelow, Jesse Shelmerdine and J Stubbs; *Labour*: E Batchelor, Leon G H Lee, F W Miller, Fred Pentelow, Charles Storey and George Underwood; *Independent*: James Adams and James Hodson.

At the quarterly meeting of the Raunds Wesleyan Circuit held on Tuesday, **24 March**, the Rev J Burrows accepted the invitation to stay on for a second year and the Rev H J Barber confirmed that he would stay for a third year.

Also today, a 12½ year old schoolboy appeared at Thrapston Petty Sessions charged with stealing a lady's silver watch, valued at 25s-0d, the property of Victoria Freeman, on 5 March. A further charge was that of stealing a lady's bicycle, value 10s-0d, the property of Ruby Rixon, between 7 & 11 March. Police Sergeant Ellingham, giving evidence, said the boy pleaded guilty to having the watch. He also showed the owner the cycle in pieces. The Chairman of the Bench said for the first charge the defendant would receive 6 strokes of the birch, and for the second charge, be placed in the hands of the Probation Officer for 6 months.

On Wednesday, **25 March**, the managers of the Church of England schools reviewed the reply from the Local Education Authority regarding the forthcoming marriages of three of the Infants Department teachers discussed at the previous month's meeting. Although the LEA conditionally approved the retention of the teachers after their weddings, it rather curiously felt the need to warn Miss George that "the managers don't like you living in Stanwick!"

Whether this was a particular dislike of the managers of that notorious settlement or just a reminder of their residence policy is not clear.

Just a week after submitting their nomination forms for the forthcoming Urban Council elections, both Walter Denton and Amos Lawrence withdrew their names for consideration, leaving 23 gentlemen to contest the 12 available seats.

On Friday, **27 March**, 8 men employed in the rough stuff room of Messrs Adams Bros factory did not return to work alleging grievances against a foreman. Councillor C Bates, president of the Rushden branch of the Boot & Shoe Operatives Union, had an interview with Mr James Adams and a deputation from the men. Mr Adams suggested he keep the foreman on for a month but the men refused to go back to work on those conditions. Referred to the Arbitration Board, the men returned to work pending the decision of the Board.

For the second time in a fortnight, Raunds Town suffered a 5-0 defeat in the Northants League on Saturday, **28 March**, this time away to Market Harborough. Elsewhere, in friendly matches, Raunds Band Lads beat Rushden CLB 1-0 while Raunds Athletic visited Wellingborough Wesleyans but lost by 2 goals to nil.

Labour candidates standing in the imminent Urban Council elections held two open air meetings on Monday, **30 March** and Tuesday, **31 March**. The first, at Top End, was presided over by Mr F W Miller and all of the candidates in turn gave an address. The following day, a crowd gathered outside Messrs Adams Bros factory during the dinner hour to hear Messrs B Batchelor and L G H Lee speak, again under the watchful eye of Mr F W Miller in the chair.

2 – April to June 1914

Tranquility at home is shattered by a royal assassination in Europe.

APRIL – It was announced in the Parish Magazine that the choir would be rendering Sir John Stainer's "Crucifixion" on Palm Sunday afternoon and Good Friday Evening.

The magazine also contained a lengthy article by J Cherry Wall on the medieval wall paintings in the parish church in which he exclaimed: "The finest example existing of the Seven Sins is that at Raunds!"

The Raunds & District Old Age Pensions Committee held their monthly meeting on Thursday, **2 April** to consider existing pensions and new claims. After review, a current pension case was reduced from 5s-0d to 3s-0d per week. There were also three new claims, one each from Ringstead, Woodford and Great Addington, these were allowed at 5s-0d, 4s-0d and 3s-0d respectively.

Raunds Town enjoyed better fortune at last in the Northants League on Saturday, **4 April**, beating Peterborough City Reserves 4-0 to move back up to 10th in the league table.

On Sunday afternoon the previously announced performance by St Mary's Church Choir of Stainer's "Crucifixion" took place in the parish church. The solo parts were contributed by Mr F E Plackett, tenor, Wellingborough and Mr W Gibbs, bass, of Raunds. Mr J P Archer accompanied on the organ.

The result of the Urban Council election of Monday, **6 April**, was declared as:

A Camozzi, 368 votes; G E Smith, 350; J Gant, 343; J Shelmerdine, 340;
L G H Lee, 325; John Adams, 308; W Asberry, 291; E Batchelor, 279; James Adams, 273; J Hodson, 263; W Gates, 262; W Agutter, 244.

This meant that the town now had a council comprising of 4 Conservatives, (an increase of 1); 4 Liberals, (a decrease of 1); 2 Labour, (no change); 2 Independent, (no change).

Saturday, **11 April** saw the continuation of Raunds Town's upturn of form in the Northants League when they defeated the bottom club Fletton, 5-0.

A "Sacred Recital" took place at the Primitive Methodist Church on Sunday, **12 April**, lead by Madame Jones Moss of Northampton. Mr A Bamford contributed 2 vocal solos to the event. On the following afternoon, a tea followed by a concert was given in the Temperance Hall. Mr Lovell of Ringstead presided and again Madame Jones Moss gave a recital. The proceeds over both days were for the "Chapel Renovation Fund".

On Monday, **13 April**, in response to the concern raised at a previous Urban Council meeting, "the custom of ringing a different bell at the funerals of Church people and Non-Conformists, which had caused considerable dissatisfaction, is to be discontinued", confirmed the Vicar.

Tuesday, **14 April**, heralded the "Annual Demonstration of the Temperance Society". Members of the "Band of Hope" assembled at 1.30pm and a procession, headed by the Temperance Band, marched through the town. Temperance melodies were sung by the children, conducted by Mr John Bass. The children, numbering 300, had tea in the Temperance Hall and neighbouring Primitive Methodist Sunday School and this was followed by a public tea at 4.30pm.

A meeting was held at 7.30pm with Mr S Smith in the chair. The Rev Sansom Iles of Desborough spoke on "Temperance Reformers and the justice of their cause." Vocal duets were rendered by the Misses Wooding of Rushden entitled "Excelsior" and "Down the vale", who were then delighted to encore with "Convent Bells". Over the tea tables, Mr J Turnbull, organiser of the "Band of Hope Union", gave a talk on "Band of Hope" work.

A spate of accidents occurred in the town during the previous week according to **17 April**'s Rushden Echo: Frank Spicer, working in Mr W Lawrence's factory, had his left forefinger smashed between the press and the knife and it had to be amputated; Mr James Lawrence, builder and undertaker, had his middle finger burst open by a coffin falling on it; and Abdon Dix was kicked by a horse and sustained a cut thigh.

By the end of April, the shoe trade dispute among the rough stuff room employees of Messrs Adams Bros factory had still not been settled successfully. About 3 weeks previously the men had come out because of some dissatisfaction with their foreman. As the action was unauthorised, Trade Union officials persuaded them to resume work pending the Arbitration Board's decision. The Board sat at Kettering on Monday, **20 April**, but were unable to come to a settlement. Therefore, the dispute was then referred to Sir George Askwith, who was expected to visit Raunds in the near future.

On that same Monday evening, a "lively passage on the chairmanship of the Urban Council" took place between Mr Gant and Mr Lee at the monthly meeting of the council. The first business of the new council session was the election of chairman. Mr Lee asked if an arrangement could be reached "whereby the chair could go round to each of the 3 parties". Messrs Asberry, Gates and Camozzi favoured the principle but Mr Gant said he could scarcely accept the proposition as he assumed the first name for the Labour Party would be Mr Lee. He added that "Anyone who aspired to fill the chair should give evidence that he took a sustained interest in the detailed work of the Council and should take a fair share in its deliberations!" Mr Lee said he was not surprised to hear that, it was what he should have expected and that "Mr Gant had no right to speak of his (Mr Lee's) capabilities". Mr Gant "I did not", Mr Lee "You did", Mr Gant "I never mentioned your capabilities". Mr Camozzi then moved that Mr Shelmerdine be elected chairman for the present year, seconded by Mr John Adams, the motion was carried unanimously.

Friday, **24 April**, was the date of the "North Northamptonshire Musical Competition" held at Oundle and resulted in success for three Raunds youngsters. Ezra Eaton won 1st prize for solo for boys under 16 with Leonard Kirk claiming 3rd prize in the same event. In the pianoforte solo class for under-16's, Edith Lawrence won 3rd prize.

The final day of the football season on Saturday, **25 April**, saw Raunds Town end their Northants League campaign with a grim 3-0 defeat at Irthlingborough, the unlucky Waller scoring an own goal, to finish tenth in the table.

And today, a baby girl, named Mabel Millicent, was born in Lawson Street. Without this young lady's contribution many years later this book would not have been possible.

On Monday evening, **27 April**, a week after the fireworks of their previous meeting, the Urban Council again sat down together. Estimates for the year were considered and it was decided to raise the amount required by setting a rate of 4s-6d in the pound, to be collected in two equal instalments. All agreed except the dissenting Mr John Adams.

That same evening also witnessed the only known sporting appearance in the town of a man destined to become a legend in both British sporting and **military** history. Northampton Town brought a strong side to play Raunds Town in an exhibition match in connection with the appearance of the former Shopmates player Bellamy in the Cobblers Southern League side. The professionals duly won the game 5-0, one of the goals being scored by ***Walter Tull*** with a penalty kick. Gate receipts totalled £7-14s-0d.

The Wesleyan Methodist Church was the scene of a festive occasion on Tuesday, **28 April**, when over 120 relatives and friends of Mr and Mrs John Horrell gathered to celebrate the couple's Golden Wedding. A meat tea was served followed by a social evening at which numerous complimentary addresses were delivered interspersed with musical items.

The Rev J Burrows presented the couple with a six volume set of "John Wesley's Journals" by the Rev Nehemiah Curnock. In accepting the gift, Mr Horrell said that although altogether unexpected, had they asked him what he would like, this would have been his choice.

The couple were married at the parish church in Higham Ferrers on April 28, 1864. Mr Horrell worked for 25 years as "confidential clerk and general manager" of Messrs W Nichols and Sons, boot and shoe manufacturers and Government contractors before setting up in business on his own in the company now operating as John Horrell and Son, under the management of his only son, Mr J C Horrell.

The **30 April** meeting of the Church of England School managers approved the proposed teachers' salary increases.

MAY – The Parish Magazine recorded that Mr Daybell was presented with a writing table at the recent congregational meeting "as a token of respect and goodwill from his friends in Raunds".

It also announced the setting up of a fund "for the purposes of erecting a stone to our late clerk and sexton, John Willmott."

The Vicar extended his congratulations to Ezra Eaton, Leonard Kirk and Edith Lawrence "for doing so well in the Oundle Singing Competition."

Advance notice was also given of the Church Garden Fete, due to be held on Saturday, 27 June. Stalls already confirmed were St Mary's Guild, Mother's Union, Girls, Rummage, Sweets, Refreshments, Flowers, and amusements in the way of Skittles and Kicking the Football. Everyone planning to take part was asked to dress in traditional Welsh costumes so as to fit in with the planned Pageant entitled "Disinherited".

There was also a plea from the Vicar that it would "help greatly if parishioners who have graves of relatives in the churchyard would cut the grass on and around them." He added that "some might like to take charge of 2 or 3 graves and keep them tidy", opinioning that "such work as this is not very difficult but is of real assistance."

The Brotherhood celebrated its 7th anniversary over the weekend of Saturday and Sunday, **2 & 3 May**. Tea was served in the Wesleyan Day School on the Saturday when nearly 130 sat down. This was followed by a well attended meeting in the Wesleyan Church. Madame Clara Streeton sang the solo "O for a closer walk with God", the Rev C J Keeler of Rushden spoke on "The relation of the Brotherhood movement to ideals, institutions and character" and the Rev David Pughe of Merthyr Tydfil, formerly of Irthlingborough, spoke on "A Manly Religion", saying that "Christianity alone has raised the inhabitants of this country from being slaves to being the flower of democracy!"

On Sunday, the sermon was given by the Rev Pughe with more solos from Madame Streeton and in the evening the choir rendered the piece with which they had been successful at the Oundle contest "Cast me not away". At the "men only" meeting in the afternoon, Mr Pughe spoke on "The religious maze of the moment" with Madame Streeton (presumably allowed special entry?) singing "The bright seraphim" and "The golden pathway". Mr J W Hall provided accompaniment at all of the meetings.

At Thrapston Petty Sessions on Tuesday, **5 May**, with Messrs George Smith and Jesse Shelmerdine on the bench, a Raunds shoehand was summoned by his wife for assault on April 21. However, the lady was not present as explained by the defendant "She says she won't appear, she is very sorry, she did it in a temper." The Clerk of the Court added that "There were bruises on her body when she arrived at our office." The Chairman ruled that she must appear at the next Court day and adjourned the case for a fortnight.

Also considered at the Sessions was an "application for an order under the Elementary Education (Blind and Deaf Childrens Act) 1893", against a Raunds shoehand, made by the schools attendance officer, Mr A Mantle. The bench made an order for the defendant to pay 2s-0d per week and 3s-6d arrears.

"Crisis in the Boot and Shoe Trade" told how the threatened trouble had been averted after agreement was reached between the Manufacturers Association and the National Union of Boot and Shoe Operatives. As a result, a new piece work system, a minimum wage and graduated scale of wages for male operatives had been established. In addition, minimum wages for female operatives and boy labour to be set at one boy per three men was agreed.

On Friday, **8 May**, Mr L G Harold Lee reported that at the Government Meteorological station in Raunds, the bright sunshine registered for April amounted to 235 hours, which was about 80 hours above the average.

And at the reading of the last will and testament of Mr Alfred Miles, shoe manufacturer of Raunds, who died on 7 December 1913, his estate value was declared as £13,580 gross, £12,640 net.

In the opening fixture of the 1914 season of the Kettering and District Cricket League – South Section, on Saturday, **9 May**, Raunds Town entertained Rushden Windmill and ran out winners by 53 runs. The Town scored 102 for 8 and then dismissed the Windmillers for 49 runs.

A memorial service, conducted by the Rev J Burrows was celebrated at the Brotherhood on Sunday, **10 May**, in memory of the late Rev Charles Silvester Horne, MP. The famous Congregationalist, who was also the Member of Parliament for Ipswich, was returning home from New York when he was taken ill suddenly and died. His son Kenneth was to become famous many years later in the world of comedy.

The Temperance Band, conducted by Mr Owen Pentelow, gave an afternoon concert on The Square. Among the items played was their test piece for the forthcoming contest at Rushden.

Celebration of the Primitive Methodist Sunday School anniversary also took place today. Mr W H Hackett preached, Miss Grace Lawrence performed a solo and Mr A Tebbutt contributed a recitation. And on Monday, **11 May**, entertainment was given by the scholars and the proceeds over the 2 days were subsequently described as "considerably above the average".

It was announced on Thursday, **14 May**, that the recent "Forget-Me-Not Day", arranged by the club in aid of the "Blind and Crippled Children's Fund", had raised £10-0s-4d.

An interesting article was published on Friday, **15 May**, telling of how Mr Horace Allen, of Wellington Road, who had been ill for some time, had constructed a model of Raunds Parish Church entirely of matches. The reporter observed that "although matchless in the ingenuity with which it is constructed, it is not so in its materials, for in its erection over 4,000 matches were utilised!" *(Plate 8)*

In the Kettering & District League on Saturday, **16 May**, Raunds Town entertained Burton Latimer 2nds and won by 11 runs. The Town scored 85 but Burton could only muster 74 in reply. In the Burton innings, J Allen took 6 wickets for 29 for Raunds.

Urban councillors, at their meeting on Monday, **18 May**, were read a letter from the Secretary to the Royal Commission on Railways requesting the council to send a representative to give evidence at the impending public inquiry, Mr John Adams was selected.

The councillors were also told that the Wellingborough Omnibus Company had advised that at present they could not make any alteration to the Raunds service.

A resolution to ask the managers of the new Council School to allow use of one of the rooms as a council chamber was carried.

The medical officer, Dr Mackenzie, reported 7 deaths and 7 births registered but no infectious diseases notified in the town during April.

At the Thrapston Petty Sessions on Tuesday, **19 May**, the court heard that in the previously adjourned case of the Raunds wife summoning her husband for assault, the good lady had since decided to withdraw the charges. A trio of cycling offenders; a shoehand and an organist, both from Raunds, and a Titchmarsh man, were each fined 5s-0d for riding their bicycles at night without lights. Another Raunds shoehand was fined 10s-0d for being drunk in the town on 12 May.

The managers of the Church of England Schools, at their monthly meeting today, agreed to write to all parents of children at the C of E School advising them that their children would have just as much access to the cookery room at the new Council School as the Council School children.

The managers also agreed to write to the clerk from the Council Schools suggesting that no child should be transferred from one school to another except during December or before the first January meeting.

"Rose Day & Radium" – at another meeting in Raunds on the Tuesday evening, it was decided to hold a "Rose Day" on 20 June. Mrs Shelmerdine presided over the gathering at which Mr C H Battle gave an address on "The need for Radium".

In the cricket match on Saturday, **23 May** between Little Addington and Raunds Town in the Kettering & District League, Raunds bowled out the home side for just 40 runs with J Allen again taking 6 wickets. The Town then reached 46 for 5 to gain victory by 5 wickets.

It was the annual festival of the Church Sunday School on Sunday, **24 May**, and prior to the afternoon children's service, the scholars marched to the church with their banners. An address was given by the Vicar and an anthem sung by the scholars. The evening service was preached by the Rev F G Bettison of St James, Northampton.

At the Wellingborough Agricultural Show in midweek, Mr W Denton, of "Northdale", took 2nd prize for his bulls.

Thursday, **28 May**, saw the birth of a baby boy, named Sidney Thomas, in the north of the county. His eventual meeting in Raunds with a young lady born one month earlier than he, and their subsequent work together, laid the foundations for this publication.

The Raunds Co-Operative Society's annual treat for members' children was held on Saturday, **30 May** when over 1,000 children from Raunds, Stanwick and the neighbourhood had a most enjoyable time. Included in the programme were a procession, tea and sports, after which the Raunds Temperance Band entertained the gathering.

On the same day, Raunds Town played Wollaston in the Kettering & District League. Raunds scored a modest 65 but then bowled out their visitors for 42 to win by 23 runs.

And on **Whitsunday**, the Church Scout Patrol met their guests, the Church Lad's Reserve & Training Corps from Northampton, at Irthlingborough station and "marched" them in to Raunds.

* * * * * * * * * * * * * * * * * * *

Your Teeth, if they are disordered,
May be the cause of those bodily ailments from which you are suffering.
Eminent medical men have expressed the opinion that septic poisoning
Is frequently the result of defective teeth and this brings in its train
Any number of attendant ills.
Do not, therefore, neglect the important question of mouth hygiene,
But consult Messrs W E Pears & Sons, the Dental Specialists,
Who attend Raunds every Friday at Mr Broker's grocery stores, High Street,
From 11.30am to 3pm. Advice given free.

* * * * * * * * * * * * * * * * * * *

JUNE – The Vicar reported in the Parish Magazine that the preparations for the Garden Fete, scheduled for Saturday and Monday, 27 and 29 June, were progressing well. Stalls and sideshows would be in the paddock and the Pageant would be staged on the lawn. Dancing would also take place on the lawn after the evening performance of the Pageant.

Entrance to the grounds would be by the West Gate only, the charge to be: Saturday, 2pm to 6pm, 6d; 6pm to 10pm, 3d; Monday, 5pm to close, 3d. The Pageant would be performed twice on the Saturday, at 3pm and 6pm, and on Monday at 6.30pm. Entrance to the Pageant would cost 1s-0d, or 6d for children, on Saturday afternoon and 6d or 3d on Saturday and Monday evenings.

A plea was made for all gifts for the Rummage Stall to be given to Mrs Camozzi.

At the meeting of the Urban Council Education Sub-Committee on Monday, **1 June**, Messrs John Adams and W F Corby were re-elected as chairman and vice-chairman respectively.

A concert was given by the Raunds Cecilia Choir on Friday, **5 June**. The work chosen was "The Death of Minnehaha" and was performed with both precision and expression. The soloists were Miss Maud Loake and Mr Arthur Trayhurn of Kettering, whose singing was greatly appreciated. The chorus also sang delightfully, and they made some thrilling effects. A word of praise was due to the band, led by Mr J F Martin of Higham Ferrers. Valuable help was given by Mr Mayes at the piano. The whole ensemble were trained and conducted by Mr J P Archer, organist of the parish church. Madame Irene Lyne charmed her hearers with several well chosen items in the second half of the programme, as did also Miss Loake and Mr Trayhurn.

On Saturday, **6 June**, Raunds Town 2nds travelled to Denford and the hosts triumphed by 54 runs despite themselves only scoring 60! The Town 2nds were dismissed for a paltry 6 runs, Denford's J Gunn taking 9 wickets for just 2 runs.

Sunday, **7 June** saw the ordination at Peterborough Cathedral of Mr W S Bethway, BA of Trinity College, Cambridge, and he was afterwards licensed to a Curacy at St Mary's, Raunds.

On Monday, **8 June**, Mr Brown of Thrapston disposed of 50 5% preference shares of £10 each in the Raunds Gas Light Company Ltd. The prices ranged from £11-15s-0d to £12-5s-0d per share. Mr Brown also offered a freehold house, workshops, outbuildings and garden or building land in Butts Road, in the occupation of Messrs Shaw. It was withdrawn at £265.

The Chairman of the Scattered Homes Committee of the Thrapston Union (Mr Smith) reported that the cottage home for children at Raunds was now complete and they had selected furniture to the cost of £200. There was accommodation for 20 children, and there were now at the workhouse, 17 children waiting to go to the new home.

The Committee recommended that an advertisement be inserted in the local newspapers for a matron at a commencing salary of £25 per annum, with rations etc. "The Delves", pleasantly situated at the top of Marshall's Road, had been purchased some time previously from the owner and occupier, Mr A Fisher. It had subsequently been enlarged and other alterations carried out, and came complete with its own gardens and grounds. *(Plate Back Cover)*

The managers of the Church of England School decided at their meeting on Thursday, **11 June**, to write to the Local Education Authority to clarify the status of the 3 newly wed female teachers. It was also confirmed that the LEA had approved the proposed pay increases. Sadly the managers accepted the resignation of Miss Curtis "with much regret" and sent her their best wishes for the future.

The funeral of Mr Frederick Lack of North Street, took place on Saturday, **13 June**. Paster S Gray officiated at the service held in the Baptist Chapel, of which the deceased was a deacon and Sunday school teacher, and at the committal at the Wesleyan burial ground.

In a bowls match at Raunds Conservative Club on the same day, the visitors, Irthlingborough Church Institute, won by 4 points, the score being 65 – 61.

Also at home on the Saturday afternoon, Raunds Town entertained Walgrave at cricket and despite J Pound taking 6 for 12, the hosts lost by 15 runs. Raunds Town replying with 33 to Walgrave's 48.

At the monthly meeting of the Urban Council on Monday, **15 June**, the assembly was read a letter from Mr Brassey, MP, saying that he would try to arrange an interview with the Registrar General with respect to additional facilities for registration at Raunds.

On the subject of housing conditions, the surveyor reported that there were currently 28 unoccupied houses in the town, with 3 other houses having recently been taken into an adjoining factory.

The County Public Health Committee had written as to whether there was "an insufficiency of houses?" But with regards to overcrowding, the surveyor said it was the smallest houses that appeared to have the biggest families, and as a rule they could not afford better ones.

Mr John Adams proposed, and Mr Camozzi seconded, that the Committee be informed that at present there does not appear to be any necessity for building additional houses in Raunds. The motion was carried but Mr Lee remained neutral!

The Highway Committee reported that steps were being taken for a traffic census upon roads in the district for the purpose of road classification and also submitted proposals with respect to widening the dangerous corners near the "Red Lion Inn".

Three births and six deaths were registered in Raunds during May advised the medical officer, Dr Mackenzie.

And a suggestion that a fire engine be purchased was also discussed, and doubt was expressed whether the supply mains near the principle factories were large enough for a steam engine. The following resolution was passed: "The Council consider it advisable to secure a fire engine, and instruct the Sanitary Committee to further report on the matter." The voting was 5-2 in favour with Messrs Gant and Lee remaining neutral.

Finally, Mr Camozzi advised of the intention of the Vicar to notify the Home Secretary of the closing of the churchyard, and gave notice to move at the next meeting that steps be taken to provide a cemetery for the parish.

At Thrapston Petty Sessions on Tuesday, **16 June**, several cases involving Raunds residents appeared before the bench made up of Mr Milligan, Mr Shelmerdine, Dr Buckley and Colonel Benyon. A father was fined 5s-0d for "neglecting to send his child to school". A young courting couple were each fined 2s-6d for "wilful damage to mowing grass", the property of Mr Jeeves, farmer.

Finally, four young shoehands (aged 14 & 15) were summoned for damage to mowing grass, the property of Mr Stanton, farmer, and also for damage to ridge tiles, to the extent of 4s-0d, the property of Mr George E Smith, builder. The bench, however, were reluctant to register a conviction against such young lads and dismissed the cases on payment of damages of 1s-3d each. One of these lads was destined to become one of the town's Great War casualties just over three years later.

In the third ballot for the election of a whole time vice-president for the local branch of the National Union of Boot & Shoe Operatives, Mr William Langley of Irthlingborough defeated Mr E Batchelor of Raunds by 821 votes to 768.

Raunds Hospital Fete was held on Saturday, **20 June**, Lord Channing of Wellingborough being the guest of honour, gave a sympathetic opening speech at what proved to be a "brilliantly successful demonstration favoured by grand summer weather". *(Plate Back Cover)*

Proceedings began with a procession forming up in the grounds of "The Crossways". The troupe, led by the Raunds Temperance Band, then paraded the streets. Following the band, came a section of the Territorials and members of the Urban Council. Next were a number of children in fancy dress followed by a large number of firemen from the neighbourhood under Captain T Yorke. Scoutmaster Bailey led the Raunds Patrol of the Incorporated Church Scouts, followed by the comic section and groups, the attire of a number of ladies from the Burton Latimer Co-Operative Society as "The Crimson Ramblers" being greatly admired. Finally came representatives of the Friendly Societies including Free Gardeners, Rechabites, Foresters, Tradesmen's Club, United Brothers and the Cottage.

After parading the village the procession moved to the grounds of "The Hall", lent for the event by Mrs Coggins. Raunds Wesleyan Prize Choir, conducted by Mr W Hall, then gave a selection.

Mr W F Corby read a letter from Mr Brassey, MP, expressing his regret at his inability to be present and enclosing a cheque for £5. Adjournment was then made to the Greenhouse field, kindly lent by Mr Amos Lawrence, where a programme of sports was carried out.

Prizes for the parade were: Childrens: 1st, Leonard Stubbs' group of pierrots; Individual get-up: 1st, Frank Whiteman, decorated cycle; Comic Groups: 1st, Burton Latimer Co-Op, The Crimson Ramblers.

Sports: 100 yards flat race (boys under 15): 1st, S Yorke; 2nd, H Childs (Rushden). 120 yards flat handicap (open): 1st, R L White; 2nd, J Butler; 3rd, B L Maddock.

The Fire Brigade Hose Cart Competition was won by Peterborough City in 25.25 seconds, Raunds No. 2 came second in 28 seconds.

Dancing to the music of the Temperance Band and a torchlight procession closed the proceedings. The total raised for the day was a little over £71, including £20-12s-3d raised by the ladies for the "Radium Fund".

Baptised on Sunday, **21 June**, at the Parish Church was one Dennis Arthur Copperwheat, who, during the World War 2, would be awarded the George Cross for his bravery in action while serving with the Royal Navy in Malta in 1942.

Raunds Wesleyan Circuit held their quarterly meeting at Denford on Thursday, **25 June**. The subject of the "Criminal Law Amendment Bill" was raised and the meeting resolved to send a note of support to the Bishop of London in his endeavours to raise the legal age of consent from 16 to 18.

The Church of England School managers met on the same evening and heard that there had been no applicants for the vacancy in the Infants Department. They also agreed to the suggestion from the managers of the new Council Schools of "continuing the old agreement as had been in use between the Church and Wesleyan Schools." It was also at this meeting that notice was received from Dr Mackenzie that he intended to offer 50s-0d for prizes at both schools in the town.

Raunds Town entertained Irthlingborough in the Kettering & District Cricket League on Saturday, **27 June**, and bowled out their opponents for 31 runs in reply to their own 103, thereby winning by 72 runs.

The Church Fete also took place on the last Saturday and Monday of the month. The centre piece of the event was a play-pageant entitled "Disinherited", in defence of the Church in Wales, in which Mrs Spicer as "Gwenfrwi" and Mr Wilford as "Meredyth", played the leading characters. Among those taking minor roles were Messrs **J Bamford (19)**, **S Brayfield (27)**, **E Ellingham (47)**, **F Shrives (103)**, and **P Stubbs (113)**, who were all destined to make the headlines within the next few years for more tragic reasons! The performance was described by the parish magazine as "recognised by all to be a great success and probably the best of anything of a like nature before produced in Raunds."

The Fete was held in the grounds of the Vicarage in aid of reducing the £660 debt remaining in connection with the comprehensive enlargement of the Church Day Schools in 1910, the total cost of which was about £2500. The organisers were most fortunate in that the weather was really fine, the stalls were tempting and the side shows did good work and proved a great attraction. Initial estimates of the total raised was "at least" £59. *(Plates 9 & Back Cover)*

However, between the Church Fete events ......

Sunday, 28 June, Archduke Franz Ferdinand, the heir to the Austro-Hungarian Empire, is assassinated in Sarajevo by Gavrilo Princip.

And the world, yes even Raunds, would never be quite the same again!

* * * * * * * * * * * * * * * * * * * *

* * * * * * * * * * * * * * * * * * * *

3 – July to September 1914

Nations glare, the first men leave for the front and the first Belgian refugees arrive.

JULY – The Vicar announced that it was still hoped to hold the annual Sunday School Treat in Feast Week on Saturday, 11 July. Children were to assemble at Titty-Ho at 1.30pm, the procession would start at 2pm (but no hymns would be sung en-route), arriving at the Church at 2.45pm. The children's tea would be at 3.15pm, followed by the public tea at 4pm, tickets at 6d. The Vicarage grounds would be open to the public at 5pm, entrance fee 2d, when the children's sports would begin. Two events would hopefully prove to be of great interest: the Old Boys race and the Tug-of-War between a team of teachers and an Old Boys team. Other amusements would be skittles and kicking the football. Dancing on the lawn would take place after the prizes had been distributed.

However, some children would not get a ticket for the Treat, namely those who had not made at least half of the possible attendances at Sunday School as the Church "did not wish to reward those who had made no attempt to be regular and do their duty!"

In a sale at Northampton on the same afternoon, 9 acres of accommodation and building land at Raunds, currently let at £120 per annum, were offered by auction. The property was subsequently withdrawn with bids standing at £350.

An inquest was held on Tuesday, **5 July**, to consider the sad case of a Raunds labourer, found by his daughter hanging from the banister rail at his home in Brooks Road. It was said that the man was one of the labourers out on strike "in connection with the Lilford dispute." He had told his daughter at Sunday dinnertime that he wanted no food but instead was going to lie down. Some time later when she could get no reply, she investigated and found him hanging on the stairs leading to the attic. When Police Sergeant Ellingham and Dr Mackenzie were summoned, they found he was quite dead. Although he had received some strike pay, the deceased had been short of money for some time which had troubled him. The jury returned a verdict of "Suicide by strangulation whilst temporarily insane."

"H" Company of the Rushden & Higham Territorials received their orders for the week with Raunds and Stanwick men told to meet at the London & North Western station, Irthlingborough, at 6.45am on Sunday, **12 July**, to parade for camp.

On Monday, **13 July**, the Annual Convention of the Raunds Wesleyan Circuit was held in the Wesleyan Church. The Rev J E Rattenbury of London preached in the afternoon to a large congregation on "Philip findeth Nathaniel". About 130 attended the tea that followed.

Thrapston Petty Sessions of Tuesday, **14 July** included two defendants from Raunds. A shoehand was doubly summoned for being drunk and disorderly on the public highway and for assaulting a young lady on the same day. Both defendant and alleged victim claimed that the other had hit them on the head with a bottle! Found guilty on both counts, the man was fined 10s-0d on the first charge and 10s-0d plus 6s-0d costs on the second charge.

In the second case, another shoehand was summoned for using obscene language to the annoyance of persons on the public highway, and had committed three previous similar offences. Sentenced to a £1 fine or 14 days in prison, the defendant said he could not pay and so remained in custody.

A teacher at the Council Infants School was involved in an accident on Wednesday, **15 July**. Whilst playing with the children, Miss Edith Hardwick slipped and broke her wrist.

During this week the town also learned that Mr S Gray, Pastor of the Baptist Chapel in Rotton Row, was about to leave the town bound for Canada. It was also announced that an application had been submitted to the Local Education Authority for approval to open an Evening School.

Finedon's Hospital Parade was held on Saturday, **18 July**, and a team of four firemen from the Raunds station took part in the Fire Brigade Hose Cart Competition also contested by 12 other brigades. Unfortunately, our boys were unsuccessful, with Irthlingborough taking the honours. However, in the Comic Band Group, the winners were the town's Andrew's Comic Band.

On Monday, **20 July**, the Urban Council met for the first time in the new Council School having previously conducted business for many years at the Coffee Tavern. A letter was read from the Co-Operative Society regarding measures to be taken to safeguard against floods and referred the matter to the Highways Committee.

Mr Camozzi then stated that the Council knew it was necessary for the town to have a new cemetery. He therefore moved that the Council take immediate steps to provide one for the parish, that part if not all should be consecrated and that one if not two cemetery chapels should be provided. Mr Smith proposed and Mr Gates seconded the motion, which was carried and referred to the Sanitary Committee.

In a report on the mortality rates throughout the county, Raunds had 13.1 deaths per 1000 of its population, this compared unfavourably against Irthlingborough with 8.3, Rushden with 8.7 and Wellingborough with 9, while Finedon with 13.4, Desborough with 13.7, Thrapston with 14.3 and Northampton with 14.7 per 1000 came out worse.

Thursday, 23 July, Austria-Hungary sends an ultimatum to Serbia.

Saturday, 25 July, Serbia refuses the Austro-Hungarian ultimatum and mobilizes its troops.

As national tensions intensified, the English summer continued with Raunds Town playing Lord Lilford's XI in a cricket friendly, running out winners by 2 runs. The Lord's XI could only muster 166 in reply to the Town's 168 who included a J Coles and G Archer in their team, names that would figure in the casualty lists later during the war.

A team from Raunds also visited Stanwick but came home on the wrong end of a 61 run defeat. C Abbott top scored for the visitors with 20.

Higham Ferrers staged their Hospital Fete on this day and two teams from the Raunds station took part in the Fire Brigade Hose Cart Competition. The town's No.1 team were third in 27.5 seconds behind victors Higham Ferrers and second placed Finedon No.1. Raunds No.2 was unplaced in 34.2 seconds.

That same afternoon in the Parish Church, eight members of the Central Northants Association of Bellringers rang a peal of "Superlative Surprise Major" in 3 hours 20 minutes. Using half muffled bells, this was a tribute to Mrs H Sharman and Mrs J W Black who had died during the previous week.

The Primitive Methodist Church held its annual Camp Meetings on Sunday, **26 July**. The venues were "Top End" at 11am, "The Hill" at 1.30pm, "Ashfields" at 2.30pm and Grove Street in the evening followed by a united service with the Salvation Army on The Square.

Elsewhere in the town, while driving in one of his fields, Mr V Woolley was thrown out of the trap by the pony suddenly swerving and he lay for half an hour awaiting assistance. A dislocated shoulder was attended to by Doctor Grainer of Thrapston. Mr Woolley suffered from bruises and shock for some days after.

Raunds Distributive Co-Operative Society held its half-yearly meeting on Monday, **27 July**, but it was very poorly attended, with less than 50 out of the total of 1066 members being present. The assembly did, however, elect Mr G T Brown to be their representative to the Northampton Hospital Committee.

In the evening, the Raunds Temperance Silver Prize Band, conducted by Mr O Pentelow, played for dancing in a field lent for the occasion by Mr Walter Denton. A collection was taken in aid of Band funds.

Tuesday, 28 July, Austria-Hungary declares war on Serbia.

"Nuisance to be Abated at Raunds" ran the headline from proceedings at today's Thrapston Petty Sessions. A Raunds butcher had been summoned by the town's Urban Council for "neglecting to abate a nuisance in his premises." Originally served in March 1914, the nuisance was created by the dripping of blood from the meat on to the floor situated below the surface of the street. The Bench made an order for the abatement of the nuisance within one month with 11s-0d costs.

And at a meeting of the Council School managers that evening, it was confirmed that the entire staff of the Wesleyan School had been transferred to the new Council School for an initial period of 6 months. It was also reported that Dr Mackenzie had given £2-10s-0d to be spent on prizes of books.

The managers of the Church of England School also met that evening and were told that there were still no applicants for the vacancy in the Infants Department. However, the Local Education Authority had written to request a reduction of Infants Department staff by one and the managers nominated Mrs Archer to be the casualty. It was also confirmed that the Schools had received £2-10s-0d from Dr Mackenzie for books for prizes in the Upper Department.

Thursday, 30 July, German troops begin to muster close to the French border.

"Success" heralded the news that both Miss Olive Clarke of Park Road and Miss Elsie Coles of Clare Street had passed the London Matriculation Examination. Miss Clarke was a pupil of Raunds Church of England and Northampton High Schools and Miss Coles a pupil of Raunds Wesleyan and Wellingborough County High Schools.

Friday, 31 July, Russian and Turkish troops are mobilized.

Today a report was published showing the infant mortality rate across the county. Raunds had 86.4 deaths per 1000 births, this compared unfavourably against Irthlingborough's impressive 46.2, Wellingborough's 69.1 and Rushden's 80.1, but the town fared better than Rothwell's 91.6, Kettering's 109.3 and Daventry's 123.2. The county average was 85 and 109 for England & Wales.

* *

* *

AUGUST – *Saturday, 1ˢᵗ, Germany declares war on Russia – the French Army is mobilized – Earl Kitchener is appointed Secretary of State for War.*

Writing in the August Parish Magazine, the Vicar reported that the Sunday School Treat had been a great success on a lovely day. The marathon race had attracted a large crowd and he hoped that it would become an annual event. The winner was W Bettles and the tug-of-war had been won by the Vestry Class.

It was also announced that the Mother's Union hoped to have an excursion to Bedford by brake on Tuesday, 18 August, the charge to be 2s-6d.

The balance sheet for the Garden Fete was published and showed that among the expenses were payments of £4-10s-0d made to the band, 6s-9d for Woodbines and 7s-1d for wigs!

On that first day of the month, Raunds Town 2ⁿᵈ XI were hosts to Denford and emerged as victors by 54 runs, the visitors only managing a score of 47 in reply to the 101 of the Seconds.

At the Baptist Chapel on Sunday, **2 August**, Miss Gray, who was about to leave this country for Canada, was presented by members of her Sunday School class with a glass & silver preserve jar and a handsome oblong tray with silver-plated rail and pearl inlay.

During the afternoon, the Raunds Temperance Silver Prize Band gave a concert in the grounds of the "Manor House" in aid of band funds. Mr and Mrs Camozzi allowed people to inspect their well kept gardens.

Monday, 3 August, Germany declares war on France and Great Britain mobilizes.

For the Bank Holiday, a large number of townspeople went to the various seaside resorts. Others, including two of Mr J Shelmerdine's daughters, even journeyed to the continent and it was doubtful when they would be able to return.

Tuesday, 4 August, Great Britain declares war on Germany at 11pm after it fails to give assurance that it will not violate Belgian neutrality.

Locally, many Raunds shoe manufacturers hurriedly returned home from their holidays and others were making their way home. Some reopened their factories that afternoon and others would start the following day in consequence of the expected rush of Government work. Already many local Army contractors had received appointments with Government officials in London. Elsewhere in the neighbourhood, Desborough and Rothwell were said to be "excited" at the prospect of war and at Thrapston there were wild scenes as men rejoined the colours.

Wednesday, 5 August, Austria-Hungary declares war on Russia.

About 20 of the Raunds Territorials, under Lance Corporal Bettles, went off on Thursday, **6 August**. Mr J Shelmerdine, chairman of the Urban Council, an old volunteer, also marched through the town with the men to the "Red Lion" where he wished them goodbye and God speed.

Welcome news for housewives came when the master bakers of the district met at Rushden and decided "not to raise the prices of bread at present."

End of term results of the Boot & Shoe classes held at the Raunds Centre were announced. At the Honours Stage, a 2nd class certificate & pass in practical pattern cutting was awarded to George L Miller; at theAdvanced Stage, F C Agutter was awarded a 2nd class certificate & pass in practical pattern cutting, Albert Firkins, a 2nd class certificate & pass in rough stuff cutting and a County Council prize for practical rough stuff cutting, and Ralph Mayes, a 2nd class certificate & pass in practical clicking; and at the Elementary Stage, Herbert Arnold, Arthur Coles, Owen Young and Ralph Sanders all attained passes with Ralph Sanders also receiving a County Council prize for a well-kept notebook.

Friday, 7 August, the first British Expeditionary Force troops land in France.

On this day the headlines included "German Army Corps Driven Back By Heroic Belgians", "Loss of British cruiser HMS Amphion", "The Bombardment of Belgrade", "Plucky Servians", "No Dear Food", "Kaiser says 'enemies are all around us'" and "Germans Found on LNWR Bridge at Conway".

And the Central Machine Company of Rushden announced today that it had been asked by the Raunds Army contractors if they could supply men for working plant and gas engines through the night for 2 or 3 shifts.

Over 100 members and friends of the "Band of Hope" journeyed to Kimbolton in brakes on Saturday, **8 August**. They took tea in the Union Chapel and also toured the castle grounds before returning home.

Public prayer meetings on "The War" were held in the Wesleyan Methodist, Primitive Methodist and Baptist Churches on Sunday, **9 August.**

On Monday, **10 August**, the funeral took place at the Wesleyan Church burial ground of Mrs Florence Annie Neal, wife of Mr Ralph Neal.

Tuesday, 11 August, Great Britain declares war on Austria-Hungary.

A review of the local Boot & Shoe trade showed that although the general trade was poor, Army boot manufacturers were hard at work. Messrs Adams Bros were already working 3 shifts, night and day and all other factories in Raunds were extremely busy, working daily from 6am to 8pm.

On Saturday, **15 August**, a meeting of the United Clubs Blind & Crippled Children's Fund was held at the Stanwick Club when notifications of new cases in Raunds, Rushden and Higham Ferrers were handed in.

In the afternoon, Raunds Town visited Cranford for a friendly fixture scoring 77 runs in reply to the home team's 90, so losing by 13 runs.

A meeting for Intercession took place on The Square on Sunday, **16 August** at 7.30pm. Paster S Gray (Baptists), the Rev J Burrows (Wesleyan Methodists), the Rev C C Aldred (Vicar of St Mary's) and the Salvation Army Captain shared the pulpit. The Rushden Wesleyan Reform Mission Band led the singing of hymns and a collection for the National Relief Fund raised £6-3s-1d. At the meeting, Dr Mackenzie announced that he would be giving free medicine and attendance to the wives and families of the men from the town who were away on active service.

Monday, 17 August, the Battle of Stalluponen, the first battle on the Eastern Front.

That evening, a recruiting meeting was held at Higham Ferrers Town Hall to meet Sir Ryland Adkins, KC MP, chairman of the Recruiting Committee of the Northamptonshire Territorial Force Association. Mr J Shelmerdine, JP and Mr John Adams, CC, represented Raunds. It was said that the Northants TFA were anxious to promote Lord Kitchener's Army of 100,000 and a Local Advisory Committee was formed that included Messrs Shelmerdine and Adams.

During the week the Army shoe trade in Raunds was described as "very brisk", all of the local contractors having received large orders for handsewn and welted ankle boots, for the British soldiers. It was forecast that the factories would be "very busy for some time" and among the new contracts placed by the War Office in recent days were those for both R Coggins & Sons Ltd and Tebbutt & Hall Bros.

Wednesday, 19 August, the Battle of Gumbinnen, the Russians defeat the German 8th Army – the USA declares its neutrality – Canada authorises an Expeditionary Force.

The Church of England School managers were read a letter from Mr Wilford at their evening meeting on Friday, **21 August**, asking for permission to join his regiment. They also received advice from the Local Education Authority that he should not yet join as "the numbers were already made up."

The managers heard that only one application had been received for the Infants Department vacancy and that "this one could not be recommended", so it was decided to continue to advertise the position.

Sunday, 23 August, the Battle of Mons begins – Japan declares war on Germany.

Miss Pulpher presided at a meeting in the Women's Adult School in aid of the National Relief Fund. An address was given by Mrs G Lee, solos were rendered by Misses Louie Smith, Winnie Pentelow & Winnie Lawrence, with Misses Grace Burton & Lily Robinson the accompanists. Recitations were given by Mrs F Lawrence and Miss March of Thrapston. A collection for the fund amounted to £2.

A public meeting was convened by the Urban Council in the Temperance Hall on Monday evening, **24 August**, presided over by Mr J Shelmerdine, chairman of the council. A local sub-committee, to act under the county committee for the relief of cases of distress, was elected. This was made up of members of the council, representatives of religious bodies and a number of ladies and gentlemen of the parish. Numerous subscriptions were promised, some as much as £50, and together they brought the total committed by Raunds to the National Relief Fund to a splendid £555-18s-10d.

Tuesday, 25 August, the Allied retreat from Mons begins.

The local press reported that owing to the high pressure in the Army boot trade at Raunds, many of the piece hands were earning "quite 50 shillings per week and some were making as much as £3."

Wednesday, 26 August, the Battle of Tannenburg, the Germans destroy the Russian 2nd Army.

On Friday evening, **28 August**, the Church of England School managers at last received an application for the Infants Department vacancy, from a Miss Lodder of Irchester and they duly invited her for interview the following Monday.

In the Kettering & District Cricket League, South Section, Raunds Town inflicted a heavy defeat on Burton Latimer 2nds on Saturday, **29 August**. The Town scored 165, of which Coles contributed 35 and Hall 34, and then dismissed the home team for a mere 34 runs, with Gibbs taking an impressive 7 wickets for just 9 runs.

That afternoon also saw about 100 people sit down to the Wesleyan Sunday School's Annual Tea held in the grounds of Mrs J Horrell's house.

The 102nd Anniversary of the Sunday School was celebrated on Sunday, **30 August**. The afternoon and evening services were led by wonderfully named W Kingscote Greenland, the famous minister, lecturer and author. In the afternoon, the Church was decorated with "a splendid array of flowers" and donations of toys, games, fruit and eggs were received for the East Ham Mission. Bibles and hymn books were presented to scholars who had attained the age of 15 since the last anniversary. Recipients included **Francis Warner (118).** At the evening service, the choir sang "Praise the Lord", accompanied by Mr J W Hall.

On the Monday evening, **31 August**, Mr Greenland gave an address entitled "The Reign of the Young People". The net proceeds of the weekend's events totalled £27-10s-0d.

The C of E School manager's interview with Miss Lodder for the Infants School vacancy resulted in her being offered the position at a starting salary of £70 per annum subject to the approval of the Local Education Authority.

SEPTEMBER – The Vicar was very forthright in his opening notes in this month's Parish Magazine as he attempted to explain to his parishioners why Britain had gone to war and what would be expected of Raunds:

"Some may still not realise why we are taking part in this tremendous struggle, why we as a nation could not stand aside. We could not do this and have a shred of national honour and self respect left to us. We were pledged and in duty bound to take our part in a war in which we are fighting for a weaker nation against a nation whose leaders have no respect for pledges, treaties or honour.

Could we as a nation have ever in the future dared or cared to raise our heads if we had stood on one side? We want now every man we can get, and at once. We want too, for those who must stay at home that there should be no panic, but a loyal trust in those to whom we have entrusted the care of our national honour. We do need to realise our position, and we do need to realise that there is a clear call for more men, NOW!"

On a slightly lighter note he looked to the forthcoming Harvest Thanksgiving: "This year the harvest seems exceptionally good, just at a time when we need the fruits of the earth so much. We shall be glad to receive any gifts of flowers, fruit and vegetables, but if these are less than usual, we shall all quite understand the reason, for we cannot be too careful in view of the present situation."

"Scholar's Success" was the headline on Thursday, **3 September**, heralding Master Harold Miles, son of the late Mr A and Mrs Miles of "Fairholme", who had been successful in passing the Senior Cambridge local examination held in July. Still under 16, young Harold was currently being educated at the East Anglian School in Bury St Edmunds.

And it was announced on the same day that the total raised from Raunds for the Prince's National Relief Fund had reached £595-2s-10d. A house to house collection was planned for the following weekend by which it was hoped that this excellent sum would be still further augmented.

Raunds Town entertained Earls Barton in the Northants Football League on Saturday, **5 September**, and were victorious by 4 goals to 1.

Sunday, 6 September, the British retreat from Mons ends at the River Marne.

The recently commenced ambulance classes run by the St John Ambulance Association under the tuition of Dr Mackenzie, had already attracted over 100 members. The Vicar, the Rev C C Aldred, was acting as honorary secretary.

The Church of England School managers received notification at their meeting of Tuesday, **8 September**, that Mr Wilford would be leaving Raunds the following day to join his regiment, the Rifle Brigade. They also approved Mrs Potter (nee Miss Ball) assuming temporary duties at 5s-0d per day, having previously had experience at Victoria Council, Wellingborough and Earls Barton C of E Schools.

On Wednesday, **9 September**, Mr Harold Lee, a member of the Urban Council and headmaster of the Council School, was accepted as a recruit for the 4th Battalion, Northamptonshire Territorials for home and colonial service.

In the evening, an Open Air Lantern Lecture, entitled "The War Against Drink", was given on The Square by Mr Turnbull, agent of the Northamptonshire Band of Hope, assisted by Mr R Desborough of Rushden, who manipulated the lantern. An immense crowd assembled and the lecture was listened to with the keenest interest.

Meanwhile, the latest figure for Raunds' contribution to the Prince of Wales' National Relief Fund was given as £667-16s-0d including £40-12s-2d from the previous weekend's house to house collection.

The death of one of the town's oldest inhabitants, that of Mr James Whitney, of Thorpe Street, aged 86, was announced on Thursday, **10 September**.

The Raunds & District Pensions Committee met today and considered four new claims, two from Raunds and one each from Barton Seagrave and Ringstead. Two were allowed at 5s-0d per week, one at 3s-0d pw and one at 2s-0d pw.

At today's meeting of the Boot & Shoe Operatives Union branch the recommendation to make grants from the National Relief Fund was approved. As a result, the Raunds committee would receive a donation of £5.

This month's issue of the Raunds Circuit Wesleyan Magazine, displaying an admirable Christian spirit, exclaimed "This war must not end until the world is completely delivered from the brutality and vandalism of the German soldier!"

Saturday, 12 September, the "Race to the Sea" begins.

During the afternoon, the "Andrews Comic Band" paraded the town and collected £3-16s-1d for the National Relief Fund.

A recruiting meeting was held in the grounds of Kimbolton Castle on Sunday, **13 September**, and 25 young men enlisted including 2 from Raunds.

There was a packed agenda for Monday, **14 September**'s Urban Council meeting. The medical officer, Dr Mackenzie reported that one death and four births were registered in the town in August. There were also 4 mild cases of scarlet fever and 3 more during the last fortnight and more ordinary sore throats had occurred in the last two weeks than in the previous six months.

The Finance Committee voted £5 to Thomas Yorke as a retaining fee as captain of the fire brigade, and accepted the tender of Mr Isaac Clark for the supply of Swanwick coal for steam rolling at 18s-7d per ton. Mr Hodson then proposed that the public should be allowed to attend council meetings, the motion was carried.

Finally, the chairman read a postcard received from Councillor L G H Lee: "B Company, 4th Northamptons, Beyton near Bury St Edmunds. Enlisted as above for foreign service. Very rough but quite contented. Kind regards to councillors at next meeting. Assure them quite safe in my keeping!"

The Council resolved to send him best wishes and a safe return, and expressed hope that other single members of the council would follow Mr Lee's example. The chairman quipped "If born bachelors, they can't help it!" – all laughed.

Tuesday, 15 September, the first trenches are dug on the Western Front.

As the lines began to be drawn in France and Flanders, a shoehand appeared at Higham Ferrers Police Court charged with being drunk and disorderly at Higham on 25 July. The Mayor said that as this was the second such charge against the defendant in the last 2 or 3 months, he would be fined 10s-0d and costs. The defendant asked for time to pay as he had been out of work for some time but had recently found employment at Raunds and was "very busy making boots for the soldiers." Superintendant McLeod did not oppose time being allowed as "the firms at Raunds were all very busy with the army boot trade." The Mayor duly allowed him 14 days to pay.

"Shocking Fatality at Hargrave", told how Dr Mackenzie had been summoned to the village to attend to an 8 year old boy, run over by the straw jack towed to the rear of a traction engine. The boy had tried to gain a ride on the jack but missed his hold and one of the wheels went right over him. The good doctor said that the boy must have died almost immediately.

On Thursday, **17 September**, the Thrapston Board of Guardians agreed, subject to the approval of the Local Government Board, to place their cottage home in Raunds at the service of Belgian refugees.

A serious accident on the evening of Saturday, **19 September**, left a cyclist unconscious. Alfred Thompson, a Raunds shoehand, was cycling home from Rushden Feast along the Stanwick Road at 11pm when he collided with a man walking in the opposite direction. Both men were taken by Wellingborough Motor Company bus to Dr Mackenzie's home, the cyclist was then taken on to Northampton Hospital on Monday, still unconscious.

The Harvest Festival was held at the Wesleyan Church on Sunday, **20 September**, when the preacher was the Rev R Heaps of Rushden, a former circuit minister.

Monday, 21 September, HMS Aboukir, Cressy and Hogue are sunk with the loss of 1,460 lives.

At their quarterly meeting, presided over by the Rev J Burrows, the Raunds Wesleyan Circuit membership was reported as totalling 433 full members with an additional 43 "on trial". The treasurer of the "Horse Hire Fund", **Arthur Groom (55)**, declared a balance in hand of £4-8s-6d.

Appearing at the Thrapston Police Court on Tuesday, **22 September**, a labourer from Raunds was summoned for stealing 2 pints of milk, value 3d, the property of William Eady, at Raunds on 9 September. The defendant, who had been in Mr Eady's employ for 8 years, was fined 10s-0d including costs.

It was revealed on Wednesday, **23 September**, that the total raised to date in Northamptonshire for the National Relief Fund was £11,365-14s-0d including £500 "from the parish of Raunds", and a concert given by the Raunds Temperance Band three days later raised £2-7s-6d for the Fund.

Harvest Thanksgiving services were held at the Parish Church on Thursday, **24 September** and Sunday, **27 September**. The Church was nicely decorated by a large body of ladies and the preacher was the Rev C Holmes of Thorpe-Achurch.

In the Preliminary Round of the English Cup played on Saturday, **26 September**, Raunds Town visited Irthlingborough but lost 3-2. Harrison scored both goals for the Shopmates. Meanwhile, in the Wellingborough League, Raunds Athletic lost by the only goal at Rushden Church Institute but remained top of the table.

The Autumnal meeting of the Northamptonshire Temperance Association & Band of Hope took place in Raunds when the Rev J Saxton proclaimed: "It is not more certain that we shall smash the Germans than it is that we shall smash the drink!"

Tuesday evening's Church of England School managers' meeting heard that although Mr Edge had rejoined his regiment, the headmaster proposed to manage without any further assistance for the present by sharing both top classes with Mrs Edge as each class was small at this time of the year. The managers decided to request a supply teacher from the start of the new school year on 1 December.

Miss Atkins, headmistress of the Infants Department tendered her resignation. Her intention was to leave on 31 December. This prompted the managers to advertise for a new headmistress.

It was decided that in future standard 1 should be adopted in the Upper School and that backward children in the top class of the Infants Department be held back for 6 months before being moved up.

And cryptically, the caretaker requested that wood be provided for him instead of him having to find it!

On the last day of September, the managers of the Council School met and Miss Beeby, headmistress of the Infants Department, on behalf of the headmaster, L G H Lee, now in the Territorials, asked the managers to accept a framed photograph of the staff of the school at the date of opening.

At the meeting, the managers appointed Mr Owen Woodman, currently of Newton Road School in Rushden, to take temporary charge in Mr Lee's absence. They also decided to interview 2 of the 3 applicants for the vacant assistant mistress's position in the Infants Department.

4 – October to December 1914

The town hears of its first casualties as the residents rally to the cause.

Thursday, 1 October, the First Battle of Arras begins.

The Vicar, in his Parish Magazine notes, observed that "News comes very slowly now from the front and as the list of those who are absent from Raunds grows, so there arises a fresh call for us who are left at home, namely to take up a little more Church work, so that the work of God may not go short."

Special Intercessions were made for all those who had left their homes in the town to do duty for King and Country.

Dr Mackenzie announced that he would be pleased to receive and forward tobacco, pipes, cigarettes, writing paper etc to the Northamptonshire Regiment and Gordon Highlanders at the front. All donations would be gladly received for the "Tobacco Fund."

The heartiest congratulations were extended to Miss Gertrude Gaunt having passed 1st Class in Division II of the Diocesan Examination in Religious Knowledge.

Today, 14 children, 12 boys and 2 girls, "flitted" from the Thrapston Union Workhouse to the new Cottage Home in Marshall's Road. They sang "It's a long way to Tipperary" as they rode in the brake and were welcomed to their new home by matron, Miss Colgrave and Mrs Lee. They soon settled in and one boy told the matron "he'd been up a tree and found an apple!" *(Plate Back Cover)*

According to an advertisement also appearing today, domestic servants were in great demand in New Zealand. "It is a rich country, the climate is good, the wages are high, constant work is obtainable. The Government promises a very cheap passage, Government protection and care on the voyage and reliable employment in New Zealand. Steamer fare only £2-16s-0d, London to any port in New Zealand."

On Friday, **2 October**, a graphic description of the war by a Raunds Lifeguard, Trooper F K Kilborn, arrived. Writing to his mother at Kingswood Place, he said "Thanks for the parcel, it's a bit off to keep on having bully beef and biscuits, so one can appreciate a little sweet stuff. I don't think myself that the war will last much longer, but we must wait and see." Sadly these hopes would not become a reality. **(Plate 21)**

It became known today that the factory formerly occupied by Mr Kingsmith was being made ready for reopening by Mr E Stanley.

And also today, the deaths were announced of Mr Thomas Knighton, 80 and Mrs Eliza Coles, 70, the wife of Mr Christopher Coles.

Raunds Town entertained Desborough in the Northants League on Saturday, **3 October**, and honours were shared in a 2-2 draw.

Mr L G H Lee, headmaster of the Council School, who recently enlisted in the 4th Battalion, Northamptonshire Regiment, was reported as having now been appointed as a despatch writer by the military authorities at Bury St Edmunds.

At Thrapston Petty Sessions on Tuesday, **6 October**, a Raunds shoe operator was summoned for failing to notify a change of ownership of a motor cycle in September. He was fined £1 with 6s-0d costs.

The inquest was held on Wednesday, **7 October**, on the death of Alfred Thompson of Marshall's Road, who had been involved in a collision with a pedestrian while cycling home on the evening of Saturday, 19 September. The hearing heard how Mr Thompson had somersaulted off his bike and fell on his head. He had remained semi-conscious for two days before he died. A verdict of "accidental death" was returned.

The managers of the Council School announced that Miss Holder of Norwich had been appointed as certified mistress in the Infants Department.

And Private L G H Lee moved quickly to contradict recent reports that he had been appointed as a military despatch writer!

The Baptist Chapel had collected nine blankets for the troops; two from Pastor and Mrs S Gray, three from the Baptist Sunday School, two from Mrs Riddle and one each from Mr W Ekins and Mr Martin. The blankets were to be promptly forwarded to the Northamptonshire Regiment.

Today, the formal appointment was announced of Mr Woodman from the Newton Road School in Rushden as temporarily in charge of the Raunds Council School while Mr L G H Lee was away on military service and the town said goodbye to its oldest male inhabitant as 88 year old Mr Lewis Bugby, of Midland Road, died.

Meanwhile, the current healthy state of the Army boot trade was confirmed with the news that numerous inquiries for boots had been made by the Russian Government. Veterans in the trade said that demand for labour was greater in the county than at any time since the Franco-Prussian war of 1870.

Sunday, 11 October, the Battle of La Bassée begins.

This afternoon, a Whist Drive was held in the Church of England Schoolrooms in aid of the National Relief Fund and at the Harvest Festival service at the Baptist Chapel, a short prayer meeting was included for the soldiers and sailors.

At the Thursday, **15 October** meeting of the Raunds Committee of the National War Relief Committee held in the Temperance Hall, offering hospitality to Belgian refugees was discussed. Considerable disappointment was expressed that the Scattered Home had not been offered by the Thrapston Board of Guardians. However, Mr T H Warth was prepared to offer two cottages and largely support their maintenance.

The Committee decided to ask Raunds Distributive Co-Operative Society if they were willing to allow "Thorpe House" to be used. A small committee comprising of the Rev J Burrows, the Rev C C Aldred, Messrs E A Milligan, JP, F W March and R Turner, was formed to review and report back.

Mr W H Wingell of Napleton Lodge, died today, aged 34. The deceased, a farmer, Churchman and Conservative, died from pneumonia and bronchitis. He left a widow and a daughter.

And the editor of the Rushden Echo asked to receive letters which had reached the district from the front. He assured readers that all letters submitted would be taken care of and returned in due course.

Monday, 19 October, the First Battle of Ypres begins.

This evening, the quarterly meeting of the Hospital Week Committee met at the "Golden Fleece" clubroom. The assembly heard that the bath chair had been procured and was now with Mr George Bass, "ready for use". The treasurer reported that receipts year to date were £128-17s-8d, expenditure (including £100 sent to the county treasurer) £101-7s-10d, with a cheque for a further £25 ready to be forwarded.

The Urban Council also met on this evening when the Sanitary and Waterworks Committee recommended the purchase for £125 of the field in Newtown from Mr J Holton, as a site for the isolation hospital.

The assembly also decided to adopt by-laws with respect to the regulation of omnibuses in the town.

Councillors also reviewed a circular letter from Royton Urban Council favouring the Government making adequate provision for soldiers and sailors' dependants out of State funds, for all dependants of men who had joined the colours, all men permanently injured, and all dependants of those killed or lost through the war. The Council were unanimously in favour of the suggestion.

"Belgian Refugees – Good Work by the Raunds Committee" was the headline leading into the story of the preparations made at that Monday evening's meeting to receive a number of Belgian refugees into the town.

The Raunds Distributive Co-Operative Society, in response to a request, had placed "Thorpe House", a large and commodious farmhouse, at the disposal of the committee for 12 months free of charge. This was believed to be sufficient to accommodate at least 20 and Mr T H Warth had also offered two cottages. The lady members of the committee, who had for some time been busily engaged in Red Cross work, undertook to arrange for the furnishing that would be required. Mr Lovell also expressed the wish of the Stanwick committee to join forces with Raunds in the scheme. Messrs E A Milligan, W H Lovell and Miss Milligan were to go to London to complete the arrangements for the sending of the Belgians.

It was also decided to open a Belgian Relief Fund and to arrange for a collection to be taken in the factories and throughout the town. Dr Mackenzie offered free medical attendance and medicine to the Belgians and a subscription of 3 guineas to the fund. Mr Milligan promised 10 guineas, Mrs Buckley £5 and Mrs T C Jeeves a ton of potatoes. In total £51-7s-0d was promised.

A meeting of Stanwick's National Relief Fund committee was held in the schoolrooms on Tuesday, **20 October** to consider the question of Belgian refugees, Mr W H Lovell presided. As no housing was available in the village it had been decided to associate with the Raunds efforts. The meeting resolved to hold a public meeting with regard to raising finances.

At Wednesday, **21 October**'s meeting of the Church of England School managers, it was reported that five applications had been received for the Infants Department headmistress' vacancy. The managers decided to wait and continue to advertise for two more weeks, but of the five applications already received, two applicants, one unfortunately named in these troubled times, Fleischmann, were discounted. The managers also reviewed the case of a scholar described as "obstreperous" but agreed to wait for the headmaster to report on how the boy behaved in future.

Dr Mackenzie, who had been actively engaged in collecting pipes and tobacco for soldiers, sent off 1,500 Woodbines, 20 packets of tobacco, 8 dozen boxes of safety matches, 3 dozen briar and cherrywood pipes, 100 packs of stationery, 100 picture postcards, 100 plain postcards, 4 dozen lead pencils, 2 dozen pairs of leather boot laces and £6-13s-6d in cash. This wonderful treasure trove was to be divided between members of the Gordon Highlanders and Northamptonshire Regiment at the front.

Saturday, 24 October, Cecil Burton (32) and Ernest Wood (134) are missing after the Battle of Langemark.

And on the day that the town's first two men were to die in the Great War, Raunds Athletic journeyed to Irchester in the Wellingborough League, only to be defeated by 6 goals to 2.

At the Palace Theatre, Raunds on Sunday, **25 October**, a concert arranged by Messrs Mitchell and Myers, the proprietors, was held in aid of the Belgian Relief Fund. There was a crowded attendance.

The Education Sub-Committee of Raunds Urban Council reported on Monday, **26 October**, that the average number on the register in the town's schools this year was 1,129 compared to 1,097 in 1913. Attendance was 89.6% compared to 91.5% in 1913.

On Tuesday, **27 October**, the Thrapston Board of Guardians met to discuss at length the failure of the Board to obtain the use of the "Scattered (Children's) Home" at Raunds for the accommodation of Belgian refugees ....

In particular, a number of committee members had taken offence at a letter received from the Raunds National Relief Fund committee in which it expressed its "deep disappointment and regret that arrangements were not made for the Scattered Home at Raunds to be placed at the disposal of the Belgian refugees" adding that "this committee feels if your Board had urged the matter upon the Local Government Board, their consent would have been obtained" and closing with "however, notwithstanding this, we intend to do our best to house a number in this district, and to be responsible for their maintenance, and thus give a practical expression of our desire to do what we can to help relieve the distress of our gallant Belgian Allies!"

After much heated debate, the Guardians decided to respond positively to the application from the Raunds Refugees Committee for the Board to lend any spare beds and bedding from the Children's Home ("The Delves") to help in furnishing Thorpe House. They granted the loan of three or four beds and bedding they understood to be surplus to current needs.

That evening, Stanwick Parish Council approved the payment of various bills including one from the Raunds Gas Company for £2-10s-3d.

Wednesday, **28 October**, saw a meeting of the managers of the Council Schools at which the appointment of Miss Ada M Holder as a certified assistant mistress in the Infants Department was confirmed. Her salary was to be £75 per annum. The managers also accepted the resignation of Miss Elsie Sykes, currently an uncertified assistant in the Infants Department.

The Liberal Literary Institute also met for their AGM in the billiard room of the Coffee Tavern this evening. The treasurer reported on a total balance for the year of £36-15s-8d including £15-15s-8d from the billiard account. Elections for the officers for the ensuing year were held resulting in Mr A Hazeldine remaining as President assisted by Messrs R Annies and H A Sanders as vice-presidents. In another example of the swell of goodwill sweeping the town, it was agreed to offer the privileges of the Institute to the Belgian refugees.

However, the national hysteria against anything sounding German reared its ugly head in the area when Mr Gottschalk, the German-born manager of the Northampton Tramways, was forced to resign as a result of public pressure and despite a Council vote of confidence. The Council offered him compensation of £300 in lieu of notice.

And at the Sharnbrook Petty Sessions on Friday, **30 October**, Pepita Eleonora Henrietta Ottilia Behrend, spinster of Sharnbrook, appeared on remand charged with being an alien enemy and failing to register under the Alien Order of 1914.

On this day it was announced that the total raised by Raunds for the Prince's National Relief Fund was now standing at £722-9s-6d. In addition, together with Stanwick, the town had collected £118-11s-8d for its own Belgian Relief Fund. The latest promises being £1 per month by Messrs Smith & Son and 10 shillings per month by Mr & Mrs W H Lovell.

During this week, the people of Raunds had been busy making preparations for receiving a number of Belgians, who were expected to arrive that afternoon. "Thorpe House", the farmhouse placed at the disposal of the committee by the Raunds Distributive Co-Operative Society, had been furnished throughout as the parishes of Raunds and Stanwick made ready to give them a hearty welcome. Currently there were five refugees in private homes in the town, and soon it was expected that quite thirty would have found a home in the district.

The month closed with a heavy defeat for Raunds Town in the Northants League at the hands of Wellingborough, who scored 4 goals without reply.

And in the Wesleyan Church, an organ recital was given by the Rev W Fiddian Moulton, MA, of Cliff College while at the Parish Church, the annual All Saints tea was held at which more than 170 people sat down, followed by a concert and recitals.

* *

England is at War, but
"Business as Usual" must be our motto
So say Yarde & Co, Seed Growers, of which
Mr Wm A Corby, Fruiterer, Raunds, is an agent.

Our Soldiers Want More Zam-Buk
Remarkable letters from the trenches:
"A box of Zam-Buk out here is like a loaf of bread to a starving man"
"I wish we had more Zam-Buk sent from home instead of so much tobacco"
"I brought 4 boxes of Zam-Buk with me when I left England"
Readers, you can do our soldier and sailor friends no better service than by sending them
1, 2 or even 3 boxes of Zam-Buk at once!

T Wingell, Family Butcher, Raunds
Good Quality Sausages & Pure Lard,
Quality Good, Prices Moderate

* *

NOVEMBER – *Sunday, 1 November, the Mesopotamian front opens.*

The winter session of the Brotherhood opened in the Wesleyan Church with an address and recital.

On Monday, **2 November**, the Boot & Shoe Operatives Union met at the Trade Union Club in Rushden. The meeting decided unanimously that the secretary should send a revision of the existing statement to the Joint Standing Committee governing Government Contractors claiming a 5% increase on piece workers total wages during the period that overtime was worked. It was also decided to support the scheme of Mr Barnes, MP, for the better treatment of the widows and dependants of soldiers and sailors.

Tuesday, 3 November, the Battle of Tanga, the Germans defeat the British in East Africa.

A letter to Mr J Shelmerdine from an un-named "Raunds Old Boy at the Front" appeared in this week's local newspapers. The writer spoke of several ex-Raunds Church School boys who had been out in France and Flanders since the beginning of the war. He himself had been present at all of the engagements, including the retreat from Mons and the battles of the Meuse, Marne and Aisne. The only local casualty he knew of was **Percy Smith (105)** who had received slight wounds. He also talked of "some rather exciting experiences up to now" including a bayonet charge on the Prussian Guards in which he thought "we did very well indeed." Other Raunds men said to be currently at the front were **Cecil Burton (32)**, Arthur Cuthbert, **Fred Cuthbert (44)**, Arthur Webb, **Sam Whiteman (128)**, **Ernest Wood (134)** and Harold York.

We now know that by the time that this letter was received, both Cecil Burton and Ernest Wood had been lost and that within the next 7 days Fred Cuthbert and Sam Whiteman would also fall.

It was also reported that Dr Mackenzie had recently sent off his third consignment for the Northamptonshire Regiment and Gordon Highlanders. Included in the sending were 5,500 cigarettes, 3 boxes of tobacco, 6 pipes and 200 cakes of chocolate. These delights had been collected from employees of Messrs R Coggins and Son, W Lawrence and other traders in the town.

Thursday, 5 November, Great Britain and France declare war on Turkey.

The Church of England School managers met on this evening to consider the applications for the headmistress vacancy in the Infants Department. Three candidates were invited for interview from the seven applying: Miss Annie Jones, 43, head of Little Bloxwich School, Walsall; Miss Hattie Cross, 36, first assistant at Clifton Road School, Southall and Miss Winifred Gooding, 27, head at Corby Council School.

A list of "Local Education Workers on Service" was published this week and included from Raunds: Pte T Edge, "C" Company, 4th (Territorial) Battalion, Devonshire Regiment, *Raunds C of E School*; Pte L G H Lee, "B" Company, 4th (Territorial) Battalion, Northamptonshire Regiment, *Raunds Council School* and Pte A E Wilford, 1st Company, 6th (Territorial) Battalion, City of London Regiment, *Raunds C of E School*.

Pte L G H Lee also contributed a lengthy piece for the local press titled "Getting Fit for the Great Day" in which he described life with Northamptonshire Territorials at their training camp in Suffolk. His previous employment as headmaster at Raunds Council Schools stands out clearly through the style and content of the article. So too does his enjoyment of the rather basic and repetitive aspects of Army life and he praises the work of the YMCA in providing small comforts such as lemonade and malted milk, gratis notepaper and envelopes and the organising of games during leisure periods.

Also included is the message that "from the Colonel downwards to the youngest recruit the men are imbued with the one thought of how they can do their best for their country at this most critical time" adding that "there will be keen disappointment if the battalion does not see foreign service somewhere" and in a reference to those who had not volunteered that "it is a huge surprise that so many young men still prefer the atmosphere of shoe factories and the monotonous tasks of modern industrialism, which clog the mind, to the invigorating drills which may tire the body, but clarify the brain and make the blood course through the veins with an exhilarating freshness."

In the Northants League on Saturday, **7 November**, Raunds Town visited Northampton Town Reserves but were beaten 3-1.

On the same day a further party of 15 Belgian refugees arrived in Raunds direct from Folkestone. This made a total of 29 who had found homes in the town. Nine were living in private homes and 20 were under the care of the Raunds & Stanwick Committee. Of those 20, there were 14 adults and 6 children. Five were housed in a cottage and 15 in "Thorpe House", the Co-Operative Society's farmhouse. Both of these residences had been furnished by the people of Raunds and Stanwick, and it was said that their guests from Belgium "appreciated most highly what had been and is being done on their behalf." *(Plate 10)*

The Brotherhood met on Sunday, **8 November**, with Mr J Gant presiding. Mr James Jackson of Northampton spoke on "Three good points for a fighter" and Foreign Missions sermons were preached at the Wesleyan Church by Mr F W Western of Sandy, Bedfordshire.

Monday, 9 November, Frederick Cuthbert (44) missing in action.

Tuesday, 10 November, Samuel Whiteman (128) missing in action.

"Raunds Private a Prisoner" headlined the story of Private J Dix of the 1st Northamptons, the son of Mr & Mrs R Dix, Grove Street, and brother of Mr F W Dix, the amateur skating champion. Pte Dix was reported as being a prisoner of war in a prison camp at Doeberitz, Germany. In a postcard received in Raunds a few days previously he said he was "all right up to the present" and asked his parents to send him cigarettes.

This week Dr Mackenzie sent off yet another supply of Woodbines etc to the Northamptons and Gordon Highlanders at the front.

"Raunds Trooper Wounded" told the tale of Trooper F K Kilborn of the Lifeguards, who was now staying with his mother in Raunds on a fifteen day furlough following convalescence. Trooper Kilborn had seen some active service at the front, having been wounded in the fighting on the Belgian border. His unit had been drafted up to Belgium from the Aisne and were driven from their trenches by the German infantry. As they left the trenches they were subjected to heavy fire over open ground and our man had been first hit in the shoulder and then, about ten yards further, in the neck. He lay for half an hour until he managed to reach the field ambulance, then he was taken to the field hospital. *(Plate 21)*

On Friday, **13 November**, relatives of Private **Cecil Burton (32)** living in Rushden, received an official notification from the War Office, in reply to their telegram, that the name of Pte C Burton was not among those whose names appeared on lists of killed or wounded. Sadly, no news was not good news.

A party of Belgian refugees from Raunds paid a visit to Stanwick in what was described as "A Red Letter Day" for the village. An address of thanks and gratitude was read by M Morel, after which he sang the Belgian national anthem and "The Fatherland" in Flemish. Mlle Margot Pfeiffenschneider sang "The Marseillaise", Mrs Richards played the Belgian and English national anthems, Miss Tarry gave a fine recitation "The Ballad of Splendid Silence", Miss Clipson sang songs and Miss Sherratt gave three recitations.

The sum of £3-10s-0d was handed to the treasurer of the Raunds & Stanwick Belgian Fund. About 20 of the refugees came to tea and stayed until 8pm. The room was gaily decorated with the flags of the Allies.

On Saturday, **14 November**, a tea was held in the Wesleyan Schoolrooms in aid of circuit funds. Upwards of 200 sat down to tea including 25 of the Belgian refugees, who had been specially invited. An excellent programme followed, to which several items were contributed by the Belgian friends. The net proceeds amounted to about £12.

At the Brotherhood meeting on Sunday, **15 November**, the Rev C J Keeler of Rushden spoke on "Facing one of the great problems of the day", Miss Hinde of Finedon was the soloist and Mr Andrew Hazeldine accompanied.

The Urban Council met on Monday, **16 November**, and the medical officer, Dr Mackenzie, reported that the district was "entirely free of notifiable infectious diseases", and that six births and six deaths had been registered during October.

The Sanitary & Waterworks Committee reported that they had obtained offers from the executors of Mr T Wingell and Mr J J Sharp for a site for the new cemetery, and recommended that the executors of Mr Sharp be asked to allow trial holes to be sunk in the field on the London Road nearest Ringstead. They also recommended that the Local Government Board be asked to sanction a loan of £250 for improved isolation hospital accommodation. With respect to the first recommendation, it was decided to meet "on the spot" to inspect the trial holes. The second recommendation was unanimously accepted.

Speaking in the House of Commons on Thursday, **19 November**, the Prime Minister said that British Military casualties in the western war area up to the end of October were approximately 57,000.

That day, the managers of the Church of England School met to interview the short-listed applicants for the Infants Department headmistress vacancy. They discovered that Miss Cross had since withdrawn her application and during discussions with Miss Jones, she declared that she was expecting the position to pay at least £110 per annum! The managers therefore decided to offer the position to Miss Gooding and asked her if she could possibly be released early from her current engagement.

An extraordinary meeting of the Rushden & Higham District Clubs was held during this week to consider the alleged misappropriation of funds raised during the effort for the Blind and Crippled Children. A Raunds man, a resident of Mapletoft Street, was invited to respond to certain elements of the allegations. He said "In reply to your letter asking for an apology from me in reference to the allegations of misappropriation of your society funds, I did not reply earlier as I was extremely at a loss to understand the purpose of your request." He then explained his view of things, and said that under the circumstances he did not think an apology was due. On hearing this, the committee agreed that he was in no way to blame and thanked him for attending.

Local imbibers would have read in horror the news that a decision had been taken for public houses in the Raunds district to be closed an hour earlier each evening to aid the war effort. The new closing times would be 10pm on week nights and 9pm on Sundays.

Members of the St Mary's Mother's Union held a meeting on Monday, **23 November** in which they entertained the wives and mothers of the sailors and soldiers "gone from Raunds to the war." An Intercession Service in the Church followed tea, afterwards the party returned to the Institute for a social evening.

Classes had been recently held by Dr Mackenzie on behalf of the St John Ambulance Association and on Wednesday, **25 November**, the results were announced with passes awarded to J Archer, J Beach, **Sam Brayfield (27)**, **Edgar Ellingham (47)**, H Ellingham, Harry Hall, George Hall, Sydney Kilborn, W Robinson, Frederick Shrives, Frank Spicer, J Spicer and **Percy Watson (119)**.

News came through on Friday, **27 November**, that two Raunds men serving with the 1st Northamptons had been wounded. Private **E Stringer (112)** was now recovering in the New Barnet Hospital while Private **W E Richards (98)** was recovering from arm wounds in the General Hospital, Rouen. Both would make full recoveries and return to the front only to be killed in action later in the war.

At the Rushden Athletic Club "Fur and Feather Show" held on Saturday, **28 November**, E Richardson of Raunds won 3rd prize in the "Poultry – Any Variety Light Breed" section.

In the evening, there was a social in the Church of England Schools so that parishioners might have an opportunity to meet the Belgian refugees. The arrangements were made by the Relief Committee, and admirably carried out by Madames E A Milligan, A Camozzi and T Yorke. Dancing commenced at 7pm and continued until 10.30pm, and was interspersed with songs by Mrs W H Spicer and Monsieurs Morel, Herrent and Empain, accompanied by Miss Marie York. The music for the dancing was supplied by members of the Temperance Band, Mr H Edwards acting as MC. The proceeds of £8 were for clothing for the refugees.

Letters of thanks were read by the Belgians during the evening, among which the following sentiments were expressed: "When we arrived at Raunds we found ourselves in the midst of strangers, but the people have made friends with us and show a friendly spirit towards their unfortunate Belgian brothers. We shall never forget our sojourn at Raunds, and we shall all feel very sorry to leave. We are all proud to be Belgians, but now we shall be pleased to be English too. Long live England, and above all, long live Raunds!"

On the following day, two of the refugees took part in the afternoon service at the Wellingborough Wesleyan Church.

The final day of the month saw a letter arrive home from Sgt Hall of the 1st Northamptons, who was in the Stationary Hospital, Boulogne Base. Writing to his mother in Hill Street, Sgt Hall said "I got wounded at Ypres. I think we left our trademark on the Germans, for we left 100's of them dead in the woods as we passed through. I thought that J Dix was killed until I heard that he was a prisoner. I don't think I shall be any good for the Army after I come out of hospital for I think the leg that got hurt will be 8½ inches shorter than the other, but that's better than being killed outright!" *(Plate 22)*

On the same day, Dr Mackenzie received a letter of thanks for the gifts sent to the front, from the Commanding Officer of the 1st Gordon Highlanders.

DECEMBER – Writing in the December issue of the Parish Magazine, the Vicar commanded to everyones notice, a new pamphlet in the church entitled "The Call of the Empire". He observed that "it is well worth reading and thinking over, the price is 1d."

In a rare entry from the "Raunds Circuit Wesleyan Methodist Church Record" regarding the war, congratulations were extended to Mr Harold Lee, on his promotion to Lance Corporal in the 4th Northamptons, and to Mr **Arnold Burrows (30)**, on his promotion to a full Lieutenancy in the 6th Northamptons. Note was also made of "our Hargrave friend, leader and local preacher" Mr Harold Nicholson, who was in training at Northampton.

As a follow on to a letter received from the Gordon Highlanders a few days earlier, Dr Mackenzie also heard from Pte J A Cuthbert, 1st Northamptons, who thanked him on behalf of his Rance pals for the sendings of tobacco and cigarettes donated by the good folk of the town.

On Thursday, **3 December**, the funeral was reported of a well-known local Salvationist, Mrs Coles of Rotton Row.

A lengthy article appeared in the local press on Friday, **4 December**, containing some fairly graphic descriptions of life at the front. Pte H Felce of Rushden was home on leave and spoke of "German Airship Trickery", "the Prussian's fear of the British bayonet" and "evidence of German barbarities".

When asked about other local men and shown a photograph of Pte **Cecil Burton (32)** he replied "Oh yes, I know him. He is all right. At least, he was when I saw him last. We were in the same trench, fighting together. We were not side by side, but I could see him quite easily as he fired at the enemy."

The annual sale of work produced by the members of the Wesleyan Church took place on Saturday, **5 December**, Mr John Adams, CC, presided. Mr Charles Lewis of Northampton performed the opening ceremony in the absence of his brother, Mr Edward Lewis, JP. The net proceeds exceeded £80.

A large attendance was attracted to Sunday, **6 December**'s Brotherhood meeting in the Wesleyan Church. The Rev A Martyn of Bedford told of "What I saw in Paris on the declaration of war". This was followed by a recital on the violin by Miss Daisy Powell of Northampton, with Mr J W Hall accompanying on the piano.

The sudden death occurred that morning of Mr Walter White of Hill Street who was found dead in bed. As he had been ill for some time, the coroner thought an inquest unnecessary.

At the monthly meeting of the local branch of the Boot and Shoe Operatives Union, held at the Trade Union Club, Rushden on Monday, **7 December**, voting took place to elect delegates to the Labour Party, General Federation and Trades Union Congress. Counting of the votes was planned for Friday, 11 December.

Tuesday, 8 December, the Battle of the Falkland Islands.

In news snippets today it was reported that Mr G Rowland Whitney, formerly a scholar and pupil teacher in the Raunds Wesleyan Day School, now a student at the Wesleyan Training College, Westminster, had gained a BSc degree. The correspondent added that "for one so young, he is 20 years of age, this is most praiseworthy"; Dr Mackenzie's latest shipment of "fags", 1,040 Woodbines, had been despatched the previous day to the Gordons and Northamptons at the front; and the "Boot & Shoe Trade Journal" advised that the sizes of Army boots now being manufactured in the district varied from 6's to 13's.

"Hospitable Raunds – How Thirty Belgian Refugees Are Being Cared For", reported on the 30 Belgians who were now residing in Raunds. Half of the party were living at "Thorpe House", including six children who were attending the Council Infants School, and noted how quickly they were picking up the English songs and nursery rhymes and how happy they seemed in their new surroundings.

On Friday, **11 December**, Mrs S Whiteman, Sheltons Row, Irthlingborough, heard "in an indirect manner" that her husband, Raunds-born Private **Samuel Whiteman (128)**, had been wounded in France. She added that she had received no official confirmation of the fact and it had been five weeks since she received the last letter from him. In this he had said that he was in good health and all right.

In connection with the Wheatsheaf Coursing Club, a match took place on Saturday, **12 December**, when Hall's "Ginger" took on Ferry's "Snowball" in a best of 7 courses. The former won "rather easily" by 4 to 2. This was followed by a handicap for £2 in prizes for which 24 dogs were entered. Mitchell's "Xmas Daisy" was 1st, Burgess's "Ium" 2nd, and Hall's "Ginger" and Hales' "Nell" runners up. Some very good coursing was witnessed by about 200 people.

An evening concert was given in the Wesleyan Schoolrooms in aid of the Belgian Relief Fund, arranged by Mrs Amos Lawrence and party of "Raunds Hall". The artistes were: Misses Grace & Ursula Lawrence, Mrs J W Hall, Messrs E R Tap, of Northampton, F D Brazier, of Higham Ferrers, O D Hall, C Olive, of Kettering and Miss Edith Adams, elocutionist. The proceeds amounted to £13-10s-3d.

An interesting meeting was held in the Higham Ferrers Wesleyan Church on Sunday, **13 December**, when an address was given to a crowded church by M Nichel Pfeiffenschneider, one of the Raunds based Belgian refugees. He "lucidly described the appalling atrocities committed by the Germans in Belgium" and also the bombardment of Antwerp, his home city. Another Belgian now living in Raunds, M Lazare Morel, an excellent baritone, rendered three solos in good style: "The Marseillaise", "The Brabancomme" and "Myn Vaterland".

At Thrapston Market on Tuesday, **15 December**, Mr Walter Denton of Raunds had several pens of fine lambhogs, which made up to 79 shillings each.

On the same day, Mrs S Whiteman of Irthlingborough received a telegram from the Commanding Officer of the Northamptonshire Regiment stating that her husband, Pte **S Whiteman (128)**, had been missing since 9 November. This was in response to a telegram she had sent to the regiment enquiring as to his whereabouts after having previously received only a lukewarm reply from the War Office to her queries. The local newspaper expressed the hope that Pte Whiteman might still be all right and only taken prisoner as he was "highly respected by a large circle of friends".

The mystery surrounding Pte **Cecil Burton**'s **(32)** fate continued when an article appeared in Friday, **18 December**'s Rushden Echo headlined "Raunds Soldier Wounded." It stated that the Raunds Steelback was unofficially reported as wounded and spoke of his father, Mr W Burton, being an accomplished violinist, his brother, P C Burton, being a well-known amateur boxer and athlete and his sister, Miss Grace, being an expert pianist. The report of Pte Burton being wounded had come from a family friend in Weymouth who had written to Cecil's mother telling her that he had heard that he had been injured and sent to England. Sadly this optimistic news was eventually to prove unfounded.

Away from the war, pre-Christmas entertainment on stage at the Rushden Palace were "Pertab Singh & Zania" – The Hindoo's Temple of Mystery, "Lulu Leigh" – vocal comedienne and "The Huntings" – juggling and ladder speciality! Meanwhile, the Royal Variety Theatre presented "Les Videos Wonders on Wheels" including "Leonie, the Juvenile Marvel".

The Northants League fixture between Raunds Town and Wellingborough Town scheduled for Saturday, **19 December**, was postponed as the Shopmates were unable to raise a team, their players being "busily engaged on Army boot orders".

That same afternoon saw the quarterly meeting of the Raunds Wesleyan Circuit with the Rev J Burrows presiding. Returns showed a membership of 431 (a decrease of 2 on the previous quarter), 43 on trial and 118 in junior classes. Mr W F Corby presented the accounts and was accorded a vote of thanks on retiring after his 3 years service. Mr Arthur Pendered, junior steward, was re-elected as was Mr John Bass. Members were then entertained to tea by Mr & Mrs Corby.

Also held on that Saturday was the annual tea and social of the Juvenile Rechabites, when about 100 members of the Juvenile Tent sat down in the Temperance Hall, presided over by sisters from the Adult Tent. After tea a "capital social of songs, recitations and instrumental music" took place.

M Nichel Pfeiffenschneider reprised his address of the previous Sunday, "The Bombardment of Antwerp", and again attracted a large crowd, this time to the Brotherhood meeting in the Wesleyan Church on Sunday, **20 December**. "Never has the chapel been so crowded" said the minister.

On Monday, **21 December**, a Raunds gentleman told of a letter he had just received from his sister, a resident of Scarborough, on the bombardment of that town by the Germans. She had informed him that "Soon after eight o'clock this morning a German boat began to shell the town from the North Bay, and we seemed to be in the thick of it, as I think they were aiming for the wireless station at Falgrave. Fragments of shell came both into our yard and our neighbours', although I am glad to say that both houses have escaped better than almost any others in the neighbourhood". She added that "It's marvellous that we should have escaped, and we feel very thankful I can assure you. We have got a trophy – a piece of shell which went clean through the middle of our washhouse door!" At least 8 people lost their lives in the attack, for some the war was no longer just a distant event.

The Urban Council met that evening and the medical officer, Dr Mackenzie, reported 2 births and 4 deaths registered in November. Although there were no instances of infectious diseases recorded there was one case of overcrowding reported, in Titty-Ho!

Monday, 21 December, Cecil Knight (67) missing in action.

Boxing Day, and in the Wesleyan Schools a public tea was held followed by entertainment, all in aid of the school renovation fund.

On Wednesday, **30 December**, another view of the Scarborough bombardment was received, from the Rev A E Oldroyd, Vicar of St James, West Hampstead, and formerly Vicar of St Mary's, Raunds. He wrote of how he and his wife had experienced a narrow escape while staying at his father-in-law's house, which was struck by two shells. These had done considerable damage to the building and severely injured a maidservant.

And during the evening, entertainment was provided in the Church School to the Sunday School scholars. Mr C Head gave a demonstration of "sleight of hand" and Mr C W Vorley gave a "magic lantern show".

So ended 1914, already five Raunds men were listed as "missing", and all were eventually to be re-classified as "presumed killed in action".

The war would be over by Christmas, but not for a few years yet!

* * * * * * * * * * * * * * * * * * * *

More Bacon For Christmas
Give One "Dennis's Lincolnshire Pig Powder" occasionally!

* * * * * * * * * * * * * * * * * * * *

5 – January to March 1915

The lights go out as the Gallipoli nightmare begins.

JANUARY – In his opening notes for the year in the Parish Magazine, the Vicar announced that it was "Goodbye" to the head teacher in the Infants Department of the C of E School, as Miss Atkins had left to marry Mr Daybell, the former curate. Miss Gooding of Corby was soon to be welcomed as the new head mistress.

He observed that the Sunday Schools had had many changes of teachers owing to the war and hoped that some parents would take a little more interest and make it their business to see that their children came regularly.

Also noted was the Church Institute's continued useful work adding that a new bath had been put in for the use of members, the facility being also open to non-members "by paying a little more!"

1914 Finances included £2-10s-0d collected for Waifs & Strays, £3-6s-0d for the War Relief Fund and 10s-0d received for grass. Expenses included £2-15s-0d spent on winding the clock and 10s-0d for ringing the Curfew Bell.

Included with the magazine was a separate "Roll of Honour" listing all known Raunds men currently serving their King and Country.

"There's A Place For <u>You</u> My Lad – Your King & Country Need You" read the large banner on page 1 of the first Rushden Echo of the year. Lord Kitchener had now obtained 900,000 recruits and was asking for just 100,000 more to make up the first million. "So Take Your Place In The Ranks Young Man!" it concluded.

On Saturday, **2 January**, the annual tea given by the Adult School for old people over 65 years of age was held in the Temperance Hall. About 150 attended, including the Belgians in the town. Mr William Peck kindly conveyed some who were unable to walk. Mr G French of Stanwick presided at the entertainment which followed and included the following contributors: Misses Winnie Abbott and Miriam Sanders, Messrs Tom Hasseldine and O D Hall, Mdlles Pfeiffenschneider and Marie De-Berghes and Mlles E Pfeiffenschneider and E & A Vligen. The Girl Pioneers performed dances.

In the afternoon, a "very pretty wedding" took place in the Parish Church between Miss Rose Gates and Mr Jack Barringer.

On the same day, the annual tea and social in connection with the St Mary's Vicarage Class and Sunday School teachers was held when about 140 sat down in the Assembly Hall and were served a "splendid meat tea."

The Brotherhood met on Sunday, **3 January**, in the Wesleyan Church when the Rev J Burrows gave an address on "Racial Ideals." Miss Winnie Pentelow was the soloist, accompanied by Miss Lilian Robinson on the piano.

And at 4.45 that afternoon, a muffled peal was rung on the church bells in memory of the fallen soldiers and sailors.

A long article, entitled "With The Territorials – How The Northants Recruits Spent Christmas", based on a letter from L G H Lee written on New Year's Eve, appeared in the local newspapers on Friday, **8 January**. "Christmas is over, and the wretched old year of 1914 has told its tale, and is going out as if ashamed of it in rain, slush and fog" he began.

He told of the joy of arrangements made for home leave, only to have them dashed by a last minute cancellation because of the Scarborough bombardment.

In a more humorous vein, he observed that "this little Norfolk town can surely seldom have seen such a parcel post as came in during Christmas week. Many of the parcels were horribly mangled, plum puddings had to be extricated from string and brown paper with the aid of a spoon, and mince pies turned up in granulated form!"

He added that among the other gifts they had received were stocking caps from the ladies of Northamptonshire, beautifully bound and illustrated Testaments for every man from the chaplain, the Rev T G Clarke of Corby, a football for each company from the commanding officer and a cheque for £30 from the boys of the King's School, Peterborough.

As the bells were ringing the old year's knell, he concluded "What will the New Year bring? What of our loved country; and what of the world at large? 'Ring out the thousand wars of old, ring in the thousand years of peace, ring in the Christ that is to be'. If that be so, ring out wild bells and let him die."

In football friendlies played on Saturday, **9 January**, Rushden Church Lad's Brigade beat Raunds Church Institute 2-0, while Raunds Boys United enjoyed a high-scoring match against Stanwick Albion, winning by 5 goals to 3.

The Wesleyan Schools, who had been showing a debt of £600, had added another £340 of expense recently through renovation of the school, reseating and the installation of hot water appliances. To reduce this liability, a tea was held on the Saturday afternoon when about 200 sat down. After the tea the Rev J Burrows outlined a scheme for clearing off the debt. Already £167 had been promised and further promises of £65 were then made. A concert followed. The proceeds of the tea and concert amounted to £8-10s-0d.

"A Great Military Problem" was the subject of an address given by the Rev H W Hart, Primitive Methodist minister, at the Brotherhood meeting of Sunday, **10 January**. The Rev H J Barber presided, Mr and Mrs Hart sang a duet and Mrs Hart contributed a solo.

A letter from Pte W Nunnely, "C" Company, 2nd Northants, was published locally, writing to his parents at Thorpe Street. "We have just come out of the trenches for three days rest. We went into the trenches for our first time a week last Sunday. My pal that enlisted the same day as I did got killed the first day. Just remember me to all the boys and tell them I am quite well ......

I saw Coles from Hargrave at Rouen. He has been sick for a fortnight; and also Mrs Smith's brother, who has been wounded. He was a cook at the camp where I spent my first three days in France. He looks fat and well!"

The Palace Theatre at Rushden this week presented: "The Dumais" – musical novelty, "Annie Estelle" – comedienne, "Sisters Wentworth" – vocal and dancing act and, best of all, "Victor and George" – dental acrobats!

While their rivals at the Royal Variety offered: "The Piquays & Imp" – Anglo-American novelty comedy artistes, "Jack Austin and Lena Lawton" – in a vaudeville tit-bit "Looking for a partner" and "The Henry Whiteley Trio" – in their original musical pot-pourri introducing "The Cake Walk Table."

At Monday, **18 January**'s meeting of the Urban Council, a request for the building of workmen's cottages was discussed. It came from a man with respect to a notice served on him to "abate a nuisance caused by overcrowding." He said he was unable to get a house at present but suggested that the Council should adopt the "Workman's Dwelling Act" and build suitable homes for the people. He would readily offer himself as a tenant! The members agreed to accept his explanation.

The question of why some street lamps were so frequently out was raised. Tampering and draughts were both suspected and the surveyor was asked to keep a "sharp look-out" and contact the police if tampering was proved.

A complaint was also received from residents in Thorpe Street who claimed that they had narrowly escaped from being flooded on December 28th. Their complaint was that they had had to clear the drains and inlets when it should have been done by council workmen.

The medical officer, Dr Mackenzie, reported 2 deaths and 3 births registered in December and 2 cases of erysipelas and 1 of pulmonary tuberculosis in January.

Tuesday, 19 January, the first attack by Zeppelins on Great Britain at Great Yarmouth and Kings Lynn.

As the bombs fell on the east coast, a concert was given in the Wesleyan Schools by a choir from Dr Stephenson's Orphanage. The Rev H J Sugden gave an address on the work of the home.

Meanwhile, another consignment from Dr Mackenzie's "Tobacco and Cigarette Fund" had been despatched.

Sunday, 24 January, the Battle of Dogger Bank.

As war was waged on the high seas the Brotherhood met in the Wesleyan Church and the Rev H J Horn from Rushden, spoke on "Round the World". Mrs S C Brightwell of Rushden, exquisitely sang "Sissy" and "There is a green hill" accompanied by Mr A W Hazeldine at the piano. Mr F Sharwood of Rushden presided.

The Hospital Week committee held its annual meeting at the "Golden Fleece" on Monday, **25 January**. Total receipts for 1914 were £193-18s-2d, £125 of which had already been forwarded to the county treasurer, with £60 more due to be sent shortly, a record for a year.

At Thrapston Market on Tuesday, **26 January**, butter was selling at 1s-3d per pound, eggs at 2s-6d per score, beef at 9s to 9s-6d per stone, mutton at 6s to 6s-6d per stone and pork at 8s to 8s-3d per stone.

Thursday, 28 January, John Arthur Webb (124), killed in action.

The Church of England School managers met in the evening and fixed the school holidays for the coming year: Shrove Tuesday – 16 February, Easter – 2 to 11 April, Ascension Day – 13 May, Whitsuntide – 22 to 30 May, Summer – 30 July to 5 September, Statute Monday – 4 October and Christmas – 24 December to 9 January 1916.

The Cambridge Local Examinations results were released this week and among those for Wellingborough Grammar School, was a pass for H Coggins of Raunds, in spoken French (Boys Seniors).

The Independent Order of Rechabites met for their annual meat tea on Saturday, **30 January** when 180 sat down in the Temperance Hall and Primitive Methodist Sunday School. The tea was followed by the "public initiation service!" in which 20 new members were initiated. Afterwards, a "capital social" took place with songs, recitals and instrumental pieces from Messrs O D Hall, A Tebbutt, R Annies, Master Willis Rands and Misses A Vorley and Mabel Lawrence.

On the same day, a Fancy Dress Ball, in connection with the Young Helpers League, was held in the Hall of the Church of England School. The dresses were very pleasing and original, floral, historical and comic being the sections in which the children dressed. The judges were Mrs T Yorke, Mrs W Adams of Stanwick, Mrs Wilkinson of Scarborough and Mrs Gillson. The event raised £4-13s-0d.

* * * * * * * * * * * * * * * * * * * *

* * * * * * * * * * * * * * * * * * * *

FEBRUARY – In his notes in the Parish Magazine, the Vicar looked back on the successful Vestry Class annual tea and social held on the first Saturday of the year. "120 members of the classes and teachers enjoyed the excellent tea provided. There were still more present for the dancing afterwards and two old favourites, Messrs H Bamford and W Gibbs, added to the enjoyment of the evening."

On the first evening of the month, the local branch of the National Union of Boot & Shoe Operatives convened at the Co-Operative Hall in Rushden. It was unanimously resolved at the mass meeting to discuss wages and conditions of labour of all workers in the boot trade.

A long discussion took place with the clickers present with respect to their wages and conditions and the clickers representatives on the Arbitration Board were urged to use every effort to improve the present unsatisfactory conditions. The men considered that they were being unfairly dealt with compared to those at Northampton and Kettering.

The Northamptonshire Union Bank Ltd, (Raunds branch open daily), released its 78th annual report which showed a net profit of £72,610-3s-9d for 1914.

And it was announced this week that the lights of Northampton would be dimmed each night, "thus rendering the town invisible to enemy aircraft in the dark!"

Thursday, 4 February, Germany announces "unrestricted submarine warfare" in British waters.

"Serious Loss – Horses Killed on Railway near Raunds" was the headline to the story that, this evening, an accident had occurred on the Midland Railway near to Raunds resulting in the loss of two valuable young horses. A number of horses, belonging to the executors of the late Mr T Wingell, escaped and strayed along the railway line towards Hargrave. A luggage train came from Kimbolton at about 8.30pm and ran into them, two were killed and three escaped, valued at £45 each.

Six boys from Raunds, aged 13 to 16, appeared at Thrapston Police Court on Tuesday, **9 February**, summoned for "playing football on the public highway" on January 29th. Two pleaded not guilty, the others guilty. PC Newberry, on duty in Park Road, had caught two, but the others had got away, and although the boys were of a respectable character, there had been so many complaints that it became necessary to bring them before the Bench as a warning.

Although the cases were dismissed, the lads were told that they must bear in mind that their conduct was not only dangerous but also a great nuisance and that they should tell their companions likewise.

At the same hearing, a former sailor, of no fixed abode, was charged on remand with attempting to obtain 6s-6d by false pretences. Giving evidence, a shoe operative employed by Messrs Lawrence Bros stated that the defendant called at the factory saying he was collecting for the Whitby Lifeboat Association ....

The witness had collected 6s-6d but his suspicions had been aroused and he declined to hand the money over to the defendant. Supt Tebbey said that to enable him to get evidence from Whitby, he would like the case adjourned for a fortnight. The adjournment was granted.

The Bench also objected to the renewal of the licenses of the "Baker's Arms" and "Forester's Arms", all other licenses being renewed.

Thursday, 11 February, the first Canadian troops land in France.

"Raunds Soldier Hopeful – Giving the 'Germ-Huns' the run", so ran the headline to a printed letter from Private Edmund Duncan who wrote thanking Dr Mackenzie for a present of tobacco "which was much appreciated by our lads." He went on to say that "things are fairly quiet at our part of the line, but the cold is very severe, likewise the wet is taking effect on many of us. We will be having Kitchener's Army up soon, no doubt, to give the 'Germ-Huns' the run, as they will be quite fresh, whereas we are completely done up with the trying weather. We have been getting long-legged rubber boots to use in the trenches amongst the water, and although they are cold, our feet are kept dry, which is a consideration."

The Temperance Band members held their annual social on Saturday, **13 February**. A large company filled the Temperance Hall for the tea. At the annual meeting Mr W F Corby presided. The Secretary, Mr J H Haynes, presented the report of the year's work, the balance sheet showed an income of £139 and a balance in hand of £14-3s-11d. During the evening songs were contributed by Mr Walter Hall, Mr Jas Vorley and Miss A Vorley and instrumental solos by Mr W Groom and Mr R Annies. Dancing was indulged in.

At the Urban Council meeting on Monday, **15 February**, the members were read the response from the Local Government Board with reference to the council's application for sanction to borrow £250 for alterations in connection with the isolation hospital. The Board advised that they would be unable to approve the application in its present form as the proposed hospital buildings were "somewhat temporary." They were of the view that the accommodation could be provided more conveniently and economically by combining with other authorities in the neighbourhood in need of similar facilities. The matter was referred to the Sanitary Committee.

The assembly was also shown the plans for the new cemetery. The layout, which included entrance gates and chapel, was to be discussed more fully at the next council meeting.

Dr Mackenzie, the medical officer, reported that 6 births were registered in January but no deaths had occurred in the town for 2 months. He added that although there had been much sickness, no infectious diseases had been notified.

In an article entitled "War & Wages", it was noted that the conflict had brought an increase in the earnings of bootmakers. On average, the weekly pay of men had risen from 30s-0d to 37s-6d, and boys now earned 9s-6d instead of 8s-0d. However, there had been no significant change to the earnings of women!

Shrove Tuesday, **16 February**, was the date of the Cinderella dance and fancy dress ball held in the Central Halls of the National Schools in aid of the Schools Building Fund. The event was arranged by Mrs A Camozzi, Mrs T Yorke and Miss Yorke. The fancy dress winners were: Ladies: 1st, Mrs Battersby, "England & France"; 2nd, Mrs W H Spicer, "snake charmer"; 3rd, Misses Lawrence & Tall, "Dutch pair"; 4th, Miss Brown (Wellingborough), "Moonstruck"; 5th, Group of Allies, "Britannia" – Miss E Yorke, "France" – Miss O L Ash, "Belgium" – Miss M Yorke, "Russia" – Mrs F A Potter, "Alsace" – Miss F Kirk. In the Gentlemen's class, Mr J Pateman, "Sunny Jim", took 1st prize.

On Wednesday, **17 February**, it was announced that Mr George E Medlock and Mr **John Bamford (19)**, who had attended Dr Mackenzie's classes during the earlier part of the winter, had been training with "C" Company of the 49th Field Ambulance at the New Barracks, Limerick, for the past 4 months. Both had successfully passed their examinations the previous week. Their training had been very hard but they "went for it with zest and goodwill".

A Whist Drive was held at the Woodbine Working Men's Club this evening in aid of Raunds Athletic Football Club. Seventy-six players took part.

And also today, Dr Mackenzie received the following letter in acknowledgement of cigarettes etc sent to the front: "1st Northants Regt, 13 Feb 1915, Dear Sir, I am directed by the CO of the 1st Northants Regt to write and thank you for the kind gift by the people of Raunds to the Regt which has duly arrived and which is greatly appreciated by the men of the Regt, Yours very truly, Stewart Lewis."

Saturday, **20 February**, saw the first reported death of a Raunds man in the war although the newspaper article itself did not mention the town. Under the headline "Pytchley Soldier Killed in Action", it told of Mrs Webb, 18 High Street, Pytchley, receiving an official intimation to the effect that her husband, Private James Arthur Webb, had been killed in action on January 28th. But this was actually Raunds-born **John Arthur Webb (124)**. He had been in the 1st Northamptons and was one of the first British lads to go into action in the war. A former regular soldier, he had previously spent five and a half pre-war years with the Regiment in India before returning home to take up agricultural work and getting married.

Home Missions services were held in the Wesleyan Church on Sunday, **21 February**, when the Rev C J Keeler of Rushden, preached to a good congregation.

Tuesday, **23 February**, was a busy day at the Thrapston Petty Sessions for Raunds cases. The previously deferred license renewal applications were again discussed, the "Forester's Arms" was duly granted a new license but the "Baker's Arms" was not and the case referred to the County Licensing Committee. The Bench commented that its judgement on the "Baker's Arms" was based on the fact that there were already 14 other licensed houses in Raunds.

A "pack" of dog cases involving Raunds caniniers were then heard. For "allowing his dog to be on the highway without a collar with the owner's name and address thereon", an "agent" was fined 1s-0d. Two cases of "keeping a dog without a licence" attracted fines of 2s-6d for a shoe operative and 5s-0d for a farmer, while another shoe operative was fined 2s-6d for "not keeping his dog under control."

In the evening, the meeting of the Church of England Schools managers received a letter of resignation from Miss Sharman, uncertified teacher in the Infants Department, owing to her forthcoming marriage. The notice was accepted and the managers sent her their best wishes and expressed regret at losing her services.

The secretary also reminded the managers that Miss Gooding would commence her duties as Infants Department head mistress on Monday, 1 March.

The question of salary increases was discussed and the following were agreed to be submitted to the Local Education Authority for ratification: Mr Potter, headmaster, £5; Miss Kirk, assistant teacher, £2-10s-0d; Miss Yorke, assistant teacher, £2-10s-0d; Miss Lodder, assistant teacher, £5.

"Dearer Shaves", heralded the controversial decision by the Northamptonshire Hairdresser's Association to raise the price of shaves from one penny to three halfpence, "in consequence of the war!"

Another article on the death of **John Arthur Webb (124)** appeared in the local press on Friday, **26 February**, under the headline "Killed in Action – Fate of a Newly-Married Raunds Man". The story stated that he was born in Raunds and the son of Mr and Mrs Thomas Webb of Francis Street, the information of his death being received from Private **Arthur Burton (31)** who was standing close to Pte Webb when he was shot down.

The Raunds Temperance Silver Band held a house to house benefit collection on Saturday, **27 February**, for Fred Hall and James Lack who, because of long illnesses, were unable to work. £11-10s-0d in total was raised including £3-7s-6d from the St Crispin Productive Society workforce.

Re-opening services were held at the Primitive Methodist Church over this weekend, "the edifice having been thoroughly renovated". The Saturday speakers were the Rev C J Keeler of Rushden and the Rev H W Hart of Wellingborough and a public tea provided, at which over 120 sat down to the trays. Sunday sermons were preached by Mr Hart and a P.S.A. was held, presided over by Mr G French of Stanwick, at which recitations and solos were rendered.

MARCH – In the March issue of the Parish Magazine, the Vicar announced that there would be several special services to celebrate the Feast of the Annunciation on Thursday, 25 March. There would be a Mother's Union Corporate Communion at 7am and he hoped that all Mother's Union members would also come to the Special Lent Service at 8.15pm. He added that any mothers wishing to join the Union should give their names to Miss Aldred before March 21st.

Advanced notice was also given that a Confirmation Service was scheduled for Thursday, 18 March, which would be conducted by Bishop Clayton.

Finally he thanked Mrs Camozzi and Miss Yorke for arranging the Shrove Tuesday Dance which had raised £3-17s-1d for the Church Schools building fund.

At the annual meeting of the Raunds Gas Company held at the Coffee Tavern on Monday, **1 March**, the directors' report was presented under the watchful eye of the chairman, Mr J Gant, JP. It showed an increase in sales of gas during 1914 of one and a quarter million cubic feet and the committee recommended a dividend of 10% subject to income tax. The chairman said that next year would be the company's jubilee, in the past year the storage capacity had been doubled and they were now equal to a two million cubic feet output. The recommended dividend was agreed and Messrs W F Corby and G E Smith were re-elected as directors.

Tuesday, 2 March, Allied troops land at Gallipoli.

On the day that the ill-fated Gallipoli campaign began, the army contractors met in Raunds in response to a claim by the National Union of Boot and Shoe Operatives for a 10% increase in wages to day workers during the continuance of the war. After some discussion, the request was unanimously agreed.

The funeral took place on Friday, **5 March**, of the late Miss Edith Evelyn Bailey, eldest daughter of Mr and Mrs H T Bailey. The deceased had been employed by the Raunds Distributive Co-Operative Society for about 12 years and was much respected. The funeral services in the church and at the graveside were conducted by the Vicar, the Rev C C Aldred.

At the Brotherhood meeting on Sunday afternoon, **7 March**, presided over by Mr J S Clipson of Rushden, Mr Softley, of the London City Mission, spoke on "Wanted, a man".

Wednesday, 10 March, the Battle of Neuve-Chapelle begins.

The Raunds and District Old Age Pensions sub-committee met to consider five new claims, including one from Raunds. All were approved at the full weekly rate of 5s-0d. An appeal was also raised on an existing pension resulting in it being increased from 2s-0d to 3s-0d per week.

"Raunds Old Scholar at the Front" headed a story that Mr George Lee had received a letter from one of his old pupils at the Wesleyan Day School. The old-boy, **G Harry Hall (59)** wrote "from the field" saying that he had recently read an article in the Wesleyan Circuit magazine on the "Old Scholar's Fund" and that it had arrived on the same day as he had been promoted from 2nd Class to 1st Class Air Mechanic. As this carried with it an increase of 14s-0d per week, he was offering his first week's rise as a contribution. He added that his brother Herbert would deliver the money to Mr Lee on his behalf and went on to say that he had seen a number of Raunds men over there in France and that he kept a good lookout for anybody who he knew as "you can never tell who may turn up".

The Rev J Burrows, superintendent minister at the Wesleyan Methodist Church, announced that his daughter had joined the staff of the United Missionary Training College in Calcutta and was currently giving lessons in Bengali.

The Belgian Relief Committee advised that steps were being taken to secure funds for the maintenance of the Belgian refugees located in the town. Among the activities planned were house-to-house and factory collections, an evening concert in the Wesleyan Schoolrooms and a football match between Raunds Town and a team of sergeants from the Scottish Horse stationed at Kettering. During the latter, the pipes would play at half-time and Raunds Distributive Co-Operative Society would provide tea.

Local football news: on Saturday, **13 March**, Raunds Athletic drew 2-2 with Harrowden in the Wellingborough League.

On Sunday, **14 March**, the Rev W Kidman of Irthlingborough, spoke at Brotherhood meeting on "England from without". Mrs Chisholm, also from Artlenock, sang "Nearer my God to thee" and "I know that my Redeemer liveth", accompanied by Mrs Bayes at the piano. Mr G Winsor presided.

The Urban Council met on Monday, **15 March**, when the surveyor reported that another analysis of the town's water supply had proved very satisfactory.

Mr Batchelor moved that owing to the high cost of living, the Council increase the wages of all its employees by 2s-0d per week. "Eventually" the question was referred to the Finance Committee.

The councillors also considered a request from Thrapston Rural District Council asking if they were prepared to supply Hargrave with water from the town's reservoir. The Waterworks Committee and the surveyor were instructed to prepare a report of recommendation.

Only three nominations were received for the four vacant seats on the Thrapston Board of Guardians: Mr John Bass, Mr J Shelmerdine, and the Rev C C Aldred. Mr W Denton, an old member, agreed to take the fourth seat.

At their meeting on Tuesday, **16 March**, the Church of England School managers were informed by the Local Education Authority that all 5 year olds and under must be excluded from school for a fortnight ending on 26 March. This was because the average age of attendants was so low. At the meeting the managers agreed to ask the LEA if Miss Gooding was entitled to a pay rise this year and also to approve a replacement for Miss Sharman in the Infants Department.

"How a Raunds Private Went to the Trenches", so ran a story on Thursday, **18 March**, on Private W Twelftree of the 7th Battalion, Hertfordshire Regiment. Writing home to his brother in Thorpe Street, Private Twelftree told of his journey across France to join his regiment, the daily routine in the billets, and how he took with him up to the front line, French bread and butter and a big chocolate cake!

The funeral took place at the Parish Church on Saturday, **20 March**, of the late Mrs Joseph Manning, who was 72 years old.

Also today, an inquest was held into the sudden death of Mr Owen Lovell, bootmaker, aged 65. The deceased's son told the coroner how his father had come home to dinner from work and had fallen down and died almost immediately. Dr Mackenzie said that Mr Lovell had suffered from influenza with bronchial catarrh over Christmas but had returned to work rather sooner than he should have done. A verdict of "death through sudden failure of the heart" was recorded.

At the Wesleyan Church on Sunday, **21 March**, sermons in connection with the Local Preachers Mutual Aid Association were preached by Mr Milner Gray, of Luton, the Liberal candidate for Mid-Herts. Mr Gray also spoke at the afternoon Brotherhood meeting when Mr Bernard Tomkins, of Rushden, was the soloist.

On Tuesday, **23 March**, a Raunds shoehand appeared before the Bench at Thrapston on charged with being drunk and disorderly on the public highway on 6 March. Found guilty, a fine of 40s-0d with 4s-0d costs was inflicted upon him.

The Church of England School managers met again on Friday, **26 March**, when they received confirmation from the Local Education Authority that Miss Gooding was eligible for an extra £5 per annum and also that the school caretaker was to receive the recommended increase of £5-4s-0d pa.

They also considered the 2 applications for the assistant, uncertified teacher's vacancy in the Infants Department. They were from Miss Florence Hall, currently employed at Great Brington School and Miss May Hornsby, of Rushden School. After discussion, the managers agreed to offer the post to Miss Hall at an annual salary of £50, subject to the approval of the LEA.

In the Wellingborough League on Saturday, **27 March**, Irchester defeated Raunds Athletic by 3 goals to 2.

Finally, the Thrapston Board of Guardians heard at their meeting on Tuesday, **30 March**, that the estimated cost of the Raunds children's home was "about £2,150".

6 – April to June 1915

Aubers Ridge despair, eggs for sick soldiers and air raid precautions.

APRIL – In this month's Parish Magazine, the Vicar thanked all members of the congregation for the Easter Offering and for all the loyal support given by the churchwardens, sidesmen and congregation during the past year.

The following names had been added to the Parochial Roll of Honour of Raunds men serving: Eric Bellamy, Harvey Bellamy, **Samuel Brayfield (27)**, George William Darlow, Ernest Gates, Harry Hall, John Stringer, Frank Spicer and **Percy Watson (119).** Any names that had been omitted were to be sent to the Vicar.

Commenting on the Confirmation service conducted by Bishop Clayton, Assistant Bishop of Peterborough, the Vicar reported that 16 of those confirmed were from Raunds, 6 from Higham Ferrers and 1 from Great Addington. He added that "none present will forget the Bishop's words".

Offertories during the winter included 26s-0d from the Sunday evening collections at the Grove Street Mission Room for new kneelers. Also acknowledged was 5s-0d from Private S Bamford for the Day Schools Building Fund, £2-5s-1d for the Belgian Fund collected in the Sunday Schools during Lent and 8s-10d raised by Miss Black's class for Waifs and Strays.

The Vicar also asked all Vestry Class members "and others" to note that a new number of "The Old Brigade" had been published, priced 2d. "Mind you secure a copy early" he added.

About 130 old people over 65 years of age sat down in the Temperance Hall to the annual tea given by the British Women's Temperance Association on Good Friday, **2 April**.

"Raunds Man a Prisoner of War" was a headline on Saturday, **3 April**. It told of Mrs A Wood of Wellington Road, who, having not heard from her son for some months, had just received this message through the British Red Cross Society: "March 19, Dear Madam, we have heard from Geneva that "LCpl" **Ernest Wood (134)**, Northants Regt, was taken at La Basse and is now a POW at Wittemberg, Germany. I enclose directions for sending letters, parcels etc to the same, yours faithfully, N Denny (Miss)".

We now know that this cruelly raised a false hope for Mrs Wood as Ernest would subsequently be listed as "missing, presumed killed on 24 October 1914", thus becoming the town's first Great War casualty together with **Cecil Burton (32)**.

The afternoon saw the local derby in the Northants League between Wellingborough Town and Raunds Town which ended in a 3-3 draw. Chambers, Harrison and Maddocks were on target for the Shopmates.

On Easter Monday, **5 April**, a social and dance was held in the Church Institute arranged by the committee of the St Mary's Guild. The event was "thoroughly appreciated" and the organisers were thanked for raising the sum of £1-6s-0d.

Raunds Temperance and Band of Hope Society celebrated its 57th anniversary on Tuesday, **6 April**. Bad weather caused the abandonment of the usual procession, the first time in its history, but at 3pm about 200 children sat down to tea in the Temperance Hall and Primitive Methodist Sunday School. A public tea at 4.30 pm followed when 80 sat down. In the evening a public meeting was held and a stirring address was given by the Rev J H Saxton of Northampton on "The Traffic in the Last Ditch".

At the Thrapston Petty Sessions, a "single woman from Raunds" applied for an affiliation order against a soldier from the 2nd Battalion, Northamptonshire Regiment, now stationed at Weymouth. An order was granted for 2s-0d per week and in addition, 2s-6d per week until the costs of £2-5s-6d were cleared.

The Square was the scene of an accident that day. A young man named Ellingham was cycling along the narrow part of the town centre, when, in order to avoid a motor car, he dashed into the plate-glass window of Messrs Palmer's grocery store. He went right through the window, but escaped with a few cuts.

The Church of England Upper School was the venue on Wednesday, **7 April**, for a "Confetti Dance" organised by Mrs Camozzi and Miss Yorke. Described as "one of the prettiest dances ever given in Raunds", coloured limelight on the lantern was provided by Mr C W Vorley, and "of the pleasure it gave there was no doubt". The School Debt was reduced by the sum of £4-5s-0d as a result of the event.

A Congregational meeting was held on Thursday, **8 April**, when members were elected to the Church Council. The Parish Warden presented the Vicar with the Easter offering of £15-10s-6d, for which he thanked all members of the congregation. The assembly decided that a Garden Fete would be held on Saturday, 12 June, if possible and scheduled a meeting on Tuesday, 20 April, for all those interested in helping at the event.

Controversy rained at Stanwick when the Parish Council wrote to the Rural District Council complaining of the condition of the footpath from Stanwick to Raunds. In reply and obviously unimpressed, the surveyor said that the Stanwick Council were asking for too much and no doubt would be shortly demanding a carpet! It was decided to leave the matter in the hands of the surveyor.

A heart warming story appeared on Friday, **9 April**. It told of a Raunds girl, Ida Broker, 13, who had sent a knitted scarf to the Northamptonshire Regiment with a short letter and had now received a reply from Corporal Sharpe of the 1st Battalion, thanking her for her gift.

Also on this day, while swinging in the trees with some of the Belgian children at Thorpe House, Elsie Dicks, 6, fell and broke both bones in her right forearm. Happily, efficient first aid was rendered by her father and Dr Mackenzie then set the limb.

At about 10.30 on Saturday morning, **10 April**, smoke was noticed arising from the slates of a house in Hill Street occupied by Mr James Asbery. The members of the Fire Brigade, under Captain Yorke, were summoned by rockets and were promptly on the scene. It was found that a chimney and some of the adjoining wood was on fire. Fortunately it was extinguished before much damage had been done. Later that day, Raunds Athletic took on Wellingborough Congregationalists in the Wellingborough League and emerged as 3-2 victors.

At the quarterly meeting of the Boot & Shoe Operatives Union local branch, held at the Rushden Trades Union Club on Monday, **12 April**, the following resolution was passed in respect to the war bonus payment to female workers: "That the bonus of 10% should be made applicable to female operatives", quoting the finding of a Government Committee "that during the war, manufacturers making Government boots should comply with the same conditions and terms as were agreed upon by the Arbitration Board in connection with Government boot and shoe contractors where the 10% bonus is payable to female operatives".

The Arbitration Board agreed that, under the circumstances, they had no alternative but to adopt these terms and the 10% bonus would therefore become payable to the female operatives where manufacturers were engaged on Army work, as from Monday, 29 March.

With regards to levellers, in conjuction with the Hercules leveller, if they were on a set wage they were entitled to the bonus, but if they were working on a piece work rate, they were not. For hand lasters, their piece work rates should be increased equal to 10%.

Doctor Mackenzie's annual medical report showed a "remarkable decrease" in the birth rate in Raunds during 1914. There had been only 58 registered, the lowest on record, as against 81 in 1913 and 80 in 1912. Compared to the national average of 23.6, the town's birth rate was only 14.9 per 1,000 of the population.

The death took place on Tuesday, **13 April**, at the age of 77 years, of Mr Francis Spicer. The deceased was the last of an old and respected family, being the son of the late Mr John Spicer of Glebe farm.

At Tuesday, **20 April**'s Thrapston Petty Sessions, a butcher from Irchester was summoned for "driving a motor car at a speed dangerous to the public on the public highway" at Raunds on 6 April. The defendant said that he had sounded his hooter 3 times, and a witness, a passenger in the car at the time, said they were only going about as fast as the motor 'buses went. The Bench dismissed the case.

In the evening, the Urban Council met and Mr Shelmerdine thanked the members for the loyal way they had supported him during his past year as chairman. Mr John Adams and Mr James Adams were then elected as the new chairman and vice-chairman respectively. A vote of thanks was expressed that "under Mr Shelmerdine's presidency they had had a very happy year".

An application was considered from the seven employees of the Council for a wage increase of 2s-0d per week to help meet the increased cost of living. The Finance Committee duly recommended an increase of 1s-0d for six of the men and that all seven should receive a 4s-0d war bonus. This was carried by 7 votes to 1, with 2 remaining neutral.

On Wednesday, **21 April**, the Urban Council responded to the previous month's request from Thrapston Rural District Council to supply water to Hargrave. They advised their neighbours that they were prepared to provide a supply to the boundary of Hargrave parish at 1s-0d per 1,000 gallons with a minimum charge of £20, but that no guarantee of water could be given to properties on land above the level of the Church due to gravity.

Thursday, 22 April, the Second Battle of Ypres begins, the Germans first use poison gas on the Western Front.

"Grateful Tommies – Thanks From the Trenches to Raunds Helpers" introduced a long article on Friday, **23 April**, about Dr Mackenzie's "Tobacco Fund". Among letters of thanks received were those from Colonel Dobbin, 1st Northants, who said "Thank you for the books and papers just received, they have been a real boon and blessing to us here, and have been greatly appraised by all". Private Morris of "D" Company added "The other day we had some cigarettes come and they said 'Who comes from round Raunds way?' I said 'I come from Tichmarsh,' and they gave me your card and asked me to write and thank you. I used to be boots at the Swan Hotel, Thrapston, before I enlisted, we have a lot of Raunds fellows in our regiment, so I'll let them know that you're sending things to us."

Another letter was sent direct to Master Stanley Archer, house-boy to the doctor, who had also collected money for cigarettes. Private W Winton of the 6th Gordons said "I wish to thank you heartily for your smokes. It was so good for a lad of 12 to collect 30s-0d, and I can assure you that it is the likes of you who provide us with our smokes that give us the strength to thrash the Germans."

A story entitled "Raunds First-Aiders", pictured four St John Ambulance men who had recently passed their first-aid examinations. **Sam Brayfield (27)**, Harry Hall, Frank Spicer & **Percy Watson (119)**, posed in their new Royal Army Medical Corps uniforms at the East Anglian Casualty Clearing Station, Ipswich, where they were now in training. Their mentor, Dr Mackenzie, commented "They are all very fine fellows, who are well up in their work, and glory in it."

Saturday, 24 April, Wilfrid Bouch (25), killed in action.

The Wesleyan Schoolrooms were packed with over 150 people attending the 80th birthday party celebrations for Mrs George Bass. Mr Bass presided and expressed his wife's appreciation on the presence of so many of her friends. Mr J Burrows congratulated her on her good health, retained in her advanced age ......

Mr Enos Smith, JP, said although she was born in the "King William Inn", she had been a temperance worker all her life. The Wesleyan Church presented her with a large framed portrait of herself with a request that she might hand it over to the trustees for hanging in the schoolroom so that it might remain as an inspiration to all who passed amongst them. *(Plate 1)*

Mr George Nicholls, ex-MP, was the principle speaker on Saturday, 24 and Sunday, **25 April**, at the 8th anniversary of the Raunds Brotherhood. On Saturday, an excellent address was given by Mr Nicholls on "Real social service: Who is doing it?" The next day he preached at the Wesleyan Church at both the morning and evening services and also addressed the men's afternoon meeting.

Sunday, 25 April, Allied troops land at Helles and Anzac Coves.

And it wasn't just in the trenches that vermin was rife as a Wollaston shoe manufacturer claimed that he had killed a rat at Chester House which measured 21 inches from its nose to the end of its tail!

The death of Mr Amos Fisher took place on Monday, **26 April**, he had been ill for some time. Married twice, he left a widow and a son by his first wife. He was for many years an overseer and inspector under the Lighting Act during the old days of parish government. One of the first members of the Parish Council, he was also a Guardian of the poor for 20 years. His funeral took place on Thursday, 29 April, the service at the Wesleyan Church being conducted by the Rev J Burrows. The coffin was borne to the grave by eight of the deceased's tenants.

Officers, men and the band of the 2nd/4th Battalion, Northamptonshire Regiment, to the number of 140, who, under the command of Lt Col Willoughby, were marching from Peterborough to Northampton, arrived at Raunds at about 12 noon on Tuesday, **27 April**. They paraded the principle streets and at 1 o'clock, a recruiting meeting was held on The Square, presided over by Mr J Adams, CC.

Addresses were given by Lt Col Willoughby and Capt the Rev Basil Stothert of Thrapston, a retired Army chaplain. The men were afterwards entertained to refreshments, cigars and cigarettes by Mr J Adams. By way of Stanwick, the men then marched to Higham Ferrers. About half a score of new recruits passed the medical officer's examination at noon, and others were waiting their turn.

While the regiment were in town, a nasty accident happened to 10 year old Ernest Marshall. As he carried another boy on his back near the Coffee Tavern, he slipped off the edge of the causeway and completely dislocated his hip joint. He was carried to Dr Mackenzie's surgery and after attention, he was taken home.

At the meeting of the Church of England School managers that evening, Miss Hall's appointment in the Infants Department was confirmed, her starting day to be 1 May. She was in fact already working in the school as a supply teacher as her old school had closed.

The Rushden Echo of Friday, **30 April**, ran a story headlined "Raunds Soldier a Prisoner – News at Last of Pte **Cecil Burton (32)** – Now in Germany". It continued that "with great pleasure we learn that Pte Burton (Raunds), 8645, 1ˢᵗ Northants Regt, is not killed but is a prisoner of war in Germany. We wish Pte Burton a safe return and hope the life he is now living will not be detrimental to his general well-being. It is still unknown at which camp he is kept, as he has not written yet – at least, his letters have not yet been received".

Alas, just as the optimistic report on Pte **Ernest Wood 134)** a few weeks earlier, this news would again prove to be untrue, for both had perished on 24 October 1914. However, Cecil's mother could not accept his fate for certain until 1921, when the last POW's returned home and her son was not among them.

* * * * * * * * * * * * * * * * * * * *

Don't forget that hundreds of Our Brave Boys at the front have died from wounds
And many from Blood Poisoning and Lockjaw.
Now we know for a fact that NO ONE would die from blood poisoning if they
Could only have their wounds dressed in
"Mrs Noble's Cure-All Ointment"
The 7½d box is the proper size to take in the trenches
Obtainable from J Gant, Chemist, Raunds or
Mrs Noble, Crumpsall, Manchester

Have you a relative fighting in the Great War?
If so you are entitled to wear our badge.
It is given only to women who have relatives serving.
So send 1s-0d for the certificate, badge, and membership in the
"Women's Branch, National Service"

W H Spicer
Plumber, Glazier, Gas Fitter & General House Decorator
Thorpe Street, Raunds

My Tired Feet Ached for "TIZ"
How glorious, how grand "TIZ" makes tired, swollen, sore, perspiring feet feel,
Just couldn't wait to take my hat off!

* * * * * * * * * * * * * * * * * * * *

MAY – This month's Parish Magazine again carried a list of additions to the Parochial Roll of Honour with **Roland Archer (15)**, Frederick Chambers, William Coles, William Hartwell, Cecil Matson, James Moules and Harry Reynolds joining the roll of local men serving with the Colours.

The plans for the Garden Fete were well advanced with the date planned as Saturday, 12 June. Stalls already promised were: St Mary's Guild, Mother's Union, Refreshments, Jumble, Sweets and Flowers plus amusements, by way of Skittles and Kicking the Football. The teachers and children had undertaken to give a Musical Operetta, which promised to be very pretty. Gifts for the Jumble Stall were requested to be sent to the Vicarage and fruit or flowers (especially pot flowers) would be most acceptable for the Flower stall.

In his "Thoughts for the Month", the Vicar observed that "Probably all of us feel we do need, just now, to pray for our land and men and allies, and also for good crops – for never before has this all come with such intensity as this year".

May Day saw a charming group of girls from the factory of Messrs Horrell and Sons, Army contractors, parading the town making a collection to buy stationery, chocolate, and cigarettes for the Raunds and Stanwick soldiers at the front. Dressed in costume and by their admirable singing of the National Anthems of the Allies, the dainty damsels succeeded in collecting £8-7s-0d with which to buy cheer for the men in the trenches. The whole affair was organised by the Misses I and F Adams, H and M Munds, and May Williamson. *(Plate Front Cover)*

Friday, 7 May, the "Lusitania" is sunk.

On the day that the world was shocked by the loss of the famous ocean liner, the Thrapston & Raunds Journal printed "a host of interesting local pictures including a splendid photograph of the Raunds girls who paraded the streets on May Day collecting for the local soldiers in the trenches".

At a meeting of the Old Age Pensions Committee, the chairman asked whether in the present demand for labour, supply could not be increased by allowing, during the period of the war, pensioners who were able to work, to do so to earn more than 5s-0d per week (the full rate pension). Adding that it was in many cases, not because they were unable to, but because there had not been a demand for them.

The newspapers of Saturday, **8 May**, all carried headlines such as "Dastardly Deed – "Lusitania" Sunk by German Pirates – Loss of 1,500 Lives Feared – Vessel Sank in 20 Minutes!", however, tomorrow an event would occur on the Western Front that would touch more local lives than these terrible events at sea.

Sunday, 9 May, the Battle of Aubers Ridge, six Raunds and Stanwick men killed.

James Brawn (26), William Webb Chambers (33), William Ernest Richards (98), killed in action.

Monday, 10 May, Ernest Parker (86), killed in action.

The first news of the local losses at Aubers Ridge came via a letter sent by Private **Ernest Stringer (112)**, "E" Company, 2nd Northamptons, to his mother, asking her to break the news to Mrs Richards of Hill Street, that her son, Private **(William) Ernest Richards (98)**, of the same company, had died from his wounds received on the 9 May. Both Private Richards and Stringer had previously been wounded, and invalided home together before being sent back to the front.

The story stated that Private Richards was the first Raunds man whose death at the front had been definitely confirmed. It would later emerge that seven of the town's men had already died before the fateful action at Aubers Ridge.

At the Bedfordshire and Northamptonshire District Wesleyan Synod on Wednesday, **12 May**, Mr George Lee was re-elected as one of the seven lay representatives of the District to the Annual Conference.

Private J A Cuthbert's letter to Dr Mackenzie appeared in the local press this week. The soldier, from "C" Company of the 1st Northamptons, thanked the good doctor for a parcel of cigarettes, chocolate etc which had arrived safely in the trenches a few days earlier. He said he was glad to hear of more men from the old town entering the war adding that he had seen some awful sights since arriving in France in August 1914. In his opinion "if our young men in England who have not yet come to the call could see what I have and still resist the call, then they are not Englishmen!" He closed with the view that they would "soon clear the dirty dogs out of the way as our artillery now has the same superiority over them as they had over us at the beginning of the war". In a "PS", **Percy Smith (105)** sent his thanks "for his fags".

Friday, 14 May, the Second Battle of Ypres ends, the BEF casualties are triple that of the Germans.

As the anger continued to rise in the wake of the sinking of the "Lusitania", the editorial in the Rushden Echo was very typical of the day: "By the carefully planned sinking of the famous Atlantic liner, the 'Lusitania', with 2,160 souls on board, the Germans have committed a crime absolutely unparalleled in the history of the world. The civilised nations of the world are horror-stricken at a crime so foul, so appalling, that it shall never be effaced from the memory of man, and the German nation can henceforth expect nothing from the world except the treatment rightly given to vipers!"

Upwards of 60 friends and relatives of Mr and Mrs Thomas Pentelow of Hill Street, gathered in the Wesleyan Schoolrooms on Saturday, **15 May**, for a meat tea to celebrate the couple's Golden Wedding. They had married at Raunds Church on 11 May 1865 and subsequently had eight children, five of whom still lived in Raunds, one son lived in Kettering, one daughter in Finedon and one daughter in Adelaide, South Australia ......

They now also had 25 grand-children and one great-grandchild. Mr Pentelow had started work when he was 9, being employed by Messrs W Nichols and Son for over 54 years.

Another account of the Aubers Ridge battle appeared on Monday, **17 May**. Private W Nunley, writing to his sister in Thorpe Street from his bed at the 2nd Northern Hospital, Leeds, reassured her that he was getting on fine now he had arrived back in England. In a brief description of his experience he said "We had the order to charge the German trenches at about 8am. I had only got about 100 yards when I fell to the ground, being shot through the left thigh. We were trying to take a village called Fromelles, and I can tell you, it was hell, our boys fell like ninepins. I lay out in the open for about 3 hours, expecting every moment to be shot again, when 2 young men of the RAMC came and picked me up and carried me into our trench."

The Urban Council considered a suggestion from the police at their meeting tonight, that "In the case of a Zeppelin raid during working hours, Messrs R Coggins and Son be asked to allow their whistle to be blown in some distinctive manner, and in the case of a raid at any other time, that the Vicar be asked to allow the big church bell to be rung". Although some members thought an attack was so unlikely and therefore it was unnecessary to take any steps, the motion was carried to accept the constabulary's initiative.

The medical officer, Dr Mackenzie, reported one case of scarlatina and a few of mild measles during April. Five deaths and three births were registered.

The Sanitary Committee advised that they had decided not to proceed with the suggestion for a Joint Isolation Hospital for the district.

The Cemetery Committee reported that two estimates had been received for the laying out of the ground, one of £1,525 and one of £1,402-10s-0d. The second had been accepted and it was now proposed to request a loan of £1,500 from the Local Government Board.

The assembly also heard that the County Council had agreed to provide a contribution towards the maintenance of the district road from Raunds Railway Station to the parish boundary with Stanwick. The sum to be received would be between £275 and £300 per annum.

At the Petty Sessions on Tuesday, **18 May**, a Raunds shoehand was summoned by the landlady of the "Robin Hood Inn" for wilful damage to a glass door. The court heard that the defendant threw a bottle through the window after being asked to leave for using bad language. Found guilty, and having previously committed a similar offence, he was fined £1 plus 4s-0d costs and ordered to pay for the damage.

Two householders were also summoned to the same hearing for not sending their children to school. One was fined 2s-6d and the other 5s-0d.

Meanwhile, Mrs Clark, landlady of the "George and Dragon", died today after a long battle against diabetes.

The chairman (the Vicar) of the Church of England Schools managers called a special meeting on Thursday, **20 May**, to consider the conduct of a Midland Road mother in the Infants Department that morning. The woman had been notified by the headmistress that she had had no right to take her child away from the playground on Tuesday, 18 May, afternoon without leave from the headmistress. She had come to the school this morning and made a scene and was abusive. After hearing the headmistress' side, the managers summoned the woman to the meeting to explain her actions. She denied everything except using bad language! However, her written apology was accepted and was to be read by the Vicar at assembly in the Infants Department the following morning.

Loyal celebrations of Empire Day took place on Friday afternoon, **21 May**, at the Council School when it closed for the Whitsuntide recess. The Mixed and Infants Departments gathered in the hall for a short concert of songs and recitations. The programme included the tableau "Britain and her colonies", the Britannic song "Red, White and Blue", a patriotic recitation by Jack Hall and Kathleen Eady, and the Empire song "God bless our native land". After the National Anthem, three hearty cheers for "The Empire" were led by the teachers and managers.

The Baptist Sunday School celebrated its anniversary on Sunday, **23 May**, when Pastor White from London, delivered the sermons.

The following day heralded the start of the Sunday School Treat season and both the Baptist and Wesleyans held their annual shindigs. For the Baptists, they indulged in a public tea followed by "outdoor amusements" held in a field made available by Mr A Camozzi. The Wesleyans meanwhile, staged a much larger event. A procession of about 380 marched through the town singing hymns, led by the Raunds Temperance Silver Prize Band. Tea was taken at 3 o'clock, followed by sports and games at Carter Hill field, kindly lent by Mr Walt Denton. The band then played for dancing until 9pm.

Primitive Methodist Sunday scholars were treated to something slightly different on Whit Tuesday, **25 May**. They were taken on a ride around by Chelveston to Hargrave. There they were served tea at the Rectory, the home of the Rev F C Boultbee.

"In the Dardanelles", Friday, **28 May**, optimistically reported how more allied troops had been landed on the peninsular and fortified positions won. The true position, however, was slightly different!

And as men continued to fight and die on several war fronts, and despite the very cold weather, the annual treat of the children belonging to members of the Raunds Distributive Co-Operative Society took place on Saturday, **29 May** …..

About 1,000 youngsters assembled at the bottom of Wellington Road and processed to The Square led by the Raunds Temperance Silver Prize Band, stopping at intervals for songs sung by the children.

Boys at the Council School, girls at the Wesleyan School and helpers, the band and Co-Operative committee at the Temperance Hall were then provided with tea. Afterwards, everyone transferred to a field in Thorpe Street, owned by the Co-Op, for a programme of sports for which the judges were Messrs W Agutter, W Woolston and W Lawrence, and the starter, Mr John Askham. An evening dance until dusk, to the music of the Temperance Band, concluded the event.

Monday, 31 May, the first Zeppelin raids on London.

* * * * * * * * * * * * * * * * * * *

A large stock of Accounts Books, Ledgers, Cash Books,
& all kinds of Business Stationery
FW March
17 High Street, Raunds

"He loved her with a devouring affection, she woman-like sought after him,
Her capture of him was his downfall, for he died cracked."
It is less trouble, if less romantic, to use
KEATING'S POWDER
Kills Bugs, Fleas, Flies, Moths, Beetles, and all Insects
In Tins, only 3d, 6d & 1s-0d, Bellows, 9d
Of all Chemists and Grocers — Send your soldier boy a tin

Zeppelins! Bombs!
Aerial risks covered by the Caledonian Insurance Company
The insurance being effected with Lloyds Underwriters
Local Agent — A Bailey, Manor Street, Raunds
For 2s-6d you are covered for 12 months to the value of £100
On household furniture etc in private dwelling-houses.

New Testaments at 1d each for the soldiers etc at cost price.
Small in size, clearly printed, can be sent to the front in quantities.
"Echo" office, 5 Park Road, Rushden. Orders by post executed.

* * * * * * * * * * * * * * * * * * *

JUNE – The Vicar reported that the "Egg Service", held on Whit Sunday afternoon for the wounded soldiers had been a great success. 746 eggs had been given and he hoped that Mr Potter (the C of E School headmaster) would be able to send each week eggs from the children in the Day School. He invited any "grown ups" who wished to join the children to do so. The egg box would be sent off on Monday evenings and as the box had spaces for 400 eggs, he hoped to send it full every week. He added that over 300,000 new laid eggs were wanted each week for the wounded soldiers.

The Vicar referred to the forthcoming Garden Fete, promising that the children's operetta "Princess Vespida" should be a real treat. Advance tickets could now be obtained to make sure of a seat in case of a crowd. The Raunds Temperance Silver Band would also be rendering selections.

Finally, he noted that the Parochial Roll of Honour of local men serving was hopefully now accurate and a copy was enclosed with this month's Parish Magazine. Any additions or corrections were to be sent to him.

On May Day, the girls from Messrs J Horrell and Sons boot factory had toured the streets collecting money for the town's soldiers at the front, and 34 parcels had been sent out catering for both smokers and non-smokers with tobacco and cigarettes or chocolate as well as milk, cocoa, sugar, carbolic soap and stationery.

Now the newspapers of early June reported that thank you letters were arriving, amongst the writers were Sergeant J Harris, Lance Corporal J W Vorley, Privates John W Bland, S Cuthbert, A Wilkins, W Twelftree, G H Hall, **P Smith (105)**, L Hodson, Walter Richardson, **A Burton (31)**, S Percival, **E Stringer (112)**, F Walden, H York, Harry Moules and R Farrer, Gunner T Askham, and Bombardier L Eady (erroneously "promoted" to Brigadier!). Several of the correspondents referred to the sad deaths of **Ernest Richards (98)**, and Tom Craven and the Felce brothers of Stanwick. Another spoke of the surprise of meeting **Harry Hall (59)** of the Royal Flying Corps, another Raunds boy destined to die.

With many local men now in the Colours, there was a boom in the job market at home, and this week the "situation vacant" columns advertised up to 50 vacancies in the shoe trade and at least 40 in other professions with two Raunds firms seeking new blood:

"Wanted – Men for edge sorting & bench, and smart youths for heel-paring & scouring, also a youth for tacking up and boys leaving school, constant employment and the best wages, Neal & Gates"

"Wanted – First class edge trimmer and also a man for benchwork, E W Stanley, Wellington Works"

A Farewell Service was held at the Baptist Chapel on Sunday, **6 June**, when the congregation said "Goodbye" to Pastor S Gray, prior to his departure for America.

On Monday, **7 June**, as the losses at Aubers Ridge were still being assessed, the entry of "2nd Battalion, Northamptonshire Regiment: Killed – **Richards**, 9581, **W E**" (98), was officially added to the local "Roll of Honour".

This evening, the headmaster of the National School sent off another 240 eggs to the Central Office, Harrods, London, for distribution to wounded soldiers.

In another despatch, Dr Mackenzie was able to forward to the 6th Gordons and 1st Northamptons at the front, 2,000 Woodbines, 250 other cigarettes, 100 pencils, 300 postcards and other stationery, also whistles, mouth organs, magazines and books. All of these delights being purchased with cash collected by two Raunds boys, Stanley Archer and Tom Nunley, who were both under 13 years old.

On Tuesday, **8 June**, the Raunds Hospital Week Fund Committee, engaged in organising the Garden Fete to be held in the Sports Field on Saturday, 19 June, invited tenders for the Ice Cream and Sweet & Fruit stalls. All applications were to be sent to Mr W F Corby.

"The Raunds Hotel & Coffee Tavern Company is seeking a man and wife as managers. Particulars from the secretary at 17 Lawson Street"

An accident occurred on Wednesday, **9 June**, when James Sutton, of Newtown, whilst getting over a fence on his way home from work, fell heavily and sustained a serious compound fracture of the shoulder joint.

The Raunds District Old Age Pensions Sub-Committee met at the Temperance Hall when six new claims were considered. Three were from Raunds, with one each from Burton Latimer, Cranford and Denford. Five of these were allowed, but the sixth was dismissed as the claimant would not be 70 until May 1916.

At the Conservative Club, the committee announced that they had received 24 applications for the steward's job and that they had appointed Mr G E Beale, who was currently manager of the Coffee Tavern.

Owing to the spread of measles in the Infants Department of the Council School, the medical officer, Dr Mackenzie, recommended its closure until 28 June. Recent attendances had been affected by up to 57%.

An article entitled "No News of Missing Raunds Soldier" appeared on Thursday, **10 June**. It was based on a letter dated 3 June 1915, from the prolific Private **A Burton (31)**, 1st Northamptons, to the parents of Private **W W Chambers (33)**, in response to an open letter they had sent to his battalion in the trenches. He says that "I have made enquiries about your son, No. 13216, and I am sorry to say that he is still missing. I am afraid it is the same as Barritt*, but to tell you the truth it is very doubtful if he is alive, as I don't think they took any prisoners that day. They even shot our wounded that made the slightest movement, they are a dirty lot, and I wish they were all wiped out" ……

William Webb Chambers was eventually listed as "missing, presumed killed" at Aubers Ridge, he has no known grave. *Barritt is probably Private Arthur Barritt, the brother of **Oliver John Barritt (21)**. He too was lost on 9 May 1915.

At the Peterborough Bankruptcy Court, a former butcher of Raunds applied for discharge from bankruptcy. The Official Receiver said that a first and final dividend had been paid and that the debtor's conduct during the proceedings had been satisfactory. The debtor said that he was not expecting to come into any money or had thought of starting in business again. His current liabilities were said to be £220 of which £140 was owing to money lenders. The Official Receiver said that if the debtor had only filed his petition instead of going to money lenders he would have been able to pay up. The debtor said that it was quite likely he would be going to war very soon. The Judge observed that it was the first time he had heard that view put before him in a petition for discharge from bankruptcy (all present laughed), but thought that he would go to fight, whether he received a discharge or not! The debtor's discharge was suspended for 2 years.

And Mr John Bass, for the Thrapston Board of Guardians, admitted today that the tender from Mr Rixon for bread for the Board's Cottage Home at Raunds was in fact 6½d per 4lb loaf, not 5d as had been previously declared.

"Local Names in Casualty Lists – 1st Northamptons – Heavy Losses": Another Aubers Ridge victim was added to the "Roll of Honour", that of **Brawn, J T (26)**.

The Garden Fete in aid of the Church of England Schools building fund took place on Saturday, **12 June**, in the grounds of the Vicarage. The stalls were: Refreshments, St Mary's Guild, Mothers' Union, work, jumble, flower and sweets.

The children of the Church schools gave 2 performances of the children's operetta "Princess Vespida". The audience included, by invitation, the wounded soldiers from the Higham Ferrers VAD Hospital and the Belgian refugees from Thorpe House, the soldiers being highly amused by some portions of the presentation.

The usual stage and scenery were dispensed with and in their stead an exceedingly pretty background of branches and foliage had been prepared by the Vicar, the Rev C C Aldred, the Curate, the Rev W S Bethway and their helpers. The children were very tastefully dressed as different characters – grasshoppers, frogs, a toad, wasps, witches, fairies, and elves. The dresses and weapons were made by the teachers and children, with the help of a few kind friends.

About 100 children took part, the principle characters being: "Fairy Queen", Mabel Bugby; "Rosebud", Doris Lawrence; "Hyacinth", Doreen Clarke; "Daffodil", Kitty Kirk; "Peachblossom", Marion Fisher; "Puck", Nelson Clarke; "Witches", Ethel Roberts, May Tidbury & Elsie Rooksby; "Wasp Princess", Doris Chambers; "Princess Vespidiana", Doris Grocott; "Vespious", Olive Scrivener; "Waspidus", Mary Finding; "Frogs", Arthur Mayes, Francis Nash, Edward Gates & Ralph Turney; "Toad", Ivor Basford; ……

"Grasshoppers" – "King", Arthur Lawrence; "Queen", Winifred Feary; "Decticus", Kenneth Spicer; "Thamnatrizon", Fred Sanders; and "Sir Tophilus", Arthur Chambers.

The infants took part in two dances performed by elves and butterflies. Miss M Yorke was the pianist and the original wasp and witches dances were the work of Mrs Ash.

The Raunds Temperance Silver Band marched to the grounds previous to the performance and played selections during the afternoon and for dancing from eight o'clock until dusk. The gross takings amounted to over £47.

A meeting under the auspices of the National Union of Railwaymen and the National Agricultural Labourers Union was held on The Square on Sunday, **13 June**. Addresses were given by Mr Walter Hall, NUR and Mr James Lunnon, NALU. Mr E Batchelor presided.

In the evening, the Raunds Temperance Silver Band gave a concert in the grounds of "The Crossways" in aid of band funds.

The Annual Convention of the Raunds Wesleyan Circuit was held in the Wesleyan Church on Monday, **14 June**. The Rev E Aldom French of Upper Tooting, London, gave a forceful sermon in the afternoon. This was followed by tea at 5pm at which more than 120 sat down. At 6.15 an organ recital was given by Mr J W Hall and a solo, "When I survey the wondrous Cross", was rendered by Mrs J W Hall. At 7pm a meeting was held, Mr John Clark of Rushden presided. A solo, "Guide me to the light", was sung by Mrs J W Hall and Mr French gave an account of his mission work. The proceeds amounted to over £15.

Another plea for information on their son, Private **William Webb Chambers (33)**, by his parents appeared in the local press this week accompanied by his photograph under the headline "Raunds Soldier Missing – The Battle of Aubers Ridge". This would be repeated for several more weeks.

On Tuesday, **15 June**, another letter from the front regarding the possible fate of Private **W W Chambers (33)** was printed. The writer was Lance Corporal C Morris of Stanwick, who said to the missing man's parents "It was a very sad day for us, as we had had to make a charge and we lost a lot of men. There were only two men left in his platoon when we came out at night. We lost about 650 killed and wounded, so you can see what we had to go through, and I think he was with those killed. I think that he is dead, for he would have written to let me know how he was getting on. Although my house is at Stanwick, I used to spend most of my time at Rushden, I only wish that I was there again".

At the Thrapston Police Court that afternoon, Mr Mitchell, cinema licensee, applied for the transfer of his current licence from the existing building in Grove Street (to become a boot factory for Mr Nicholls) to another old factory nearby. The case was adjourned while inspection of the new premises took place.

More eggs were despatched today by Mr F A Potter, headmaster of the Council School, when 136 went oeuf to the central depot of the National Egg Collection for Wounded Soldiers.

The members of the Women's Adult School decided at their meeting on Wednesday, **16 June**, to each make a garment for the refugees in France.

And yet another letter from Private **Arthur Burton (31)** was published today, this time to Mr Albert Barritt of Beech Hill, the brother of Private Arthur Barritt (and Private **Oliver J Barritt (21)**). Again concerning events at Aubers Ridge, he mentioned recalling a conversation with Albert at Kettering the previous Christmas when they talked of his brother at the front. He went on to say that as soldiers they often used to have a joke together, and that they were talking only a few minutes before the fateful charge, when Private Barritt was in high spirits. The family were natives of Hannington, near Kettering, but Arthur's two brothers, Albert and Oliver, had subsequently moved to and worked in Raunds.

It was announced on Thursday, **17 June**, that among the boot contracts recently placed by the Army were ones with R Coggins & Son and Tebbutt & Hall Bros.

The Council School managers decided on Friday, **18 June**, that the whole school should be disinfected prior to re-opening after the measles epidemic. It was also determined that the summer holiday be fixed so that older children "might be useful in the harvest field". Finally, in the light of headmaster L G H Lee's promotion in France, the managers agreed "to forward their congratulations".

It was "Hospital Week" in Raunds culminating in the annual parade and sports day on Saturday, **19 June**. Local opinion was that the town "possessed an excellent record for its enthusiastic efforts on behalf of the Northampton Hospital" and this year fully maintained its reputation. The large and representative committee carried out the arrangements with characteristic thoroughness aided by no lack of willing helpers. Moreover, the ladies of the town again undertook a "Rose Day" in which they were very successful.

The procession, including numerous parties of fancy dress competitors, formed at about two o'clock in the grounds of "The Crossways", the residence of Mr E A Milligan, JP, in beautiful weather. The order of parade was: the Raunds Temperance Silver Prize Band; members of the Raunds Urban District Council; representatives of neighbouring Hospital Week Fund Committees; tradesmen and other residents of the town; the friendly societies: Foresters "Rose of Sharon", Free Gardeners, Boot & Shoe Operatives, Raunds Tradesmen's Club, Rechabites and Raunds Cottage; Belgian refugees, with emblematical representation; fancy dress competitors and members of Raunds and other Fire Brigades in uniform. *(Plate 12)*

The route followed was Wellington Road, Grove Street, Thorpe Street, Primrose Hill, Clare Street, Lawson Street, Hill Street, to The Square, where the total concourse numbered nearly 3,000 and a selection was played by the band ......

It then proceeded by way of High Street, Bridge Street, Rotton Row, North Street, High Street, Brook Street, to the grounds of "The Hall", kindly placed at the disposal of the committee by Mrs Coggins. There, the opening ceremony was carried out by Sir Ryland Adkins, MP, ably supported by Sir Charles Knightley.

Over 70 entered the various classes in the fancy dress competiton, the winners being: Individual Children – W Cyril Betts, (3s-0d); Children's Group – Mabel Bugby's party of 10, (3s-0d); Adult get-up – Fred Bugby, 7s-6d); Comic Group – H Allen, (7s-6d); National or Artistic Group – Florrie Pentelow and party, (7s-6d).

Sports winners were: 100 Yards Flat, boys 10-15 years – S D Yorke, (6s-0d); 120 Yards Flat Handicap, open – Victor Roberts, (15s-0d); Cycle Musical Chair Race – J Ball, (5s-0d); 120 Yards Obstacle Race – T Bettles, (10s-0d); Skittle Handicap – T Mumford.

Kettering Clothing Society Fire Brigade won the Hose Cart Drill in a time of 26.3 seconds, for which they received the Challenge Cup, £1 prize money and a silver medal for each member.

A torchlight procession through the town, starting from the sports field, closed the most successful proceedings arousing great interest. The total receipts exceeded £100, which, after the deduction of expenses, resulted in a profit of over £80.

On Sunday, **20 June**, the employees of the Raunds Distributive Co-Operative Society went to Oxford by motor omnibus for their annual summer outing. The college gardens at this time of the year were said to "present a picture most beautiful to behold". The party arrived home at around midnight.

Mr John Bunyan of Peterborough, Provincial Grandmaster of the Peterborough District of Oddfellows, was the subject of a fine photograph and biography in this year's "Oddfellows" magazine. Brother Bunyan was born in Raunds in 1867 and went to Peterborough in 1874.

At the Urban Council meeting of Monday, **21 June**, the surveyor (Mr Yorke) reported that the tar painting of the streets had begun and suggested that it be continued right through the town. The chairman favoured this so that no section of ratepayers would have cause to complain. Mr G E Smith said the decision was to cover that section of the road covered by the buses. A move that the work be completed was carried on division.

The Highway Committee recommended that the lighting for the season commence on August 28, that the lamps be put out at 10pm, that upon the nights intervening between the first quarter and full moon lamps be not lit, that tenders be invited for the two men to light and clean the street lamps for the same districts as last year. Opponents to the proposed lighting timetable pointed out that in the past it had been pitch black on some nights there should have been a moon, so felt it a step backwards. However, those in favour said that economy needed to be practiced and all of the recommended suggestions were carried after discussion.

The medical officer, Dr Mackenzie, reported that three deaths and six births were registered in the town during May. He also advised that the current epidemic of measles had necessitated the closing of the Council Schools.

The Local Government Board had previously intimated to the council by letter that they were prepared to "at once" consider an application for a loan for the cemetery if the council desired it, but that sanction would not be given at present unless "urgent necessity could be shown". At tonight's meeting, the assembly resolved to press the matter forward as one of urgent necessity.

Another resolution passed was the congratulating of Councillor Harold Lee on his promotion to the rank of sergeant.

The question of air raid warnings arose again and both the Vicar and R Coggins & Son had replied to requests for assistance. The Vicar confirmed that he would be willing to ring the Parish Church's big and little bells at the same time and proposed "test rings" during next Thursday and Friday's dinner hour. And although R Coggins also indicated their willingness to help, they felt their whistle could not be relied upon, so it was agreed to proceed with just the church bells.

Finally, a plan for the conversion of a portion of a disused factory in Grove Street into a "picture palace" was provisionally approved by the Sanitary Committee.

And today it was announced that a proposed amalgamation of the National Union of Boot & Shoe Operatives and the Amalgamated Society of Boot & Shoe Makers had been agreed, subject to ratification of the respective members.

Yet more eggs for wounded soldiers were despatched on Tuesday, **22 June**. The 138 sent off today making a total of 561 in the past 3 weeks.

Another name was added to the local Roll of Honour of those Northamptons now officially classified as "missing" after the Battle of Aubers Ridge – **Chambers**, 13216, **W W (33).**

"Rain At Last" reported the local press as the first rain fell in the district for 37 days, although only very small amounts fell in some areas.

There was good news for housewives on Friday, **25 June**, when the Thrapston, Raunds and Oundle district of bakers announced a reduction in the price of a 4lb loaf from 8d to 7^1/2d.

But there was disappointment for residents looking forward to seeing the 1st/4th Battalion of the Northamptonshire Regiment march through the town on Tuesday, **29 June**. Owing to the measles outbreak, the visit was cancelled and the town bypassed by the boys in khaki.

At the weekly Thrapston Market, the prices were: butter at 1s-2d per pound, eggs at 2s-0d per score, beef at 7s-4d to 7s-6d per stone, mutton at 7s-0d to 7s-2d per stone, and pork at 9s-6d to 10s-0d per stone.

Also today it was announced that all schools in the town were to be closed for a further fortnight owing to the measles epidemic.

The month closed with a story of a Raunds lady's nephew serving with the Australian contingent in Egypt. Mrs E J Whitney's nephew, Ernest Lucas, was from Derby, Tasmania. He had written to his aunt from his training camp saying that he had recently been in hospital for five weeks suffering from influenza. Although there were beautiful buildings to see, it was a country where one needed plenty of money as everything was very dear. He had visited Turkish prisoners and wounded Indian soldiers and observed that the former were a rough-looking crowd but the latter were very pleased to see their Australian visitors. Of the Tommies, he said they were great chums, coming out on Sundays to tea, but felt sorry that they were only paid 1s-0d a day compared to the 6s-0d a day of the Australians.

* *

* * * * * * * * * * * * * * * * * * * *

PROMINENT CITIZENS

1) Mrs G Bass, a staunch temperance worker, who became an octogenarian in April 1915.

2) Mr Charles Groom, a founder of the Raunds Co-Operative Society, who died in August 1915.

3) Mr Jesse Shelmerdine, the former Church of England School headmaster, appointed a Justice of the Peace in December 1915.

4) The Rev E Percy Blackburn, appointed Wesleyan Methodist Superintendent Minister in September 1916.

(All Kettering Leader)

5) Raunds Athletic Football Club, 1913-14, including
John Henry Bamford (19), back row, 4th right.
(Vorley/SJB)

6) St Mary's Vestry Class, 1914 – many of these boys would soon find
themselves wearing khaki, and at least three would not survive the war.
(Vorley/SJB)

7) The new Council Schools in Park Street, 1914. Mr L G Harold Lee was the first headmaster. (Vorley/SJB)

8) Raunds Parish Church made from matchsticks by Horace Allen, May 1914. (Vorley/Kettering Leader)

9) A chorus line from the 1914 Church Pageant. (Vorley/SJB)

10) The Belgian refugees arrive, November 1914. (Sharpe/Kettering Leader)

11) A Co-Operative Society window display of neckwear patriotically embellished with literature, photographs and flags of the Allies, c1915. (Vorley/SJB)

12) The Belgian refugees in costume at the 1915 Hospital Week Demonstration. (Clarkson/Kettering Leader)

13) Five generations of the Stubbs family: Ann, 92 (centre); son Henry, 68 (left); grandson William, 45 (right); great-grandson Corporal John Henry, 25 (back); and great-great-grandson John, 2 days (baby), October 1915. (Kettering Leader)

14) The Vicarage and grounds, the scene of many Church fetes, c1916. (Vorley/SJB)

15) The Rt Hon Arthur Henderson, front row centre, and party at the 1916 Hospital Week Demonstration. (Kettering Leader)

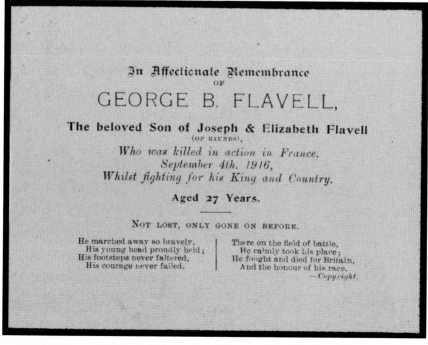

In Affectionate Remembrance
OF
GEORGE B. FLAVELL,

The beloved Son of Joseph & Elizabeth Flavell
(OF RAUNDS),

Who was killed in action in France,
September 4th. 1916,
Whilst fighting for his King and Country.

Aged 27 Years.

NOT LOST, ONLY GONE ON BEFORE.

He marched away so bravely,
His young head proudly held;
His footsteps never faltered,
His courage never failed.

There on the field of battle,
He calmly took his place;
He fought and died for Britain,
And the honour of his race.
—*Copyright.*

16) A Memorial Card dedicated to **George Benjamin Flavell (51)**, September 1916. (Courtesy of Kevin Varty)

17) "Forget-Me-Not" Day collectors, September 1916.
(Clarkson/Kettering Leader)

Front Row, l to r: Ivy Desborough, Grace Hall, Rose Sale, Elsie Weekley, Ivy Richards, & Kate Shrives. *Second Row:* Kate Whiteman, Edna Burton, Winnie Smith, Nellie Walters, Kathleen Richards, Violet Bunting, Gertrude Gilbert, Doris Lawrence, Edith Smith, & Ada Wade. *Third Row:* Minnie Hodson, Elsie Lawrence, Emily Butler, Doris Foster, Lillie Lawrence, Doris Bunting, Alice Cuthbert, Ethel Eaton, & Ida Adams. *Back Row:* Nellie Cuthbert, Ada Nunley, Doris Hodson, & Amy Burton.

18) The "Dodgers Comic Band" in one of their many guises, c1916. (Vorley/SJB)

19) The Church of England Upper School "Pierettes", who won 2nd prize in the fancy dress competition at the 1916 Red Cross Flag Day & Sports.
(Clarkson/Kettering Leader)
Left to Right: Ethel Roberts, Kitty Kirk, May Cuthbert, Edna Marriott, May Tidbury, Mary Finding, Winnie Barker, Edith Green, Olive Scrivener, & Rose Stringer.

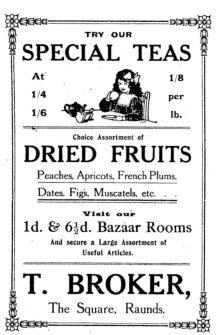
20) Advertisements from the 1915 "Raunds Almanack & Business Directory"

21) Trooper Frederick Kilborn,
Lifeguards, November 1914.

22) Sergeant Hall, 1st Northamptons,
November 1914

Both were wounded in the first few months of the war.

23) Privates Frederick Shrives,
Edgar Ellingham (47), &
Sydney Kilborn, new recruits for
the Royal Army Medical Corps,
July 1915.

24)   Sergeant Frederick Gates,
6th Northamptons, awarded the
Military Medal in November 1916.

(All Kettering Leader)

7 – July to September 1915

Raunds Feast and the "Royal Edward".

JULY – The Vicar began his monthly notes with a look back at the Garden Fete held in June, "on an ideal day and proving to be a great success" he observed. He thanked everyone who put in such hard work, especially the teachers and children whose efforts made the operetta "such a very pleasing entertainment." The stalls and sideshows had done an excellent trade and very nearly cleared everything out, the band played to an appreciative audience and a large number of dancers, and total takings on the day amounted to £41-12s-4d.

Sunday, 4 July, would be the Dedication Festival at the church. However, the Childrens Services had been cancelled owing to the Day Schools being closed for measles although the children were still to assemble in the school playground at 1.30pm to receive their tickets for the Sunday School Treat on Saturday, 10 July. The children were asked to bring eggs instead of the usual flowers, fruit or toys, so they could be sent to the wounded soldiers.

Arrangements for the Sunday School Treat were that tea would be held in the open air if possible. The public tea at the schools would be at 4pm, the Vicarage grounds would open to the public at 5pm, entrance 2d, the children's sports would commence at 5pm, with the Vestry Class Marathon at 7pm. The Raunds Temperance Band would be playing for dancing on the lawn afterwards.

Thanks were extended to Mrs Coggins for the gift of a new carpet for the pulpit. New hassocks had been bought for the Church but more were needed, or rather the money to buy them. And 650 eggs had been sent from the Day Schools during June and it was hoped that the schools would re-open at 9am on Monday, 12 July, the message being "Remember the Eggs".

Finally, 13 more names had been added to the Parochial Roll of Honour of men serving: Sidney Archer, **John Ashby (16)**, George Bottoms, Joseph Chambers, Richard Chambers, **Cyril Clarke (38)**, **George H Hall (59)**, Arthur Jacobs, William Nunley, Charles W Price, John W Robinson, William Sansome and Thomas Everitt Tansley.

The winners of medals and prizes awarded to boot and shoe making students in the county were announced on Thursday, **1 July**. Students from Raunds receiving prizes (worth 10s-0d each) for practical work were: Machine finishing – Garner Matson; Rough stuff cutting – Thomas Marlow; Advanced stage – J Arnold; Elementary stage – Sidney E Coles.

Also today, the new master and matron took up their duties at the new Cottage Homes in Raunds. Instead of a domestic servant being engaged, two "big girls" aged 14, who had gone to the Homes from the Workhouse, and were capable of doing domestic service (but were not yet "very domesticated") were to be kept for 6 months to a year to assist in the work of the Homes and trained for domestic service. A seamstress and washerwoman would also be engaged as required.

Raunds Feast commenced as usual on Saturday evening, **3 July**, when Messrs Thurston, the well known amusement caterers, opened their various sources of attraction, including motors etc, in the Carter Hill Field. The attractions were open every night during the following week, and with the trade of the town being brisk, good business was done.

The Temperance Silver Prize Band gave two concerts on Feast Sunday, **4 July**. The first took place on "The Hill" at 4.30pm, when there was a fair gathering, the second followed on The Square at 7.30pm. However, after two pieces had been played, a thunderstorm burst over the town causing both bandsmen and their listeners to beat a hasty retreat.

Anniversary services were held at the Wesleyan Church on the Sunday when the Rev Thomas Kirkup preached. The young women of the church arranged a garden party on Feast Monday afternoon in the grounds of "The Maples", by kind permission of Mr John Horrell. About 100 sat down to tea at 5 o'clock after which games and amusements were indulged in until dusk. The proceeds, nearly £16, were for a new piano for the girls Vestry Class.

The managers of the Church of England school met on Tuesday, **6 July**, and received notification from the Medical Officer of Health, Dr Mackenzie, that he had extended the closure of the schools for a further fortnight ending on Monday, 12 July, owing to the measles in the town. During the closure, 6 of the school's teachers had been sent out on supply duty. The managers also received an application from Miss Hall for an increase in salary.

At the quarterly meeting of the local branch of the Boot and Shoe Operatives Union on Wednesday, **7 July**, the minimum wage was on the agenda. The proposed increase of 1s-0d for males of 22 and above in the lasting, finishing, clicking and press departments was discussed. However, there was a disagreement with the manufacturers on when the new rates should become effective, the union expected it to be from 1 July but the manufacturers insisted on 1 September as 3 months notice was required under the existing agreement. The issue would be discussed again at a future meeting.

The branch agreed to adopt a minimum wage scale for male day workers in the heel building department and the stock or shoe room, with not less than 2 years experience prior to attaining the age of 18, of 16s-0d per week at age 18, up to 27s-0d per week at 23 and over. For female workers, the rate would be 14s-0d per week at 18, up to 17s-0d per week at 20. Both males and females would receive an additional 10% bonus on these rates during the period of the war.

The branch executive authorised the trustees to invest £100 of branch funds in the War Loan. The secretary reported that membership as at the end of June 1915 stood at 4,929, contributions received were £1,700, and sick and funeral pay amounted to £552. About 500 members were now on active service, with some having been killed in action for which deepest sympathy was offered to relatives.

Two Raunds youngsters heard on Thursday, **8 July**, that they were to receive County Council scholarships. A 2 year scholarship "to enable the pupil to proceed to secondary school" was awarded to Ralph Burton of Sackville Street, currently at Raunds Council School, while a 1 year scholarship "to enable the holder of an existing 1 year scholarship to continue at secondary school" went to Edna Pendered of Coleman Street, a pupil of Wellingborough County High School.

"To Aid The Wounded – More Raunds Lads Join the RAMC" proclaimed the Kettering Leader on Friday, **9 July**. It told of three more St John Ambulance pupils who had passed their first-aid examinations and joined the RAMC, making nine men from the town, all of whom had been trained by Dr Mackenzie. The three, Privates **Edgar Ellingham (47)**, Sydney Kilborn and Frederick Shrives, were said to be "most anxious to go away and do their bit!" The young fellows had arrived at Southampton on the day after the great battle at Aubers Ridge, and their work had begun at once, carrying wounded soldiers from the transports from morning till night for many days. The paper observed "like the whole of the men of the British Army, they deserve all the praise we can give them." *(Plate 23)*

That evening, the Church of England School managers met again to discuss the consequences of the measles epidemic and a proposal from the Local Education Sub-Committee for the summer holidays to run from Monday, 12 July until 16 August. The managers were concerned that this would mean a Christmas term of 18 weeks, giving the teachers almost no time to make their arrangements. It would also be hard on parents who hoped to send their children into the harvest fields. After discussion, a letter was drafted to both the Local Education Authority and Sub-Committee which saying "we recommend that the summer holidays continue to 23 August owing to children being probably employed in the harvest fields."

On Saturday, **10 July**, it was reported that Mrs Annie Bamford of Spencer Street, a regular subscriber to each consignment of cigarettes etc forwarded to the front by Dr Mackenzie, had received a letter of thanks from Sergeant F Harris, "O" Company, 1st Northamptons. He said "May I be permitted to express, on behalf of the non-commissioned officers and men, their warm appreciation and gratitude to you for your great kindness in sending and getting so many cigarettes for us. I can confidently say it would be very miserable indeed or the majority of us were it not for the acts of kindness some of our country people have shown us".

Mrs Bamford had also received a postcard from Private John Horne of the Gordon Highlanders in which he said "They comfort us in more ways than one, and it is nice to think that we still have some friends that are doing all they possibly can to provide us with such luxuries."

Feast Saturday saw the annual treat for scholars from the Church of England Sunday School. Tea was provided for the scholars at 3.15pm and the public at 4.30, afterwards the party retired to the Vicarage grounds for the usual outdoor sports and games ......

A "marathon", upwards of 4 miles, was run in the evening for Vestry Class members. This was won by W Bettles, who received a pair of brushes and case donated by Messrs Sanders and Head. Second was A Groom (a watch), and third, J Archer (a clock). The Temperance Silver Band played for dancing in the evening after the sports.

A nasty accident happened to Mrs Corby, of Brook Street, on Sunday, **11 July**. She left with her husband in the afternoon to cycle to Wollaston Feast and while going down Stanwick Hill, she lost control of her bicycle and dashed into the wall of the Barn at the bottom. The unfortunate lady was thrown to the ground heavily and her machine was badly buckled. She was picked up in a semi-conscious condition and conveyed to Mr Freeman's house nearby. It was found that she had sustained nasty wounds about the face and a badly bruised hip. Internal injuries were also feared. First aid was rendered by local St John Nursing Sisters, and later the injured lady received attention from Dr Mackenzie.

This was the fifth accident to have occurred on the hill during the past fortnight. Two of them had been serious, those of Mrs Corby, above, and Mr Pullen of the "Live and Let Live Inn", Wellingborough, the previous day. Stanwick parishioners suggested that the powers that be should provide storage for broken bicycles and a hospital for the wounded!

The medical officer, Dr Mackenzie, confirmed the closure of all of the town's schools for a further three weeks owing to the spread of measles and the indications of an outbreak of whooping cough. As the summer holidays were nearing, it was decided that these three weeks would be part of the holidays.

Another clutch of Raunds cases came before Thrapston Petty Sessions on Tuesday, **13 July**. A shoehand was summoned for being drunk and disorderly on the public highway on 28 June. Sergeant Ellingham said he understood that the defendant got drinking every Monday and did not work, adding that several others in the town were also doing that again. Pleading guilty, the defendant was fined 10s-0d with 4s-0d costs.

A London man, of no fixed abode, who came to Raunds for the Feast, working for the show people, was summoned for breaking into a factory and stealing 6 pairs of Army boots, the property of Messrs R Coggins and Son. He was subsequently committed for trial at the next Quarter Sessions.

An 11 year old Hargrave boy was found guilty of stealing a silver watch, worth 30s-0d, from the blacksmith in Hill Street. He was put on probation for two months and his mother was bound over for his good behaviour during that period.

Finally, a 14 year Raunds lad, a shoehand, was charged with stealing four tins of cycle repair outfits from a local cycle and motor agent. He pleaded guilty and was bound over on probation for 12 months.

Confirmation of the registration of a new company was announced on Wednesday, **14 July**. The Regulation Boot Co (Raunds) Ltd, (140,892), was registered with a capital of £3,000 in £1 shares, "to carry on the business of boot and shoe manufacture in Raunds or elsewhere". The subscribers were named as J H Nicholls of Raunds and G H W Gibbs of Kettering.

"W F & F A Corby – House & Estate Agents, have the following properties placed in their hands for sale by private treaty: 3 dwellings in Marshall's Road; a cottage on The Square; 6 cottages and 7 houses in Hill Street; 4 houses in West Street; 9 houses in Rotton Row; a building plot in Manor Street."

On Thursday, **15 July**, the Urban Council sent their good wishes to Sergeant L G H Lee, a council member, on his appointment as assistant meteorologist to the BEF. He had previously been acting as secretary to Lieutenant Colonel Curtis, Commanding Officer of the 1st/4th Northants, but was leaving almost immediately to take up his new duties. Sergeant Lee was well known locally for his knowledge of meteorology, and it was expected that one important phase of his work would be connected with aviation conditions.

Interesting statistics were published on Friday, **16 July**, on the death rates in the county in 1914. In urban areas, Raunds had an average of 12.1 deaths per 1,000 of the population, compared to Rushden's 8.9, Higham Ferrers' 9.7 and Daventry's 12.2, the only one higher than Raunds. The average for the county was 11.97 and for England & Wales, 14. The low averages for Rushden and Higham Ferrers was put down to "the magnificent water supply and efficient drainage".

Another Raunds name was included on the latest War Office Casualty List issued today, that of **F Cuthbert (44)**, 1st Northamptons, missing since 9 November 1914.

The annual camp meetings of the Primitive Methodist Church took place on Sunday, **18 July**. There were gatherings at "Top End" in the morning, at Newtown in the afternoon, and on The Square at 5 o'clock. These were followed by an evening evangelical service in the Primitive Methodist Church.

Down the street at the Wesleyan Church, special sermons were preached by the Rev H J Barber of Thrapston, and collections were taken for Northampton Hospital.

At Monday, **19 July**'s, Urban Council meeting, the assembly were read a letter from Sergeant L G H Lee, council member, serving with the 1st/4th Northamptons. He said he was perfectly well in health and thoroughly enjoying military life. His only regret was that his division was still in England, as they were itching to get somewhere more exciting. Since the letter was written, Sgt Lee had been promoted again and was now in France in connection with the Meteorological Office.

The medical officer, Dr Mackenzie, reported that 3 deaths and 12 births had been registered in the town during June and there had been 3 cases of mild scarlet fever.

On the Local Education Sub-Committee, Messrs John Adams CC, and W F Corby, were elected as chairman and vice-chairman respectively.

The suitability of the site for the proposed new cemetery was also discussed. A "numerously signed petition" asked that a portion of the new cemetery be consecrated by the Bishop of Peterborough.

Wednesday, **21 July**, was the Belgian National Day, and some of the refugees in the town had the idea of arranging a collection on behalf of the Wounded Soldiers Fund. M Lazare Morel, assisted by Mme Morel, Mme Stroobant and children raised £8-13s-1d.

Thursday, 22 July, severe Russian losses result in the Great Retreat.

At Wellingborough Police Court, a lieutenant in the 2nd/1st Herefords was charged with driving a motor car without a licence in Wellingborough. The vehicle had knocked down and killed a child. Found guilty, the defendant was fined 10s-0d!

"Boot and Shoe Machinery for Sale, for disposal as displaced by new Royalty Machines, contact Messrs Adams Bros, Spencer Street"

Among local contractors securing orders from the War Office during June were Messrs John Horrell and Son, Tebbutt and Hall Bros and the St Crispin Productive Society. Tenders were now out for 600,000 boots for the Serbians and the winter requirements for the British Army in footwear were expected to be announced within the next fortnight.

More local health statistics were released this week, with the county infant mortality rates for 1914 made public. The figures were based on the deaths of infants under 1 year old per 1,000 births and Raunds had a rate of 86.2. This compared with the 26.3 of Brackley, 55.5 at Higham Ferrers and Rothwell's 133.3. The county average was 73, England & Wales, 105 and 114 for "Large Towns". The exceptional result for Brackley was attributed to "the great benefit of having health visitors working in the homes of the poor".

A meeting of the town's school managers discussed the apparent staffing mismatch in the Infants department of the two schools. Although there were 30 more scholars in the Council School than in the Church of England School, there was one less teacher. Mr Shelmerdine observed that this needed to be put right.

The number of scholars on the district register now totalled 1,133, which was 13 up from last year. However, attendance had dropped from 90.9% to 86.3%, chiefly due to the epidemic sickness in the town.

On Friday, **23 July**, it was announced that the Rev E E Law, formerly the Vicar at Raunds, had been appointed an Army Chaplain.

At the quarterly meeting of the Hospital Week Fund Committee at the "Golden Fleece", the treasurer announced that the annual demonstration and parade had produced a profit of £81-5s-0d. As the balance in hand was now £117-14s-6d, it was agreed to forward £100 to the county treasurer.

In the entertainment world, the Palace, Rushden, was offering "Tillie's Punctured Romance", a 6-reeler featuring Charlie Chaplin, while the Royal Variety Theatre presented "Frank Sylvo", the quaint comedy juggler, "Honri Foden", acrobatic hand balancer and jumping equilibrist, and "Maidie and Gent", a laughing hit on four continents.

On Saturday, **24 July**, a fete was held at Denford in aid of the "Denford Soldiers Comforts Fund". The fancy dress competition brought success for two Raunds entries, winners of the "Decorated Bicycle – Adult (not less than 5 in group)" class were the "Dodgers Ragtime Band", while in the "Individual Get-Up, Children" class, Miss K Kirk took first place as "Cupid".

At a meeting of the Government Army Boot Contractors Association at Raunds on Monday, **26 July**, it was decided to close the factories for the whole of the August Bank Holiday week.

The half yearly meeting of the Raunds Distributive Co-Operative Society was also held on this day. In the absence of the president, Mr Charles Groom, through illness, Mr T Pentelow was elected to the chair. Mr Groom had written tendering his resignation, but it was not accepted and instead a vote of sympathy was passed.

The balance sheet showed that sales for the first half of 1915 were the largest on record, exceeding last year by £4,527 or 38%. The balance after expenses and provisions was £1,634. Disposal of this was agreed as follows: dividend to members, general, butchery and coal, 2s-0d in the £1; dividend to non-members, 1s-0d in the £1. Retiring members Messrs Askham, Annies and Miller were all re-elected to the committee.

The death occurred suddenly on Tuesday, **27 July**, of Albert Martin, the youngest son of Mr and Mrs Enos Martin of Park Street. The deceased was out and about on Sunday as usual, but was taken ill during that evening. The cause of death was scarlet fever and meningitis.

The Rev C C Aldred officiated on Thursday, **29 July**, at the wedding of Miss Elsie May Denton, eldest daughter of Mr and Mrs Walter Denton, to Mr Leonard Arthur Thomas, eldest son of the late Mr H P and Mrs Thomas, of Rushton. The bride, given away by her father, was attired in a dress of white satin, veiled with shadow lace, with a veil of Brussels net and orange blossom. The bridesmaids, Misses Edith and Mildred Denton, sisters, and Miss Constance Thomas, sister, were dressed in white voile and satin relieved with pale pink, and wore gold brooches, gifts of the bridegroom. Mr J Curtis of Kettering was best man.

And today, the Wesleyan Methodist Church Annual Conference confirmed that the Rev J Burrows should remain at Raunds.

On Friday, **30 July**, Wellingborough Grammar School announced that the fees for boarders had been raised by £1 per term.

It was "Forget Me Not Day" on Saturday, **31 July**, and there were a large number of young ladies selling flowers during the day in aid of the "Blind & Crippled Children's Fund". In the afternoon, the Temperance Silver Band paraded the town, and the total sum realised was about £11-10s-0d.

Cricket – In the afternoon, Lord Lilford's XI entertained Raunds Town in a friendly fixture and emerged as victors by a massive 347 runs to 75. A feature of the game was the brilliant all round work of Wells, who in addition to a fine innings of 112, took 5 Raunds wickets for 36. For the Town, D Turnock scored 25 and took 4 wickets.

* * * * * * * * * * * * * * * * * * * *

* * * * * * * * * * * * * * * * * * *

AUGUST – Writing in the Parish Magazine, the Vicar looked back on the Sunday School treat which passed off very well, making a good finish to Feast week. He was grateful to all who helped in anyway, especially Miss Wingell and helpers who did the catering and attended to the teas, all who undertook to manage the sweet stall, hoop-la, and skittles, and all who gave prizes or gifts of money. The marathon race had been even better than last year's event and W Bettles was congratulated on coming first again. Expenses for the treat included 1s-2d for the hire of tablecloths, 4s-8d for the washing of tablecloths, and £2-8s-0d for the band.

It was expected before many more months had elapsed that the new cemetery would be opened and, as a result, the churchyard would be closed except for those plots of ground which had been purchased by faculty, or in the case of 8 foot graves, where one more internment was possible. Although it was sad that the closing should have to come, it was realised that after some 900 years, "necessity knows no choice."

During August there would be Children's Services each Sunday at 1.30pm instead of Sunday School. The collections would be in aid of the Waifs and Strays Society. It was hoped that more eggs would be brought for the wounded soldiers.

A party of about 60 of the St James, Northampton, Church Lad's Brigade would be in camp in Raunds later during the coming Bank Holiday week, being accommodated in the Church Institute and in tents on the lawn.

The Raunds Temperance Silver Band gave two concerts on Bank Holiday Sunday, **1 August**, in aid of band funds, the first at 4.30pm at "The Hill", and the second at 7.30pm in the paddock adjoining the "Manor House". The grounds of the house were thrown open to the public by kind permission of Mr & Mrs Camozzi.

At the Primitive Methodist Church, the preacher was the Rev W B Bache of St Neots and at the evening service a solo was rendered by Miss Miriam Sanders with Miss Edith Sanders accompanying at the piano. On Monday, 2 August, a service was held at 3 o'clock when a sermon was also preached by the reverend gentleman. A tea followed and in the evening a meeting took place when Mr S Pettit of Stanwick presided and addresses were given by the Rev Bache and the Rev H W Hart of Wellingborough.

The Thrapston Board of Guardians were asked on Tuesday, **3 August**, by the committee of the Children's Home at Raunds for money to buy games such as drafts, chess and dominoes, as "at present the children have nothing they can do to amuse themselves". The Guardians agreed to allow £2 "to be spent appropriately".

Wellingborough and District Band of Hope had their annual outing today when arrangements were made for tea in the grounds of the Manor House, Stanwick. Unfortunately it had to be held in the large barn owing to showers. Over 230 partook of an excellent tea provided by the Raunds Distributive Co-Operative Society.

A very pretty but quiet wedding took place at the Wesleyan Church on the afternoon of Wednesday, **4 August**. R Walter Janes of Burton Latimer married Miss Emmeline Dora Lee, the youngest daughter of Mr and Mrs George Lee of "Kingswood". The bride was given away by her father, the bridesmaids were Miss Pauline Smith (cousin) and Miss Doreen Stevenson (niece), and Mr Chamberlain of Wellingborough, the best man. The Rev J Burrows officiated and Mr Cyril Groom played festal music as the guests arrived and Mendelssohn's "Wedding March" at the close. The couple were recipients of many handsome and useful presents and left for their honeymoon in Ilfracombe by the 5.45pm train.

The successful students from the local "Shoe Classes" were announced on Friday, **6 August**, and the Raunds Centre congratulated the following: *Honours* – County Council prize for practical rough-stuff cutting, Thomas Marlow; *Advanced* – 1st class certificate and pass in practical pattern cutting, Fred C Agutter; 1st class certificate and pass in practical machine finishing, Garner Matson (with County Council prize for practical machine finishing); 2nd class certificate and pass in practical rough-stuff cutting, Albert Firkins; County Council prize for well kept notebook, Herbert Arnold; *Elementary* – pass, Sidney E Coles (with County Council prize for well kept notebook), Horace Lawrence and Garner Matson.

Another set of health statistics were issued today, "Victims of Consumption in Northamptonshire in 1914", and they made grim reading. Calculated as deaths per 1,000 of the population, Oundle had the lowest with 0.36, Higham Ferrers, 1.08 and Irthlingborough, 1.48, however, Raunds, with 2.32, was by far the worst of the urban districts.

It was also reported today that a recent volunteer in Northamptonshire for enlistment in the Army had eleven children but only one tooth!

At the monthly meeting of the Boot & Shoe Operatives Union local branch, held at the Rushden Trade Unions Club on Monday, **9 August**, there was discussion on the payment date of the 1s-0d increase to the minimum wage for 22 year olds and upwards.

The manufacturers were insisting that it could not be paid before 1 September despite the national agreement to the contrary with the Board of Trade. Some disrest was predicted by the committee who felt that it was bound to cause dissatisfaction and trouble to the members although everything was being done to avoid friction with the employers. The committee also received three funeral claims for members "killed in action" and extended their sympathy to their friends.

More Raunds transgressors appeared at the Thrapston Petty Sessions on Tuesday, **10 August**. A fine of 5s-0d was inflicted upon a shoehand who was found guilty of being drunk on the public highway on 31 July. PC Newberry, giving evidence, said that at about 10pm he saw the defendant lying helplessly drunk in the middle of Stanwick Road.

A soldier from the 2nd Northants, who did not attend the hearing, was summoned for being drunk and disorderly on the highway at Raunds on 24 July. Supt Tebbey stated that the defendant had been home for a month on sick furlough but had since gone back to his regiment. The charge was reduced to one of drunkenness, in order to deal with it on the day, and the defendant was fined 5s-0d.

Finally, a Raunds labourer was summoned by his farmer employer in respect of a claim of 18s-0d, one week's wages, in lieu of one week's notice. Supt Tebbey read a letter from the defendant, who enclosed the amount of the claim and costs. Under these circumstances, the complainant withdrew the summons.

Concern was expressed on Thursday, **12 August**, on the wellbeing of Private **Cecil Burton (32)**, who, although officially reported to be a prisoner of war by the German Government, had still failed to communicate with his relatives and a postcard sent to him at his supposed camp at Gottengen had been returned.

Friday, 13 August, the troopship "Royal Edward" is sunk, Sam Brayfield (27) and Percy Watson (119), drowned.

On this sad day, a Raunds resident from High Street was found guilty at Wellingborough Police Court of riding a bicycle without a light at Stanwick on 31 July. He was fined 3s-0d.

It was "Rose Day" at Irthlingborough on Saturday, **14 August**, when Artlenockians strove to raise money for the Red Cross and various Raunds groups made their contribution. The Firemen's Hose-Cart competition attracted a good deal of attention, with the silver challenge cup going to the winners, Wolverton, in 27.35 seconds, Raunds No.1 team came third in 30.1 seconds. In the preceding parade, led by the Irthlingborough's Silver Prize Band, the "Dodgers Band" from Raunds, under Mr H Harding, caused much amusement with their "grotesque costumes and instruments". And during the afternoon a highly appreciated musical programme was given by the Raunds Temperance Silver Prize Band.

That same afternoon, the annual fete of the Stanwick branch of the British Women's Temperance Association was held in the grounds of the "Manor House", Stanwick, and guests included the Belgian refugees from Raunds, and nurses and wounded soldiers from Higham Ferrers VAD Hospital. Of the 23 entries in the fiercely contested "Brown & Polson's Home Baking Cake Competition", Mrs F Pentelow of Raunds, was highly commended and received a certificate of merit.

After seven weeks holiday, and with the measles epidemic practically ceased, all schools in the town reopened on Monday, **16 August**.

"Transport Lost – Royal Edward – British Vessel sunk in the Aegean" was the leading headline on Tuesday, **17 August**, as the scale of losses from 3 days previous began to emerge. It was now estimated that 32 military officers, 1,350 troops, and 220 crew had drowned, and approximately 600 men had been saved.

Those aboard included members of the Royal Army Medical Corps, but at this stage no names were released so the fates of **Sam Brayfield (27)**, Harry Hall and **Percy Watson (119)** were unknown.

The Local Government Board inspector held an inquiry at the Council School on Friday, **20 August**, into the application from the Urban Council for sanction to borrow £1,500 for a cemetery, proposed to be erected in "Ringstead Road". Although there was no local opposition to the scheme, the inspector explained the need to cut expenditure to the lowest possible limit under the present war conditions. The clerk then read letters from the Vicar and Wesleyan Minister showing the scarcity of grave spaces in the burial grounds.

In the churchyard there was now only room in previously purchased family plots or 8 foot graves with currently just one occupant, whilst the trustees of the chapel burial ground had recently unanimously agreed that its future use be reserved for Raunds Wesleyan Methodists or "strictly Methodist adherents". The clerk also described how the grave diggers were now turning up human remains!

The inspector said that there was no doubt a cemetery was wanted but it should be done with the smallest loan possible at present, adding that there was no urgent need for a chapel at £620. He also thought that it would have been desirable for the Council to have found a field nearer to the town but the Cemetery Committee chairman advised that this was absolutely the best they could get. The inquiry then closed and the inspector left by motor, with the surveyor and others, to view the proposed site, about three-quarters of a mile away.

Local fruit growers would doubtless have been concerned to read in the London Gazette of Saturday, **21 August**, that an "Infected Area Order" had been scheduled in Desborough owing to an outbreak of gooseberry mildew.

"Harvest Operations at Raunds" were reported on Thursday, **26 August**. It told of the weather of the last week or 10 days having been very good and that the farmers had taken advantage of it to get on with the harvest. They were hoping the weather would hold fine for a few more days as the owners of some of the larger farms had complained of a shortage of labour.

Saturday, **28 August**, saw the coming of age of Miss Edith Jacobs, the only daughter of Mr and Mrs Robert Jacobs of Wellington Road. At 4.30pm about 40 relatives and friends sat down to a splendid spread in the grounds of "The Maples", kindly placed at their disposal by Mr and Mrs John Horrell. Miss Jacobs was the recipient of a large number of handsome and useful presents.

Also that afternoon, the members of the Thorpe House Tennis Club held a tournament at "Thorpe House" in which eight couples took part. Tea was provided during the afternoon and a very pleasant time was spent.

On Monday, **30 August**, the death of Mr Charles Groom of Lawson Street, after a long and painful illness, was announced. The fifty-one year old was well known in Co-Operative circles, and the current president of the Raunds Distributive Co-Operative Society, having been one of its founders. He was also one of the founders of the St Crispin Productive Co-Operative Society, and was manager at the time of his death. A local preacher of the Wesleyan Methodist Circuit, he was also one of the Wesleyan School trustees. He had been a member of the first Town Parish Council and then the Urban Council, at one time being chairman. A director of the Raunds Hotel & Coffee Tavern, he was also actively associated with the "Beehive" Tent of the Independent Order of Rechabites. Charles Groom left a widow, a daughter and six sons, one of whom was **Arthur Groom (55)**. *(Plate 2)*

In the evening, an accident happened to 10 year old Tom Nunley of Brook Street. He had climbed up an elm tree opposite the Post Office, and when near the top took hold of a rotten bough, which gave way and he fell to the ground. He was bruised all over, but no bones were broken.

* *

* *

SEPTEMBER – The Vicar, in his monthly Parish Magazine notes, previewed the "Service of Thanksgiving for the Ingathering of the Crops" on Thursday, 30 September, asking that gifts of flowers, fruit and vegetables be brought to the Church on the previous day. The usual sale would take place on the following Monday evening in the Church Institute. The collections during the Festival would be for the Churchwardens funds. He observed that "we might well remember that our Diocesan quota has been raised to £18 this year but as we know well that money is not exactly scarce in Raunds, we trust that this appeal for the Church Expenses Fund will be well responded to".

The visit of the St James Church Lad's Brigade from Northampton during August was looked back on. They had all thoroughly enjoyed their stay and the thought was pondered that "perhaps in time we may have a similar company in Raunds".

Congratulations were offered to Private **C A Vorley (117)** and Sergeant Vincent Sykes on their recent promotions to 2nd Lieutenant, and also to Private H York for being "mentioned in despatches".

The first meeting for the winter season of the Church of England Men's Society would be held on Monday, 27 September, at 8.15pm in the Vicarage. A paper on "Miracles" would be read by Mr C Head.

The magazine also noted the marriage on Thursday, 29 July, of **William James Askham Smith (109)** to Miss Minnie Pettit.

Finally, the Vicar spoke for all of the grief felt when it was heard that a member of the congregation and R.A.M.C., **Samuel Brayfield (27)**, had been reported as missing as a result of the sinking of the "Royal Edward". Sympathies were extended to his relatives and friends. He added that "his mission and work was to minister to the sick and suffering, and of him it is true to say – Greater love hath no man than this that a man lay down his life for his friends."

The funeral of Mr Charles Groom took place at the Wesleyan Church on Thursday, **2 September**. The service was conducted by the Rev J Burrows and the principle mourners included his son, Private **Arthur Groom (55)**. Owing to the prominent position which the deceased had occupied in the town for many years past, the obsequies partook of a public character, and the large and representative gathering of sympathisers and considerable number of floral tributes testified to the high esteem in which he was held. *(Plate 2)*

"Raunds Men On The Lost Transport" introduced the news on Friday, **3 September**, that Mr and Mrs A Hall of North Street had received official intimation that their son, Private H Hall of the R.A.M.C., who was on the "Royal Edward", was amongst the survivors. However, the family and friends of Privates **Sam Brayfield (27)** and **Percy Watson (119)**, also of the R.A.M.C., had heard nothing and so the worst was feared.

Two Raunds men, who were home from the Front, also featured in articles today.

Second-Lieutenant V Sykes of the 2nd Sherwood Foresters, son of Mr W B Sykes of Grove Street, had been home on five days leave after serving in France for six months. He had been called out on the outbreak of the war, at which time he belonged to the 7th Middlesex, and was a member of the first Territorial Battalion to leave England, proceeding to Gibraltar on garrison duty. From there he went in February to France from where he had just returned on leave.

Private **G H Hall (59)**, son of Mr and Mrs James Hall, now of Higham Ferrers, of the Royal Flying Corps, was also home on leave, after eleven months in France. He told the reporter that he had had the experience of flying over the German lines.

Both visitors were said to be looking fit and well, and during the interview with the latter he gave the opinion that "it will be a long time before the war is over". The writer hoped they both be spared to see it fought out to a successful finish!

And it was announced today that the members of the Red Cross Committee of Raunds, as at the end of the first year of the war, had sent to the Northampton depot, 821 articles including 134 body belts, 124 pairs of day socks, 102 day shirts, 104 scarves and 56 pairs of mittens. Many of the scarves and nearly all of the mittens had been made by school children. Blankets, sheets, hand towels and handkerchiefs had also been sent. In addition to the above, several of the Raunds soldiers had been provided with socks, shirts etc, when they were home on leave.

A tribute to the late Mr Charles Groom appeared on Saturday, **4 September**, in the Raunds Wesleyan Methodist Circuit Magazine. "Not his family alone, but Raunds and the whole church deeply mourn his loss. As a local preacher he was welcome wherever he went, and always had the welfare of the Church at heart. As a society steward and church worker, especially as secretary of the School Trust, he was a most devoted servant of God in the church and will be greatly missed."

The Debt and Renovation Fund of the Wesleyan Sunday School had now reached the sum of £512-19s-11d, and £150 had been paid off the debt, saving £6-15s-0d per annum in interest. The scholars of the Sunday School had started out to raise £100, and so far had collected the fine sum of £43-17s-1d.

Also at the Wesleyan Church, for some time past, Misses Louie Smith and Bertha Tebbutt had been collecting for a new piano for the lower vestry. For two years and more the old harmonium had been used, so a new instrument would be greatly appreciated by the large Young Women's Bible Class meeting there on Sundays, by the week-evening congregation, and the classes meeting in the vestry. The cost would be £20, and nearly £17 had now been collected. The balance, it was hoped, would be raised by a concert and the instrument would shortly be in use.

"Wanted – Pressman for Army Middles etc, and also boy for rough-stuff room – Apply, J Horrell and Son."

In another Saturday, 4 September event, the Dodger's Mixed Comic Band paraded the town, when a collection was taken for the benefit of Raunds soldiers. Starting from the "Red Lion Inn", the amount raised was £8-12s-0d, which would be equally divided between the town's soldiers at the front.

The Temperance Silver Prize Band gave a concert in the grounds of "The Hall", by kind permission of Mrs Coggins, on Sunday afternoon, **5 September**, at 4.30, when a large number attended. Amongst the various items given was the selection "A Soldier's Life", which was very well played, and was much appreciated by those present. The sum of £2-4s-8d was collected in aid of band funds.

Celebrating its 103rd anniversary today was the Wesleyan Sunday School. In the afternoon there was a Young People's Flower Service at which Bibles and hymn books were presented to scholars who had attained 15 years of age during the previous year. A collection of eggs was made and nearly 850 were given, these and fruit, sweets and books were sent to the VAD Hospital at Northampton. At all of the day's services, Mr R H Hughil preached in the absence through illness of the Rev J Williams Butcher. In the evening, the choir sang the anthem "Great is the Lord". The annual tea was held the day before at "The Maples", residence of Mr and Mrs John Horrell, when approximately 100 sat down. The net proceeds of the anniversary weekend were £28-13s-0d.

Topping the bill in the week commencing Monday, **6 September**, at the Kettering Coliseum were "Frank Cumminger & Frances Colonna" – the world record sand dancer from the London Pavilion and the tallest lady sand dancer. And among the forthcoming attractions were "The Decors and Tomato" – an original animal act, introducing "Tomato", the finest trained Donkey the world has ever seen!

"Wanted – Edge Setter, also Laster on Welded Army – apply, Adams Bros."

Mrs Ward of High Street was found dead in bed on Wednesday morning, **8 September**. The sad discovery was made by the deceased's daughter-in-law when she came home to breakfast. Dr Mackenzie's examination found that she had been dead for some hours.

Today's papers urged readers: "You Have Got a Penny, Then Buy a Flag on Ambulance Saturday, 11 September".

A memorial service was held in the Wesleyan Church on Thursday, **9 September**, in memory of the life and work of the late Mr Charles Groom, the Rev J Burrows officiated and the choir sang the anthem "What are these arrayed in white?"

On Friday, **10 September**, a Roll of Honour summary report stated that 851 men had been lost from the "Royal Edward" including 142 from the Royal Army Medical Corps.

More eggs from the Rev C C Aldred and the Wesleyan Sunday School were acknowledged today by the VAD Hospital at Higham Ferrers.

The factory outing season began on Saturday, **11 September**, when employees of the Wellington Works (E W Stanley Ltd) went to Stratford-upon-Avon. The party of about 160 had an early start, leaving the Crossways at 5.45am in a fleet of 'buses, and arrived home just before midnight. A very pleasant time was spent.

And on this day, Mrs Cleavely, the oldest inhabitant of Wellingborough at 97, died. A native of Raunds, the deceased was the daughter of Mr Cleavely, farmer.

Harvest Festival was celebrated at the Primitive Methodist Church on Sunday, **12 September**. The service was taken by Sister Rachael of the South East London Mission. An afternoon meeting included solos by Miss Travill of Wollaston and selections played by the String Band. After tea and the evening service, the fruit sale took place with the proceeds going to Circuit and Trust Funds. On Monday afternoon, a tea was provided in the schoolroom and at the meeting afterwards, Sister Rachael spoke on her work at St George's Hall.

Meanwhile, at the Wesleyan Church, the day's services were taken by the Rev Harry Shaw, the new minister at Thrapston.

A new registered company was announced on Monday, **13 September**. "The Raunds Palace Kinema Company Ltd – 141539" had a registered capital of £1,000 in £1 shares, with J Mitchell and E Myers trading as the aforementioned Palace Kinema Co. The named subscribers were J Mitchell, E Myers, and Mrs L A Mitchell, with one share each. The first directors were to be J Mitchell and E Myers (subject to holding 10 shares), each on a remuneration of £130 per annum.

The employees of Messrs Tebbutt and Hall Bros. had an outing on this day which proved to be "of a very interesting character". Leaving Raunds soon after 6am, the party of 124 travelled by motor omnibus via Olney, Newport Pagnell, Woburn Sands, Leighton Buzzard and Tring to Chesham where a substantial dinner was waiting. They then voyaged on to Berkhampstead, Dunstable and so to Luton, where tea was provided by the local Co-Operative Society. After tea, the homeward journey passed via Bedford, arriving back in Raunds at 11.30pm. Despite the long day all appeared to have had a thoroughly enjoyable time. The principles of the firm and their wives accompanied the party.

"Death of Raunds Footballer Confirmed", headed the story on Tuesday, **14 September**, that the family and friends of Private **Fred Cuthbert (44)**, of the 1st Northamptons, had just received information that he was killed in action on 9 November 1914. Private **Sam Whiteman (128)** had suggested in a letter as long ago as November 1914 that his pal had been killed, but nothing further had been heard until the official intimation arrived from the War Office four days ago.

At Thrapston Police Court, Mr Mitchell applied for the transfer of his cinema and theatrical licence from the old premises, now being used as a boot factory, to his new building. The request was approved and the licence granted.

The School Managers had a meeting this evening at which it was noted that there were currently 180 pupils in the Council Infants Department but only 143 on the roll of the Church of England Infants.

"Wanted – Youth for Pounding Up Machine, also youth for tacking insoles – Apply to Messrs C E Nichols."

News emerged on Friday, **17 September**, that Private H Hall, R.A.M.C., had written to his parents from Port Said, Egypt, stating that he was saved after going down with the transport "Royal Edward". He described how the ship sank in four minutes, and that he stayed on board till the water was level with the second deck and then jumped into the sea. When the ship sank most of the men in the water were drawn under by the suction. He thought he was never going to see daylight again, but when he did he saw around him lots of men and wreckage. He then got hold of a door, and was afterwards taken into a collapsible boat. After just over three hours, they were picked up by a hospital ship. Of **Sam Brayfield (27)** and **Percy Watson (119)** he added "Poor old Sam and Percy are missing. I didn't see either of them after the ship was torpedoed. You can guess how I feel about Sam. He has been my pal for ages, and I feel as if I have lost a brother!"

The factory outing for the employees of Walter Lawrence took place today and it also proved to be of a very pleasing and interesting character. The party of between 70 and 80 left the town at 6.30am in two motor omnibuses and three private cars. Their itinerary was the same as that undertaken by their colleagues from Messrs Tebbutt and Hall Bros, four days earlier.

The Picture Palace opened in its new premise in Grove Street on Saturday, **18 September**. In the afternoon there was a performance for children, and in the evening, two more performances, at 7pm and 9pm, both of which were crowded.

Over this weekend the Wesleyan Church held its Harvest Festival. On Saturday afternoon there was a public tea. Special services took place on Sunday at which Mr George Nicholls preached and on Monday evening, the sale of fruit and vegetables was held in the schoolrooms with Mr A G Brown, the auctioneer.

A recruiting meeting was held on The Square on Monday evening, **20 September**, with Captain Stocker, recruiting officer for the 8th Northamptons, presiding. An address was given by Captain P Humphreys, 3rd Northamptons, home on leave from Flanders. Mr George Nicholls, formerly MP for North Northants, who was staying in the district, also spoke "by invitation". There was a large crowd present.

However, the men from Messrs Neal & Gates missed the meeting as they were off on their annual factory outing. The 50 employees went via Biggleswade and Letchworth to Norton, where dinner "in fine style" was enjoyed at the "Three Horse Shoes". Tea was taken at Luton, provided by the local Co-Operative Society, and they returned via Woburn and Bedford, arriving home at 10.30pm.

The Urban Council also met in the evening and appointed Mr T W Jones, of Lyme Regis, the new Inspector of Nuisances, out of 36 applicants.

The chairman noted that since the last meeting, two Rounds men, Privates **Sam Brayfield (27)** and **Percy Watson (119)** of the R.A.M.C., had, it was feared, gone down in the sinking of the ill-fated "Royal Edward". He therefore moved that the Council send to their relations an expression of sympathy. And as another town man on the same ship, Private Harry Hall, had had a miraculous escape, he also moved that a letter be sent to his parents expressing pleasure at his safety.

The estimate for the second half-year was approved and a rate of 2s-3d in the pound agreed upon. It was also resolved that the street lighting be curtailed in the coming winter.

And "somewhere in France", Sergeant L G H Lee wrote of witnessing an air duel in which "the German airmen were outdone". "I had the thrill of my life" he said, "there was the usual whirr of an aeroplane overhead, but I hadn't noticed that it was German. All at once an English plane appeared and there was a splendid manoeuvring for position. Then came a quick staccato of machine-guns and the German's tail went up and the machine came down like a stone, but at about 300 feet off the ground it pulled up and settled down in a field within our lines. Some of our men went to take the Germans prisoners, but they machine-gunned them, killing one man and wounding several others. Of course they were instantly shot – Such is war!"

Also today, another consignment of cigarettes was sent by Dr Mackenzie to the Gordons and Northamptons at the front. It numbered in all, 1,870 Woodbines and other cigarettes, given by Miss Bessie Warner, Mrs Harry Bamford, Mrs W Allen, Mr John Allen, and Stanley Archer. Miss Mackenzie, by the sale of lavender flowers, provided another 500 Woodbines, and Mrs E A Lawrence of Newark, USA, sent 10s-0d through Mrs Sam Nunley, her mother.

The following day it was the turn of the workers from Messrs C E Nichols to sally forth. Travelling via Rushden, Olney, Newport Pagnell, Woburn and Dunstable, to Luton, for dinner at "The Wheatsheaf", they came back via Bedford, arriving home at 11pm. The weather was "all that could be desired."

At the evening meeting of Stanwick Parish Council, the tender for painting lamp posts was accepted, it was also decided that the crop from the sewage farm be sold by tender, and lastly, a bill from the Rounds Gas Company was ordered to be paid.

Tuesday, **21 September**, also saw a concert being given for the wounded soldiers at the Higham Ferrers VAD Hospital by the Rounds Quartette Party, assisted by Mr and Mrs Jethro Hall. Quartettes were contributed by Messrs C Coles, O D Hall, W Coles and W Hall, and songs by Mrs J W Hall, Messrs C and W Coles and O D and W Hall. Messrs Coles were also associated in a duet, Mr J W Hall ably accompanied, and thanks were accorded the artistes by Councillor A Pack.

Good news for local housewives emerged on Thursday, **23 September** when the Northampton Grocers Association today fixed the price of lump sugar at 6d per pound and granulated sugar at 4d per pound.

Employees of Messrs R Coggins and Sons went on their annual factory outing on Friday, **24 September**, when over 200 travelled in six omnibuses to Stratford-upon-Avon. The party left The Square at 6am and journeyed via Northampton, Daventry, Leamington Spa and Warwick. On their return, tea was taken at Banbury, then on through Brackley, Towcester and Northampton, arriving home soon after midnight. Unfortunately they encountered rain at Banbury which spoilt an otherwise splendid outing. Their employers generously provided the omnibuses and refreshments and also paid them for a day's work!

Saturday, 25 September, the Battle of Loos begins.

The Friendly Societies Councils of Finedon, Kettering, Raunds and Rushden held a meeting on this Saturday, in Raunds Temperance Hall. Brother C B Marshall, of Derby, president of the Midland Federation, gave an address on the Friendly Society Council movement, and Brother O Thompson, of Rushden, presided.

The Independent Labour Party held a meeting on The Square this evening when Mr H Croft, of Northampton, gave an address entitled "No Conscription".

It was Rushden Working Men's Club's 19th Annual Show of Flowers, Fruit & Vegetables over the two days of the weekend, "giving proof" their chairman exclaimed "that working men employed their time much more usefully than just drinking beer." Among the successful entrants was Mr W Lack, of Raunds, winner of the "Class A (Open), Eschalots".

Monday, 27 September, William Whiteman (130), killed in action.

This evening, the Belgian Committee met with Mr Camozzi in the chair. The secretary, Mr W F Corby, reported that £246-19s-10d had been received, and expenditure was £247-15s-1d, leaving an adverse balance of 15s-3d, but this would be more than met by the sum of £10 due from Stanwick. The committee recommended that the catering at "Thorpe House" be dispensed with, instead each family should be granted a sum to be determined by the necessities of each case. This was adopted and Stanwick promised to contribute one fifth of the money.

"Wanted – a Good Organiser for Boot Factory. One with a thorough knowledge of Bottom Stock desired. Apply, stating previous experience and wages required, not later than Wednesday morning, 6th October to: St Crispin's Ltd, Raunds."

Yet another factory outing took place on Tuesday, **28 September**, when the employees of Messrs Owen Smith also ventured to Stratford-upon-Avon. One hundred merrymakers left Raunds at 6am in three omnibuses, dinner was enjoyed on the firm in the River Restaurant, after which cigars were handed round. Some intrepid folk then had a trip on the river. The party arrived home at 11.30pm.

8 – October to December 1915

The Vicar leaves for the front and fine tegs take the prizes.

OCTOBER – Speaking in his opening notes in this month's Parish Magazine, the Vicar had no doubt that the people had heard that he felt it his duty to volunteer for work as an Army chaplain, either at home or abroad. The Bishop had now given his consent and Mr Bethway, the Curate, would try to carry on the work while he was away.

The Church Council had decided that the All Saints meeting would be held on Saturday, 6 November. Tea would be at 5pm in the school, with the meeting directly after, followed by the usual social. People willing to be givers of trays or half-trays were asked to send in their names.

Congratulations were extended to Private Alfred W Merrill of the Royal Fusiliers and Corporal Charles Shelmerdine, 6th Northants, on their promotions to Sergeant. Private Sam Bamford of the Royal Marines was welcomed home on leave after a long absence. The ringers had known his fondness for the bells and had arranged a short peal on the Sunday evening "so that he might enjoy something more than the ringing of the ship's bell."

On 26 October there would be a Lantern Lecture for children at 6pm in the Institute on the work of Prevention of Cruelty to Animals.

Additions to the Parochial Roll of Honour were William Farrer, RFA; Jack Lilleyman, RE; Cyril Mayes, Yorkshire Regiment; **Stanley Nunley (84)**, Expeditionary Force Canteen; Felix Pentelow, RE; Peter York, Northants Regiment and Herbert Sidney Hall, RN Sick Bay.

The number of eggs sent to the wounded soldiers during the previous month by the school children and a few friends, had been 209.

The scholars of the Vestry Class had decided to make an offering of eggs and cigarettes on the first Sunday of each month. The eggs would go to wounded soldiers and the cigarettes to those class members who were on naval or military service. And as thirty of the boys were now in khaki, as many cigarettes as could be collected would be easily disposed of.

On Friday, **1 October**, it was reported that four local men engaged in Army boot nailing were said to be earning between £3-1s-3d and £4-6s-11d a week!

The Wheatsheaf Coursing Club arranged a handicap in **Mr Pettit's** field on Saturday, **2 October**, for which there were 32 entries. The result was victory for Hall's "Ginger", second was Desborough's "Spider" from Wymington. Runners up were Mitchell's "Christmas Daisy" from Rushden, and Allen's "Jack".

Mr Joseph Heirs, aged 86, died suddenly on Monday, **4 October**, causing profound regret throughout the town. Mr Heirs, who lived with his daughter at 45 Hill Street, went into the wash-house during the afternoon and was there taken very ill, dying almost immediately and before medical assistance could be called.

"Raunds Officer Wounded", headed the story today of 2nd Lieutenant V Sykes who had been wounded in the arm and head. He had been removed to a base hospital and it was hoped that he would be back in England soon. Previously a schoolmaster in London, he had joined the 2nd Middlesex at the outbreak of the war, and was subsequently given a commission in the Sherwood Foresters. In the summer of 1913, he had married Miss O Webb of Denford.

In the evening, the local branch of the Boot & Shoe Operatives Union gathered for their monthly meeting. The treasurer reported a gain in the branch funds for the last quarter of £231, sick and funeral pay totalled £376 and out of work pay, 18s-4d. In his address, the chairman said that although substantial advances in wages had been secured for the members through organisation, the present high cost of living and the indirect, if not direct taxation of their wages, made it very necessary for the workers to be thoroughly united. He added stingingly that the upper and middle classes had "such a 'cute' way of shifting the burden off themselves on to the workers!"

The Church of England school managers met on Tuesday, **5 October**, and the Vicar advised that the Archdeacon of Oakham had sanctioned the appointment of Mr Bethway as temporary correspondent and school manager while he was away.

Mrs Edge had given notice of her resignation with effect from 30 November, this was accepted "with regret" and she would be thanked for her service. In view of this, the Local Education Authority would be asked to advertise the vacancy.

Miss F Hall was to be asked to go to Hargrave as a supply teacher on 11 October. Ominously for Miss Hall, the LEA had decided to reduce the staff of the Infants Department by one uncertified teacher and she had been "selected for reduction"!

The following day, the Vicar left Raunds for France to take up his new role of Army Chaplain. The esteemed gentleman observing that "one cannot decide on such a step as leaving a parish for a time unless the circumstances are exceptional, and no doubt we all feel that the present time is exceptional and we are all realising the principle of giving up some things and doing a little more individually than perhaps we have been accustomed to".

A "Thrift Campaign Week" throughout the county was announced by the Northamptonshire Education Authority on Friday, **8 October**. Demonstrations of economical cookery in the schools would be attended by the older girls, and their mothers would also be invited.

Employees of Messrs Adams Brothers went on their annual factory outing today. About 400 happy folk set off for Leamington Spa at 6.30am in various motor buses and charabancs, travelling via Northampton and dining at Rugby before arriving at the Spa in the early afternoon. At 4pm they began their return journey, taking tea at Franklin's Gardens, Northampton. All expenses were paid for by the firm and the weather was exceptional for the time of year.

On Saturday, **9 October**, the Temperance Silver Prize Band, conducted by Mr O Pentelow, gave a concert on "The Hill" at 4.30pm, in aid of band funds.

Second Lieutenant V Sykes had now arrived home on a month's convalescent leave and was staying with his father-in-law, Mr Alfred Webb, in Denford. He had apparently been wounded at night by shrapnel, his injuries being two wounds on the head, a cut upper lip, two or three teeth knocked out, and a wound to his right arm. He told friends that had he been standing up he would, in all probability, have had his head blown off, but he happened to be sitting on a box at the time. He then had to lie low for the remainder of the night before being carried half a mile to the dressing station.

Anniversary services were held at the Primitive Methodist Church on Sunday, **10 October**. The Rev J McKinney of Peterborough preached at both morning and evening gathering, and also at a pleasant afternoon service at which a duet was rendered by Messrs C and E Gray of Ringstead and a trombone solo was given by Mr H Bugby.

The Sunday afternoon service at the Wesleyan Church was in aid of local Red Cross funds. Previous to the meeting the Raunds Temperance Band paraded the town and the church was quite filled. Mr John Adams, CC, presided, the Rev H Shaw gave the address, the Wesleyan Prize Choir led the singing, Mr E T England of Rushden sang two solos, and Second Lieutenant V Sykes, who read the lesson, was also congratulated on his narrow escape at the front from more serious injury. The collection realised £11-2s-10d.

Tuesday, 12 October, Edith Cavell is executed by the Germans.

On this sad day, a fatal accident occurred at Raunds station when a guard from Kettering, was crushed to death during shunting operations. Harry Edwards was the acting guard on the train from Cambridge to Kettering which reached Raunds at 4.20pm, and whilst engaged in shunting was crushed between a horse box and the landing stage. His injuries were most serious and arrangements were made at once for his removal to Thrapston Infirmary, where he died soon after. The 50 year old had been in the service of the Midland Railway Company for 32 years. He left a widow, two sons (one of whom was in the RAMC) and two daughters. The inquest was held at the Thrapston Workhouse on Thursday, **14 October**. After hearing the testimony of witnesses, the coroner's jury returned a verdict of "accidental death". The funeral took place two days later at Kettering cemetery.

On Friday, **15 October**, it was announced that the Berrywood Asylum in Northampton would shortly be taken over by the War Office for use as a military hospital. In future years, two Raunds men, **Cornelius Robins (100)** and **John James Coles (40a)**, would spend their last days there. It was also noted that the asylum was currently the home of a Wellingborough inmate who would be 100 in March 1916, having spent the past 40 years in its care!

Late that evening, the death occurred of Mr Henry Gaunt, landlord of the "Red Lion Inn". Mr Gaunt, who had been ill for several weeks past, had been staying with his niece at Northampton and visiting the hospital for treatment. He returned home on the 5th of this month and had not kept to his bed at all, being out on this very morning as usual.

Coming to the Royal Variety Theatre, Rushden next week, by special engagement and at enormous cost, were "The Original Ten Loonies!" – That Crazy Comedy Crowd of Comical Musical Comedians.

"Raunds Soldier Invalided Home", this story appeared on Saturday, **16 October**, and told of Private Horace Reginald Sykes, 69th Co (MT) Army Service Corps, who had been in France for just over twelve months but had recently been sent back to England suffering from kidney trouble. The son of Mr and Mrs William Sykes of Vicarage Place was now in the VAD Hospital, Shrewsbury. Before the war he had been a motor bus driver for Coventry Corporation, and he lived in that city with his wife and four children. Whilst in France he was attached to the Lahore Division of the Indian Contingent and said that he found their soldiers to be a pleasant lot of fellows, willing to do anything for their English pals.

The Urban Council met for their monthly meeting on the evening of Monday, **18 October**. It was pointed out that none of nineteen lamps to be kept alight for the coming season had meters. However, the Raunds Gas Company had offered to supply gas for the restricted lighting for £12. Their offer was accepted.

The medical officer, Dr Mackenzie, reported 4 deaths and 8 births registered in September and that the district was "quite free from notifiable infections".

The assembly reviewed a plan submitted by Mr E Chambers for a proposed galvanised iron shed to be erected in Park Road, the application was approved.

The Waterworks sub-committee reported that certain parts of the equipment at the pumping station needed overhauling, and were given the go ahead to proceed.

The organisers of the Serbian Relief Fund had written asking the Council to arrange a Serbian Flag Day in support of funds. The request "found favour" and a public meeting to discuss the subject was arranged for the following Monday.

The funeral of the late Mr Henry Gaunt, landlord of the "Red Lion Inn", took place at the Parish Church on Tuesday, **19 October**. The Rev W S Bethway officiated.

And at the Thrapston Petty Sessions, a 24 year old Aldwincle woman, a domestic servant, was charged with stealing a quantity of clothing worth £2-10s-0d from her Raunds employer on 9 October. A witness, the plaintiff's daughter, said that she noticed the clothing was missing after the defendant had left her mother's employment. Later she saw the defendant wearing some of the articles. Pleading guilty, the accused was bound over to be of good behaviour for 12 months. Her mother was also bound over and ordered to pay costs of 15s-0d at 2s-6d per week.

At the same session, a Raunds shoehand was fined 10s-0d with 4s-0d costs, for being drunk on the highway in the town on 3 October. The Bench was told that this was the defendant's third similar offence in less than a year.

The Church of England School managers, at their evening meeting, accepted that they would have to write to Miss F Hall regretting that they were compelled to dispense with her services owing to the enforced reductions of staff. Likewise they would also write to Miss Gooding informing her that her proposed salary increase would have to be considered by the County Education Committee.

The managers also rejected the Education sub-committee's proposal that the Christmas holiday be reduced from two to one week to give a longer summer holiday. They considered that, in view of the long term from 16 August to 23 December, the teachers would need the usual two weeks holiday and that, if only one week was granted, attendance would suffer considerably.

On Friday, **22 October**, the annual meeting of the Liberal Literary Institute was held in the billiard room of the Coffee Tavern, with Mr Hazeldine presiding. The secretary, Mr W F Corby, presented the treasurer's accounts showing receipts for the year of £26-4s-3d and expenditure £34-10s-0d, a deficit of £8-5s-9d. However, this was nearly offset by a surplus of nearly £6 from the billiards account. During the evening's discussions, the group decided not to hold an annual tea this year but instead to make a collection to buy Christmas gifts for Raunds soldiers.

Sunday afternoon, **24 October**, saw the opening meeting of the Brotherhood season, the entertainers being a party of friends from Rushden. Miss Catlin, accompanied by Miss Sanders on the piano, gave 2 solos, "Here and There" and "Through Love to Light", the String Band was in attendance and led the singing.

The town meeting to consider the Urban Council suggestion that a Serbian Flag Day be arranged, took place in the Temperance Hall on Monday, **25 October**, with Mr John Adams, CC, in the chair. Mr Agutter proposed, and Mr Haynes seconded, that a flag day be held on Saturday, 13 November. This was carried. Messrs W F Corby and W H Lawrence were elected secretaries, and Mr Walter Gates was appointed treasurer. The Temperance Band offered their services and asked thus to parade round the town in the afternoon, playing selections at intervals, collecting en route. An apology was received from Mr and Mrs Warth of "The Grange" who sent a cheque for £5 in aid of the fund.

Miss Mackenzie had collected a sufficient amount of money during the past 2 or 3 weeks from the people of the town to pay for comforts for the 1st Northamptons. On Tuesday, **26 October**, the goods were handed over to Quartermaster Sergeant H Bull, who happened to be at home from the front for a week, and had called in to see Dr Mackenzie. The comforts thus sent comprised of 1,500 Woodbines, 10 khaki worsted helmets, 6 pairs of khaki mittens, 250 envelopes, 10 quires of writing paper, and 2 dozen lavender bags made by Mrs Warth of Raunds Grange.

At the VAD Hospital, Higham Ferrers this evening, a party of Raunds folk, led by Mrs Lawrence of Raunds Hall, entertained the wounded soldiers. Mr Jethro Hall sang "Keep your toys, laddie boy" with pleasing effect, Miss Edith Adams recited "The magic of a kiss", and Miss Ursula Lawrence sang "When you come home" to much well-merited applause. The first half closed with Mr O D Hall's humorous "Mary Anne" which brought the house down. The second half began with an amusing sketch "Paddy's Mistake", Mrs J Hall rendered "Rosebud" and encored with "Tired Hands", Miss E Adams recited "A Border Story" and encored with "Business as usual", and O D Hall finished with "My wedding", the patter of which was very funny, and was forced to encore twice with the same to satisfy the audience. Mr Jethro Hall accompanied on the piano.

A letter from Miss Gooding was discussed at the Church of England School managers meeting on Thursday, **28 October**. She advised that a scholar had taken the bunch of school keys from a nail outside of the Infants Department door and thrown them into "The Pits". They decided that "Gambull" should make up three new keys and a padlock, and that the cost should be borne by the boy's mother.

They also issued instructions that, in future, the caretaker should take the keys away with him after locking up the school.

The managers also considered an application from Miss Edith Emma Tregardine for the vacant post of Certified Assistant in the Mixed Department. It was decided to write to the applicant asking if she was still interested in view of the salary being considerably lower than her present one at Derby. In the meantime they would also write to the Rev Sore of St Werburgh's, Derby, for a testimonial.

A list published on Friday, **29 October**, of recent recruits for the Northamptons included Raunds men: J W Hall, **Fred Norris (81)**, G W Norris, S Partridge, A Willmott, and Ralph Wood.

Today's "London Gazette" recorded the appointment of the Rev C C Aldred as a "Temporary Chaplain to the Forces, 4th Class".

The story, "Raunds Soldier in Cambridge Hospital" also appeared today. It told how Mr and Mrs William Archer, of Midland Road, had received a letter from their son, 17 year old Private **R Archer (15)**, of the 1st Northamptons. He told how he had been wounded on 25 September in the action around Lens and Loos, and after a fortnight in a hospital in France, had now returned to England "where I hope to stay for a rest".

Another Raunds correspondent aired his views today from a military camp in Norfolk. Corporal Wesley Lee, Royal Bucks Hussars, wrote "The cold-blooded murder of Nurse Cavell has filled me with hatred of German militarism. In all sincerity I do hope I shall soon have the opportunity of taking part in the avenging of this crime. The Kaiser and his warlords' wicked ambitions have brought so much agony, physical and mental, into this world".

The managers of the Council Schools met in the evening and discussed the problem that although they had nearly 200 on the register and the average daily attendance was 180, the staff was only qualified to teach up to 160. Despite this, their request for a fifth teacher had been declined by the Local Education Committee. They therefore proposed to put these facts to the LEA and ask for an explanation as they knew of other schools with less pupils but had five teachers. They also heard that their application to the Authority for a full fortnight's holiday at Christmas had been agreed to.

And speaking in Parliament, Mr Asquith announced that the total British losses in the war up to 9 October were:

On the Western Front: Killed – 4,401 Officers, 63,059 Other Ranks; Wounded – 9,169 Officers, 225,716 Other Ranks; Missing – 156 Officers, 61,134 Other Ranks; Total – 363,635.

In All Fields: Killed – 6,660 Officers, 94,992 Other Ranks; Wounded – 12,633 Officers, 304,832 Other Ranks; Missing – 2,000 Officers, 72,177 Other Ranks; Total – 493,294.

Saturday, **30 October**, St Luke's Fair, Wellingborough – Thurston's "Best Scenic Railway" and Sedgewick's "Wild Beast Show".

"Five Generations – Remarkable Family Record at Raunds", ran the headline to the story that the town could boast a unique family record, that of Mrs Ann Stubbs and her four direct descendants. Mrs Stubbs, the matriarchal head of the family, was still sprightly and active, despite her 92 years. She was born in 1823 and had thus lived in no fewer than five reigns – George IV, William IV, Victoria, Edward VII, and George V, and just remembered the celebrations at the accession of William IV, when she was seven, and distinctly remembered his death seven years later. Her son, Mr Henry Stubbs, 68, was the current sexton at Raunds Parish Church and a well-known campanologist. His son, Mr William Stubbs, 45, was a former well-known handbell ringer. His son, Corporal John Henry Stubbs, 25, of the 10th Middlesex, was a teacher at Higham Ferrers when war broke out. Finally the grand old lady's great-great grandson, Master John Stubbs, was two days old when this story was written, making a grand five generation total of 230 years. *(Plate 13)*

Foreign Mission services were held at the Wesleyan Church on Sunday, **31 October**, when a Public Tea was provided and Mr J C Horrell presided over an unusually large attendance. Hymns and prayers were led by the Revs J Burrows and Harry Shaw, and the Rev C A Bone gave an interesting talk on his 35 years as a missionary in China. Misses Felicia Pendered and Edith Lawrence gave missionary addresses, a recitation was given by Miss Doris Coles, and the collection speech was taken by Master Willis Rands.

NOVEMBER – Writing from France in this month's Parish Magazine, the Vicar said "As you know, I am out here trying to take a little share in this great work. Please try and make as much as you can of All Saints-tide. It can also be a great help to all those who have given of their dearest since last All Saint's Day."

Dancing classes were to be held in the Institute on 8 and 22 November, at 8pm.

Final notice was given that the All Saint's tea and social would take place on 6 November in the Upper School. Preparations were said to be "well in hand" and tickets were now available: Tea only, 6d; Dance only, 6d; Inclusive Tea and Dance, 9d. Tea would be served at 5pm with dancing from 7.30pm to 10.30pm.

Anyone who wished to help by doing work for the Northamptonshire branch of the Red Cross Society was asked to contact Mrs Milligan of "The Crossways" for plain sewing or Mrs Jeeves of "Grove House" for knitting.

The number of eggs sent from the Church of England School to the wounded soldiers in October was about six dozen.

A Grand Concert was arranged by the committee of the Woodbine Working Men's Club on Monday, **1 November**, for the benefit of all Raunds soldiers and sailors serving in His Majesty's Colours. The event was held in the large club room, which was filled to capacity. Mr John Adams, JP, CC, was in the chair and the following artistes kindly gave of their services:

Mrs J W Hall, contralto; Misses Grace Lawrence, Louie Smith, V Lawrence, sopranos; Miss Edith Adams, elocutionist; Mr W W Hall's Quartette Party; Mr O D Hall, comedian; Mr W Gibbs, bass; Mr G H Pateman, tenor; Mr R Pentelow, baritone; Messrs Walter Smith and J Shatford, of Rushden; Mr Harry Smith, of Ringstead, comedian; and Mr George Drage, of Irthlingborough, euphonium soloist. The proceeds amounted to upwards of £18 and in connection with the same cause, a corresponding "number competition" was also taking place.

The Hospital Week Committee also held their quarterly meeting this evening at the "Golden Fleece" clubroom when Mr G Bass presided over "a fair attendance". The treasurer reported that receipts year to date were £178-1s-9d, expenditure (including £125 sent to the county treasurer) was £125-17s-2d, leaving a balance of £52-4s-7d. It was therefore decided to send another £50 to the county fund.

In a speech to Parliament on the progress of the war on Wednesday, **3 November**, the Prime Minister, Mr Asquith, said that conscription would be introduced if necessary, as a matter of expediency. However, the Allies were still confident of victory and were carrying a righteous cause to a triumphant issue.

That evening, Raunds Woodbine Working Men's Club took on Higham Ferrers Athletic Club in the Club Union Cribbage League, and winning by 30 to 25.

And today it was announced that Mrs E A Milligan had been elected Guardian and Rural District Councillor for Covington, succeeding the late Major Barnett.

At their meeting on Thursday, **4 November**, the Church of England School managers were advised that although Miss Tregardine had now withdrawn her application, Mrs Edge was willing to postpone her resignation until 31 December.

The Local Education Authority suggested that in the cause of economy of fuel and light, the interval between morning and afternoon school be curtailed to save lighting and coal. After discussion, the managers unanimously agreed to recommend that the afternoon session should in future commence at 1.30pm.

With the exceptional need for strict economy still in mind, they also agreed not to recommend any furniture requisitions except for two blackboards.

A Raunds bridegroom took his marriage vows in London today. Mr George A Farey, son of the late Mr John Farey and Mrs Farey, wed Miss Florence L James of Manor Park, at St Edmund's Church, Forest Gate. After the reception, the couple left for Raunds, the bride's travelling dress being a blue cloth costume with picture hat trimmed with ostrich feathers. There were many beautiful presents.

And at the Wellingborough Police Court this afternoon, a 45 year old Raunds shoehand of Wellington Road pleaded guilty to being drunk and disorderly in Rushden on 31 October. He was fined 19s-6d.

News emerged on Friday, **5 November**, that the Vicar, the Rev C C Aldred, at present a chaplain to the Forces "somewhere in France", had been back in England for a few days following receipt of a telegram informing him that his mother was seriously ill. The gentleman had arrived back in this country just in time to see her before she passed away. After the funeral, he paid a brief visit to Raunds, before departing once more for France.

The latest published list of recruits joining the 8th Northamptons included Raunds men J W Hall, W H March, S F Partridge, and A G Smart.

Ambulance classes for both men and women were announced on Saturday, **6 November**. They would be held in the Church of England School, with lectures by Dr Mackenzie, assisted by Dr McInnes.

The annual tea, concert and dance in connection with the Dedication Festival of the Parish Church took place this afternoon. A business meeting followed, presided over by the Rev W S Bethway.

The Brotherhood meeting on Sunday, **7 November**, was one of the most successful open meetings held. The Temperance Silver Prize Band had paraded the town prior to the meeting, the Wesleyan Church was quite full and both the Wesleyan Prize Choir and Brotherhood String Band were in attendance. The special object of the meeting was the raising of funds in order to send out practical greetings to the men at the front at Christmas. The Rev C J Keeler gave an address and his description of his work in the trenches made a great impression and left few of the large congregation unmoved. The collection raised £10-1s-8d.

A recruiting meeting was held in the Temperance Hall on Monday, **8 November**, to arrange to canvass in connection with the proposals of Lord Derby. Mr John Adams, CC, presided. The following volunteered to canvass: Messrs John Adams, J Shelmerdine, W F Corby, J Gant, JP, G E Smith, A Camozzi, W Agutter, Enos Smith, JP, G Lee, J Bass, R Lawrence, W Cobley, T Broker, W Shrives, A Tebbutt, H Betts, and Mrs Lee.

At Northampton Crown Court on Tuesday, **9 November**, Messrs Adams Bros, of Raunds, sued a Walgrave man for the return of a truck loaned to him, or its value, £3-10s-0d. Mr Fred Adams, giving evidence, said that the defendant's truck had broken down and he asked for the loan of theirs, but he had not returned it. Judgement was found in favour of the plaintiffs for £3-10s-0d and costs.

On Wednesday, **10 November**, the "Raunds Circuit Wesleyan Methodist Church Record" voiced in appropriate terms the regret felt by many throughout the district at the news of the death from pneumonia of Private Harold W Nicholson, of Hargrave, at Gallipoli on 21 October.

On this same day, Mr Tom Coggins, son of Mrs Coggins of "The Hall", left for Boulogne, as a motor ambulance driver.

News of the registration of a new company was published on Thursday, **11 November**. Tebbutt & Hall Bros Ltd (141061) was registered with a capital of £12,000 in £1 shares to carry on the business of boot and shoe manufacturers, leather merchants, dressers and tanners, manufacturing and dealing in boots, shoes, and machinery apparatus, tools, goods, leather, rubber and materials used in connection therewith. The initial directors were W W Hall, J W Hall, and J P Hall, with the registered office in Clare Street, Raunds.

Another item appearing in the "Raunds Circuit Wesleyan Methodist Church Record" stated that the friends of Lieutenant **A H Burrows (30),** of "Berrister House", would be pleased to hear that on Wednesday, 27 October, he was promoted to the rank of captain, the promotion being backdated to 26 July. Lieutenant Burrows was reported as being with the 6th Northamptons in France "in a hot place!"

The "Victims of the War" column on Friday, **12 November**, included in the "Missing" list, the name of **William Whiteman (130)**, 15127, 7th Northants.

The Serbian Flag Day was held in the town on Saturday, **13 November**, "in aid of our Serbian Allies", and proved most successful. A committee, of which Mrs V Spicer was convenor, arranged for every house and factory in the town to be visited. In the afternoon, the Temperance Band paraded the town, taking a collection. In all £31-14s-0d was raised.

"Wanted – Operator on Rapid Stitcher – Good wages to first class man – permanent employment – Apply to: Owen Smith, Raunds"

Mr H W Allen, confectioner of Wellington Road, had held a "guessing competition" in his shop during the past few days, the proceeds of which were to be sent to the "Daily News Christmas Pudding Fund", and the competition closed on Monday, **15 November**. Mr Allen had filled a bottle with small sweets, and the one who guessed the nearest number was to be given a prize of a 2lb box of chocolates. On counting the number of sweets, the bottle was found to contain 1,906. Two persons guessed 1,902 (the nearest number), so each received a 1lb box of chocolates. The amount raised by the effort totalled £1-13s-0d.

Colonel Stopford Sackville and Sir Ryland Adkins, MP, addressed another fine recruiting meeting this evening. Mr John Adams, CC, was again presiding, supported by (in khaki) Mr C Kenneth Murchison, JP, of Hargrave, Lieutenant V Sykes, and Mr J Shelmerdine. The Colonel remarked that it was about forty-seven years since he first presented himself for participation in the county regiment of militia but that the lapse of years now made him rather unwilling to turn out at night, but in this national crisis all must put personal feelings on one side. Now was not the time for speeches, but for action!

At the Thrapston Petty Sessions on Tuesday, **16 November**, the request to transfer the license of the "Red Lion" "fully licensed house" from the late Henry Gaunt to his widow, Annie Gaunt, was approved.

"Wanted – Capable man to take charge of a new 50hp Tangye gas engine, latest type, gas plant and dynamo – Apply to: Regulation Boot Co (Raunds) Ltd"

A meeting of the Raunds and District Friendly Societies Council was held at the "Axe and Compass", Ringstead, on Thursday, **18 November**, when Brother J T Pettit of Raunds presided over a very good attendance. The subject of "Consolidation and Centralisation" was ably opened for discussion by Brother H W Lawrence of Raunds.

On Friday, **19 November**, the Urban Council released a letter received in acknowledgement of the cheque for £31-14s-0d, the proceeds of the "Serbian Flag Day": "I wish to tender our warmest thanks for the splendid contribution, and trust you will convey to the many kind helpers our gratitude for their efforts in raising such a healthy sum for this deserving cause. As you imagine, funds are now urgently needed for us to carry on relief work to alleviate the sufferings of many thousands of refugees that are flocking daily into Greece and Romania."

In another recruiting session for the Northamptons at Rushden today, enlistments included Raunds men: Thomas Knight, of Newtown Road, in the 3rd/4th Battalion, Bill Stringer in the Depot and W J Annies in the 8th Battalion. Meanwhile in Irthlingborough, it was claimed that great efforts were being made to raise a "Pals" section!

"Wanted – At once, Operator on Consol Lasting – Government work – Apply to: Regulation Boot Co Ltd, Raunds"

Writing home on Saturday, **20 November**, Sergeant L G H Lee told of how he spent an "exciting birthday" earlier in the month. "There was nothing eventful until midday although during my observation work I did notice a German aeroplane out scouting, and heard the whistle of enemy shells. However, after finishing my work I went for dinner, bully beef and toothpicks, toothpicks are an essential after a course of bully beef! I was just coming away from the hutments when there was a scream of an approaching shell, which came hurtling through the park trees over my head, bringing down a big branch, and finally landing plump in the middle of the centric hut. Fortunately the occupants, except for one or two who had been on all night duty, had just gone on parade, or there must have been considerable loss. In the evening we had our birthday supper, the sergeants, and no shell disturbed our innocent convivialities. Selby's sausages sizzled in the frying pan, and never tasted so well at home. The biggest of the Smeathers' pork pies positively gleamed at us, as if proud to be 'doing its bit'. A plum pudding, mother's make, pronounced by one to be the 'best bloomin' plum pudding he had ever had,' was the 'plat du jour'. Tea, with some of those many smokes sent over by Dr Mackenzie, concluded our meal."

Mrs A Lawrence of "The Hall" organised a concert in the Wesleyan School today in aid of the Belgian Relief Fund today, raising £16.

At the Wesleyan Church on Sunday, **21 November**, the Rev T Ashley, of Handsworth College, was the preacher, and Miss Grace Lawrence was the soloist.

The Brotherhood meeting in the afternoon saw Mr Haselby, of Northampton, give an address on "History and the War". Miss Miriam Sanders was the soloist, and Miss Edith Sanders accompanied her at the piano. During the meeting, letters were read from two Brotherhood members now serving their country in France.

Monday, 22 November, the Battle of Ctesiphon, the Anglo-Indian advance up the Tigris is halted by the Turks.

As our boys battled the heat and flies of Mesopotamia, a town meeting was called this evening in the Temperance Hall to consider the call from Mr Herbert Dulley, Battalion Commandant of the Wellingborough and District Volunteer Training Corps, for the Council to try and form a Volunteers Corps in Raunds. Mr John Adams, JP, CC, presided, with support from Mr J Shelmerdine and Mr A G Henfrey. The "rather limited attendance" heard Mr Dulley explain that with many men already away on military service it was the duty of every man who remained to do what they could. What was needed was a Corps in the town to help protect the railway bridges etc in the district, and the more that joined then the lighter the duties for all. Mr Shelmerdine then proposed that a Volunteer Corps for Raunds be formed. This was carried and several gave their names to join. Mr Adams responded by donating £5 towards the equipment that would be needed.

Leaving Raunds on Tuesday, **23 November**, were Monsieur and Madame Deberghes and their little daughter Marie. The Belgian family had been entertained by the Raunds and Stanwick Belgian Relief Committee since October 1914, but now M Deberghes had secured a position on the railway in north west France. Before the invasion of his country, he had been a porter superintendent of the luggage department at Antwerp station. Before leaving, the family called on the secretary of the committee, Mr W F Corby, to express their grateful thanks to the people of Raunds and Stanwick for the great kindness shown to them. Following this departure, there were still 16 refugees under the care of the committee in the town.

It was announced on Wednesday, **24 November**, that after the end of the month, the public could not send any parcel over 7lb in weight to a soldier on active service. To reach troops by Christmas, letters had to be posted by 17 December, and parcels by 13 December as the War Office needed to limit the amount of parcel traffic during the Christmas period. The rates for the Salonika Force were: postcards, 1d; letters, 1d per ounce; newspapers, ½d for two ounces; parcels up to three pounds, 1s-0d; and between three and seven pounds, 1s-9d. Parcels for the Mediterranean Expeditionary Force needed to be posted by 1 December, and in view of the exceptional conditions of transit, transhipments, and weather, parcels should be very carefully packed. Wooden or metal boxes had to be well padded with no sharp corners.

A serious accident occurred at Messrs Stanley and Company's boot factory on Thursday, **25 November**. A young girl named Hall, from Stanwick, got her left hand trapped in the splitting machine, splitting four fingers from end to end. Dr McInnes attended to the injury at once, and she was sent home by motor, and was later seen by Drs Mackenzie and McInnes, who redressed the wounds. It was hoped that the patient would eventually regain the use of her fingers.

In the evening, the managers of the Church of England School met and heard that no applications had been received for the Certified Assistant in the Mixed Department. It was therefore unanimously agreed to ask for a Supply Teacher when the school reopened after Christmas and that Miss Florence Hall should be brought back.

The headmaster of the Mixed Department, Mr F A Potter, asked the managers' opinion on what course of action he should take under Lord Derby's Recruiting Scheme. However, they felt they could not advise him and left it to his own discretion.

Regarding the proposed date of 4pm, 24 December, to start the Christmas holiday, letters from head teachers Mr Potter and Miss Gooding, on behalf of the staff, were read out. They pointed out the serious inconvenience of the proposal which prompted the managers to agree to send letters and minutes of the meeting to the District Sub-Committee asking that the date be brought forward to 23 December.

On Friday, **26 November**, it was announced that Mr F W Dix, the town's famous athlete, cyclist, and skating champion, together with his brother, had joined the Motor Transport section of the Army Service Corps.

In the Rushden and District Billiards League, Rushden Athletic Club played Raunds Conservatives on Saturday, **27 November**, winning by 596 to 454. Mr A Lawrence captained the Raunds team comprising of Messrs A B Couzen, W Bailey, H Nicholls, J Chambers, and H Sykes.

That evening, intense cold in the district was especially felt by the motor 'bus drivers. The fog made the cold even more piercing, and one of the drivers was so overcome that he was assisted off his 'bus in a semi-conscious condition.

Two deaths occurred in the town on Sunday, **28 November**. Mr Ernest Wingell, aged 38, the second son of the late Mr Thomas Wingell, succumbed after a long illness of about 18 months. And in the morning, at the residence of her daughter, Mrs Miles, of "Fairholme", Mrs Mary Adams, 80 years old, the mother of Mr James Adams and Mr John Adams, CC, died from an attack of acute bronchitis.

The local recruiting officer under Lord Derby's current scheme, Mr John Adams, attended the Council Schools on Tuesday, **30 November**, to receive attestations. Accompanied by Lieutenant Young of Wellingborough, and Mr W F Corby, the honorary secretary, they had a brisk time. Dr Mackenzie and his assistant Dr McInnes were kept busy from 9.30pm conducting medical examinations. Seven men, however, went away un-enrolled, owing to the numbers in waiting. The attestation would open again on Thursday evening, 2 December, from 6 o'clock.

The managers of the Council School also met this evening to consider a letter from the Education Committee regarding their request for an increase in staff in the Infants Department, pointing out that staffing was below average. However, due to the number of scholars moving to the Upper School at Christmas it was decided that the current levels should remain.

The number of cases of irregular attendances was discussed and several parents appeared before the committee and promised regular attendance in future. Finally, six exemptions for employment under the new laws were submitted and agreed to.

* * * * * * * * * * * * * * * * * * * *

* * * * * * * * * * * * * * * * * * * *

DECEMBER – The final Parish Magazine of the year opened with a letter from the Vicar, the Rev C C Aldred, from "somewhere in France", who said "Your fellow men out here and elsewhere need your prayers. It is a tremendous help to know that you are frequently praying for the men and the work on this side. May this coming Christmas bring you all dear friends, the lasting joy of real service in prayer."

The collection at the Parish Church on Christmas Day would be distributed between the Church of England "Waifs and Strays Society" and the Parochial Sick and Poor Fund.

A letter from the relatives of the late John Wilmott written in November to the Vicar, Churchwardens, and all subscribers said "Will you please accept our hearty thanks for the handsome memorial you have placed in the churchyard in memory of father. It's very pleasing to know that his services as Parish Clerk and Sexton were so highly appreciated, on behalf of the family, Mrs J Driver and Mr A Wilmott."

It was decided that the Vestry Class of 5 December would be designated as "Cigarette Sunday" and the organisers hoped to get enough to send each of the soldier members a few "smokes" for Christmas.

Wednesday, **1 December**, "Wanted – Operator for Rapid Stitcher – Good wages to first class man – Permanent employment – Apply to: Owen Smith, Raunds"

Today, it was announced that from Monday, 6 December, the post box at the Post Office would be cleared at 7.45am instead of 8am as at present. All other despatches and deliveries would remain as before.

The funeral of Mr Ernest Wingell was held at the Parish Church this afternoon.

And in the evening, the girls of the closing department at Messrs E W Stanley's factory arranged a social and dance in the Central Hall of the Council Schools at which nearly 300 attended. Songs were contributed by Messrs A Tebbutt, A Barford, and L Morel and three of the Belgian children resident in the town. A piano and mandolin duet was also given by Misses Betts and Bailey. Miss Foster ably contributed pianoforte selections during the interval and games and amusements were enjoyed by all. A "doll guessing" competition was also arranged, raising 11s-0d. Later, dancing was indulged in, the music being supplied by Messrs W C Green on the piano and Bert Clark on the violin while Mr H Betts acted as MC. In all, the proceeds of the evening amounted to £9, which was to be used to provide New Year's gifts for the Raunds soldiers at the front.

At the final Church of England Schools managers' meeting of 1915 on Thursday, **2 December**, they considered a request from the Council School managers that the Christmas holidays should begin on 22 December. After discussion, they decided to adhere to the previous meeting's resolution for the holiday to begin on 23 December.

An application from Mrs A E Potter for the managers' recommendation that she be put on the staff of the Mixed Department was referred to the Local Education Authority.

The LEA was also to be sent a reminder that Miss Gooding had still not yet received her agreed salary increase.

Laid to rest today was the late Mrs Mary Adams. The cortege left "Fairholme", residence of the deceased's daughter, Mrs Miles, at 2.30pm for the Wesleyan Chapel. The service was conducted by the Rev J Burrows who also read the committal service at the graveside. The coffin, placed in a bricked grave lined with ivy, was of panelled oak with brass fittings, and was carried by eight of the employees of Messrs Adams Bros.

A meeting of the Raunds Recruiting Sub-Committee took place in the Council School on Friday evening, **3 December**. The result of the recent canvass in the town revealed the fact that 495 cards had been returned out of the 518 to be accounted for. On the motion of Mr J Shelmerdine, seconded by Mr R Lawrence, it was decided to issue another poster calling attention to the need of all persons with badges being enrolled. It was also decided to have the attestation station open again in the Council School during the coming week on Tuesday and Thursday to give further facilities for enrolment. Attesting officials and doctors had already been appointed for the county's temporary enrolment stations, and for Raunds these were Mr John Adams, JP, and Dr W Mackenzie.

Acknowledged today was another donation of eggs for the VAD Hospital at Higham Ferrers, from the Raunds schools; while in Stanwick, a plea went out asking "the gentleman who bought some apples on the Raunds road, to please return the bags!"

The Brotherhood met as usual in the Wesleyan Church on Sunday afternoon, **5 December**, when the speaker was Councillor James Jackson of Northampton. He gave a splendid address on "What the War means". Mrs J Hall was the soloist and rendered "God, who madest Earth and Heaven" and "There's a Lord", in her usual artistic style, accompanied by Mr J W Hall at the piano. Mr L W Sheffield presided over a good attendance and an interesting feature of the meeting was the reading of letters from three members now serving at the front.

A young fellow experienced a painful accident at Raunds on Monday, **6 December**. Arthur Hall, of Red Row, was going down the steps at the bottom of Coleman Street, to his home for dinner from one of the factories, when he slipped and fell and his left hand was caught by a spike fixed to the wall. The spike entered at the wrist and completely divided the hand in two, right up to the forefinger which was also split open. The cut extended between the metacarpal bones almost to the skin at the back. Dr Mackenzie dressed the wound and sent him off to Northampton General Hospital.

A Thanksgiving Day was held in the Wesleyan Church this afternoon, the proceedings being enlivened by musical items. The effort was staged instead of the annual Boxing Day sale of work, which it was thought advisable to drop this year owing to the various calls being made upon the public through the war. Refreshments were provided and vocal items were contributed by the Rev H and Mrs Shaw of Thrapston, and Mr A Tebbutt, and piano solos by Miss Doris Green. Mr J W Hall accompanied the solos and the proceeds of the event totalled £30.

And a concern to working folk in Rance would have been the alleged suggestion today by the Central Liquor Control Board that the closing of all licensed houses on Christmas and Boxing Days was under consideration!

Tuesday, 7 December, the Siege of Kut begins.

The Raunds Old Age Pensions Sub-Committee met today and four new claims were reviewed, one each from Raunds and Twywell and two from Burton Latimer. Two were allowed at the full rate and another at 1s-0d per week, the fourth was disallowed on the grounds of "excessive means". Three new claims for dependency allowance were also considered, one each from Raunds, Ringstead and Burton Latimer, and an allowance of 5s-0d in each case was agreed to.

Mr W Denton, of "Northdale", enjoyed a very successful day as an exhibitor at Tuesday's Thrapston Christmas Fat Stock Show. He took first prize for five lambhogs in Class 6, first prize for three lambhogs in Class 7, and first and second prizes for two lambhogs in Class 3.

Wednesday, 8 December, the Allied evacuation from Gallipoli begins.

Recruiting officials were engaged for four hours at the Council School on Thursday evening, **9 December**, and at the close there were still more who had to go away than the officials had been able to deal with. Consequently, it was agreed to re-open for attestations again on Friday evening, and if necessary, on Saturday. Already many more than the number of those who promised had been attested and there was every evidence that when the final figures were known it would be seen that a very good percentage of the "eligibles" had responded to the call.

A new Arbitration Board for Northamptonshire met for the first time today at the offices of Messrs Cattell & Favell, of Rushden. Comprising of six employers and six employees, of whom John Adams, CC, and A Hazeldine of Messrs C E Nichols represented Raunds, its purpose was to fix prices for Government boot and shoe work.

It was announced on Friday, **10 December**, that collections for the Wesleyan War Emergency Fund throughout the Raunds Circuit had realised £9-12s-9d, which had been sent to the Rev Simpson, secretary of the Conference. Individual chapel contributions included £4-14s-9d from Raunds, 10s-5d from Ringstead, £1-2s-4d from Thrapston, and £1-1s-9d from Denford.

The latest league table for the Rushden and District Clubs' Billiards League published today showed Raunds Conservatives lying fourth and Raunds Woodbine occupying eighth and last place.

On Saturday, **11 December**, a Flag Day was arranged by Mrs A Camozzi and Mrs A Lawrence, in aid of the funds of the local Red Cross Committee. The splendid sum of £19-4s-6d was raised. A number of ladies were allotted the various districts to collect in and hearty thanks were given to those ladies for the fine financial result of their efforts.

In the evening in the Wesleyan Schoolroom, there was an exhibition of limelight views of the war. Dr Mackenzie was unable to take the chair owing to the recruiting boom, so in his absence Mr George Lee presided over a fairly good attendance. A fine series of pictures included scenes from the home country, France, Belgium, Romania, Poland, the Dardanelles and Serbia. The Rev J Burrows briefly explained and commented upon the pictures, Mr L W Sheffield was the lanternist, assisted by Mr A Tebbutt. Solos were rendered by Miss Winnie Pentelow entitled "My Dear Soul" and "Cuckoo", accompanied by Miss Lilian Robinson at the piano.

Coming into force today was the final clause of the 1914 National Agreement for the minimum wage for National Union of Boot and Shoe Operatives. Members over 23 years of age would receive an increase of 1s-0d per week and were urged by their union to make sure that this was complied with by the manufacturers.

NUBSO duly extolled: "So Non-Unionists – Here we are again! Bobs! Bobs! Bobs! – Why don't you Bob up and Bob into the Union Office!"

The latest issue of the "Raunds Circuit Wesleyan Methodist Church Record" commented on some interesting drink statistics given at a recent temperance conference held in the town. "The Government is preaching the absolute necessity of saving money instead of spending it. Frequenters of public houses in Raunds could, if they would, save more than £12,000 a year!" This was based on the estimated per home annual spend of £13-17s-0d for each of the town's 900 houses.

The Rushden and District Clubs' "Helping the Blind and Crippled Children Association" meeting was held at the Windmill Club, Rushden, today, including delegates from Raunds. The 1915 accounts showed total receipts of £180-12s-1d, including £11-2s-4d raised by the sale of Forget-Me-Nots in Raunds. Of the total expenditure of £93-14s-6d, £1-5s-0d was granted to a Raunds blind person, and 4s-0d towards surgical appliances and treatment of a crippled child in the town. In the elections of officers for 1916, Mr John Adams was appointed auditor and Raunds Woodbine Working Mens Club would supply two delegates for future meetings.

Lieutenant V S Sykes, Sherwood Foresters, gave a very interesting address on "The British Tommy's Religion" at the Brotherhood meeting on Sunday afternoon, **12 December**. The Lieutenant had been out to France twice, but was currently home recuperating from wounds received in the service of his country. Miss Grace Lawrence was the soloist, rendering "Jerusalem" and "O Divine Redeemer", accompanied by Mr W Cyril Groom. The large attendance generously contributed to the Benevolent Fund.

"Closing Rush at Rushden", "Boom at Thrapston", "Wellingborough Willing", "Finedon's Good Finish", "Bedford Busy", "Burton Booming", and "Raunds Ready". In common with many other places, it did prove to be a very busy last long weekend of recruiting in the town, with the local recruiting officer, Mr John Adams, JP, CC, and his assistant Mr W F Corby, being indefatigable in their efforts to meet the calls. As already planned, all who had promised to enrol had done so by Thursday evening, but on Friday there were still many coming forward, and although the office was open from 6pm to 11pm, that did not suffice. On Saturday from 2 o'clock to 11.30pm many more came up and on Sunday evening a good number more were attested. Sixty percent of the town's men (exclusive of those who enrolled elsewhere) in total attested, this was five times more than those who had promised. Dr Mackenzie and Dr McInnes, the local medical men, consequently also had a very busy time. Amusingly at Rushden, two doctors were sworn in under Lord Derby's scheme, and each medically examined the other!

On Monday afternoon, **13 December**, an inquiry was held at the "George & Dragon Hotel" into the death of John Harris Elliott, who was found dead in his house in Marshall's Road the previous morning. Witnesses told how he had last been seen alive on 25 November and Sgt Ellingham testified that he had been drawn to the deceased's house by the sight of a crowd gathered there. After forcing an entry through a window he found the body lying on the downstairs floor. There was no sign of a struggle, and there was money and watches on the mantelpiece, and food on the table. The man appeared to have been dead for some time. Dr Mackenzie stated that when he was called, he found no marks of violence and that the deceased appeared to have died from an apoplectic stroke. A verdict was returned of "death between 25 November and 12 December from apoplexy".

Buckingham Palace announced on Tuesday, **14 December**, that despite a serious loss of weight after his accident on 28 October, the King was now able resume work with certain limitations.

And after his success at the previous week's Thrapston Fat Stock Show, Mr Walter Denton of "Northdale" had some fine tegs on sale at today's Thrapston Cattle Market. The highest price realised was 79s-0d, and the average (for 12 animals) was 72s-7d.

Wednesday, 15 December, General Sir Douglas Haig replaces Field Marshall Sir John French as Commander-in-Chief of British forces in France.

Under the auspices of the Independent Labour Party, a musical evening was arranged in the Temperance Hall this evening, when "Casey" (Walter Hampson) paid a return visit. Although the attendance was somewhat affected by another attraction in the National Schools, those present were well rewarded with the splendid items provided, and those contributed by "Casey" were evidently greatly enjoyed. Miss Dolly Pickard was the efficient accompanist.

The rival event that reduced the attendance at the Temperance Hall was a grand dance held in the central hall of the National Schools in aid of funds of the local Red Cross Committee. The evening was arranged by Mrs A Camozzi of the Manor House, and Mrs A Lawrence of The Hall. Included in the company were staff and the wounded soldiers from the VAD Hospital, Higham Ferrers, under the charge of the Matron, Mrs T Patenhall, Mayoress of Higham Ferrers, who had been motored over by Messrs A Camozzi, A Lawrence, H W Lawrence, and J W Coggins.

The music for the dancing was gratuitously supplied by the members of the Raunds Temperance Silver Band. Mr H Edwards acted as MC, and refreshments were provided during the interval by a committee of ladies. Songs were also given by Mrs Adcock, Mr O D Hall, and the Rev W S Bethway, Mr J W Hall accompanying at the piano. At the far end of the hall hung a large Union Jack and the words "God bless our Khaki Boys and our Sailor Boys". The proceeds of the dance augmented the funds by nearly £14.

The annual distribution of prizes to the successful students attending the Raunds Evening Schools took place on Friday evening, **17 December**. Mr John Adams, CC, was unable to attend to present the prizes, so Mr J Shelmerdine officiated. The awards, about 40 in number, were of a very useful nature, the girls receiving writing cases and musical cabinets, and the boys Tennyson's poems and other works. The prizes for students in the Boot and Shoe classes consisted of size sticks, grading tools, and compasses, and for students in the woodwork classes, a selection of woodwork tools. At the close, a vote of thanks was accorded to Mr Shelmerdine, and in reply he moved a similar vote of thanks to the head teacher and staff which was accorded by three ringing cheers from the students.

It was also the annual prize giving today at the Wellingborough County Girls School, and Edna Pendered of Raunds was three times successful, receiving awards for Form IVa, Mathematics; Holiday, socks; and Toy Show, knitting.

And former town shoe operative, Private A S Lawman of the 1st/4th Northamptons, was reported as being in hospital suffering from wounds.

There was excitement at midday on Sunday, **19 December**, when an aeroplane passed over the town and alighted near Mr Ratcliffe's farm, in the parish of Ringstead. The aviator was Lieutenant Gilmour, of the Royal Flying Corps, who was accompanied by his mechanic. They came down as they had run out of petrol.

The Lieutenant went into Raunds, where he soon got a fresh supply from Mr C Masters, who then motored the aviator back to the scene. When everything was ready to resume their journey, the aeroplane circled round, and the occupants waved farewell to the large number of spectators who had visited the spot. The machine was quickly out of sight.

The pulpit at the Wesleyan Church was today occupied by the Rev Harry Shaw of Thrapston, who preached two very interesting sermons. At the evening service the reverend gentleman took for his subject "Creed and Character" and delivered a very fine sermon on the subject. Mrs Shaw rendered the solo entitles "O rest in the Lord" and the choir also contributed the chorus "How great are the depths", Mr J W Hall being at the organ.

In the afternoon, the Brotherhood held their annual musical service when there was a large attendance. In addition to the usual carols, solos were performed in a very creditable way by Mrs Shaw entitled "How lovely are thy dwellings" and "The Lord is my light". The Wesleyan Prize Choir sang a selection entitled "O Father" with Mr J W Hall again presiding at the organ. An instrumental quartette was also given by members of the Temperance Band (Messrs E Vickers, H Bailey, W Groom and R Annies), conducted by Mr O Pentelow. The Brotherhood String Band, conducted by Mr F Jeffkins, played a selection while the collection was taken, which was in aid of the Northampton General Hospital, and realised the splendid sum of £5-5s-3d.

In Northampton, women tram conductors made their first appearance and a lady "postman" in Kettering was said to be "attracting much attention".

On Monday, **20 December**, it was announced that the total amount raised by the Flag Day and dance in aid of local Red Cross funds was the most satisfactory sum of £32-15s-9d. The organisers expressed tremendous delight with the support accorded to both events by the general public. The flags were generously provided by Mr Fred Adams, and Mesdames Milligan, Lawrence and Camozzi.

Also today, additions to the County's Commissioners of the Peace were published and they included Mr Jesse Shelmerdine, of "Wirkfield", Raunds. His credentials were listed as: retired schoolmaster, Urban Councillor, Northamptonshire Education Committee member, trustee of the Church of England School, guardian and overseer, churchwarden, chairman of the Conservative Club, prominent Freemason, and Past Master of the Chicheley and Lilford Lodges. *(Plate 3)*

The following notice of the Raunds Temperance Silver Prize Band's annual prize distribution appeared in the local press on Tuesday, **21 December**: "Winning numbers .... We, the undersigned, certify that the above draw has been carried out in a straightforward and satisfactory manner, Fred Abbott and J W Jones, Scrutineers. Prizes to be claimed on or before 30 December from the Secretary, Mr Joseph Vorley, Marshall's Road, Raunds."

In the evening the Urban Council met and Mr Shelmerdine reported that the recent public meeting to consider the formation of a Volunteer Corps for the town attracted an attendance that was not very encouraging. The council agreed to leave the matter with him to develop for further discussion at a later date.

The medical officer, reported six cases of scarlet fever in November, five of which, all mild, were in one house, and two deaths and six births registered in the town.

A letter had been received from the captain of the Fire Brigade asking that certain necessary items might be purchased in connection with the equipment of the Fire Brigade, to this the councillors agreed. They also agreed to the appointment of Mr Bert Bailey as a fireman in place of Fireman Coles, now with the forces.

Also reviewed was a letter from the Local Government Board enclosing their formal sanction to the loans of £305 and £178, which upon reconsideration they had decided to grant for the provision of a cemetery in accordance with the modified application. The Board stated they had been advised that an area of about two acres would meet all reasonable future requirements of the district as far as could be foreseen. However, they stressed that any surplus land purchased should be resold as soon as possible to reduce the debt.

During the meeting Mr G E Smith asked that his name be withdrawn as a member of the Local Tribunal under Lord Derby's recruiting scheme for personal reasons. Mr W F Corby then asked for the same action but for reasons of workload. After much debate Mr G E Smith reluctantly agreed to stay but Mr Corby's resignation was accepted and Mr W Agutter was chosen to fill the vacancy. Mr Shelmerdine added that he had been asked by the Officer in Charge at Northampton to act as the military representative on the Raunds committee, and had accepted the request.

At the close of the meeting the chairman, on behalf of the council, offered congratulations to Mr Shelmerdine on his appointment as magistrate. He also wished the members the compliments of the season and upon his suggestion, it was decided to send a message of good cheer to Mr Gant, who was absent through indisposition, and Mr Lee, who was serving "somewhere in France".

An important meeting took place at the Coffee Tavern on Wednesday morning, **22 December**, when the Joint Standing Committee governing Government contracts met to discuss two payment issues. The talks were presided over by Mr C Bates, representing the manufacturers were Messrs John Adams, R O Neal, A Hazeldine and A Lawrence, and representing the workers were Messrs W Langley, E Batchelor, and A Robinson. First it was agreed that the proposed extra 1s-0d per week, for men at 23 years of age and over, should be paid as from 4 December. With regard to the 10% war bonus paid on the Home Service Blucher, it was stated that, although the boot was being manufactured in a number of factories, in some it was being lasted by hand at piece rates. It was therefore agreed that the 10% should be paid for this operation "in accordance with the price fixed for boots, ankle, screwed aloft, as provided for on page 16 of the Green Book."

And a tip for readers: "Among your Christmas gifts to the boys at the front, don't forget tomorrow's Christmas number of the Thrapston & Raunds Journal".

The following day, the staff of the Higham Ferrers VAD Hospital were invited to a dance at Raunds.

As in previous years on **Christmas Eve**, members of the Temperance and Salvation Army Bands visited various parts of the town and played Christmas carols and other seasonable music. Unfortunately, owing to the unsatisfactory weather, they had to leave off before going right round. The Primitive Methodist Carol Singers also visited various areas of the town. The bands reconvened to play appropriate music at many locations in the town on **Christmas Day**, when a collection was taken in aid of their funds.

The usual service was held in the Parish Church on Christmas morning when the preacher was the Rev W S Bethway. In the afternoon a carol service was held at 3pm. On Boxing Day the services were again conducted by the Curate and the collection, in aid of Northampton General Hospital, amounted to £3.

A young people's party was held at the Wesleyan Schools on **Boxing Day** and was largely attended. The proceedings commenced with a tea at 5 o'clock when about 140 sat down to the trays presided over by Misses B Groom, L Hazeldine, E Sanders, D Green, L Walker, E Cuthbert, N Finding, M Abbott, L Smith, and E Ball. After the tables had been cleared, a social was held when vocal and instrumental music was contributed and various seasonable games and amusements were provided. The young people entered heartily into the various games etc and a very pleasant and happy time was spent together.

Monday, **27 December**, severe gales passed through the district, and although no-one was injured, they were responsible for a good deal of damage with chimney pots and roof tiles dislodged and several large trees uprooted.

At the Temperance Hall in Ringstead a sale of work took place arranged by the Wesleyan Methodist Church. Mr John Adams, JP, CC, came over from Raunds to open the proceedings and, in a most suitable manner, made a donation of £2 to the funds. About £17 was raised for the piano and restoration funds.

The St Mary's Guild arranged a dance in the Church Institute on Tuesday evening, **28 December**, there being a fair company present. Dancing was indulged in from 7pm to 10.30pm, with an interval for refreshments which were handed round by Mesdames J E Barringer, J P Archer, J Pentelow, R Mayes, and Mesdemoiselles Aldred and N Barringer. The music was supplied by Mrs W Spicer and Mr R Cox.

Also today, the death took place of a highly respected inhabitant, Mr George Warren, of Grove Street, at the ripe old age of 84 years. The deceased, a staunch non-conformist, was an attendant at the Wesleyan Church. For many years he had been farm bailiff to the late John K Nichols, and later gardener to Mr John Horrell.

The Church Sunday School teachers and the members of the Vicarage and Vestry Classes held their annual tea and social in the central hall of the National Schools on Thursday, **30 December**. Tea was served at 5 o'clock, when about 150 sat down to a capital spread provided by the Raunds Distributive Co-Operative Society. After the tables had been cleared the social evening commenced, when songs were contributed by Messrs W Gibbs, W S Sykes, W March, H Bamford, and S Wright (comic); recitations by the Rev F C Boultbee of Hargrave; and "sleight of hand" performances by Mr C Head. Refreshments were provided during the evening, and dancing was indulged in, the music being supplied by Messrs F Reynolds (piano), and Bert Clarke (violin). Messrs R Mayes, W Gibbs, and S Wright acted as MC's. An enjoyable evening terminated at about 12.30.

On **New Year's Eve**, the employees of Messrs Tebbutt & Hall Bros held a social in the Wesleyan Sunday School room, about 160 employees and friends being present. The proceedings commenced with a substantial meat tea at 5 o'clock, the catering for which was again admirably carried out by the Raunds Co-Op. The company re-assembled after the tables had been cleared when an excellent programme of music and dancing was contributed, including songs by Messrs W White, O D Hall, W Gibbs, Mrs J W Hall, Misses Louie Smith, Winnie Pentelow, and Grace Lawrence, and Mr and Mrs H Baker; monologues by Mr A Tebbutt; and Mr Barker gave an exhibition of the magician's art with "living marionettes" and card tricks. The dancing was led by an efficient band, comprising Messrs W Cyril Groom (piano), W Burton (violin), M Drage (euphonium), and H Bailey (cornet). Messrs O D Hall, W Gibbs, and H Millard were the MC's.

And today the clerk to the District Education Sub-Committee, Mr Arthur Mantle, reminded parents via a notice in the local press that the Raunds Schools would re-open after the Christmas holidays on Monday, 10 January.

Year-end entertainmental delights included "Maudie and Gladys", in their speciality Toe Dancing and Quick Change act, and "Ward and Welsh", the sensational Balancing and Comedy eccentrics, appearing at the Rushden Palace.

The second war-time Christmas had now been celebrated with no end in sight to the hostilities. "Only" fourteen Raunds men had so far given their lives for King and Country, the last one more than three months earlier, but next year would not be so kind to local families!

* * * * * * * * * * * * * * * * * * * *

For men in khaki, For men in blue, For men in mufti, For women too!
The "Swan" Fountain Pen, is a splendid Christmas Gift

* * * * * * * * * * * * * * * * * * * *

9 – January to March 1916

Conscription comes and so do the blizzards.

JANUARY – In his first Parish Notes of the New Year, the Vicar announced that this year's confirmation service would be on Thursday, 16 March. He stated that the responsibility was laid on parents and godparents to see that their children were brought forward for confirmation. He added that "if your child is old enough to go out to work, he or she is old enough to be confirmed, and you are neglecting your duty if you send them to work in factories for a year or two without the help of the Holy Ghost the Comforter". Classes would be held at the Vicarage, on Tuesdays for boys and on Thursdays for girls.

Dates for the diary were dance classes in the Institute from 8pm to 10pm on the 10 and 24 January.

The Parish Magazine featured the report on the review of Religious Instruction at the Church Schools, as carried out by A E A Jones, Diocesan Inspector. Of the Mixed Department he observed that "teaching in this class has evidently been most carefully given and the children seemed to delight in the subject. In the three groups examined, the Bible facts were generally well known and the children showed a fair appreciation of their meaning". Of the Infants Department his view was that "the infants in classes 2 and 3 were bright, intelligent, and interested. They showed a good knowledge of facts, and though in some portions of the repetition the longer words were not quite accurate in pronunciation, otherwise it was excellent". His overall conclusion was that "altogether, the school has well maintained its reputation".

Also in the magazine were the 1915 Churchwarden's Accounts. Total income and expenditure was £139-19s-5d, this included £2-10s-0d for "organ blowing" and £1-8s-6d for "washing surplices".

The annual tea given by the Men's and Women's Adult Schools for old people over 65 was held in the Temperance Hall on **New Year's Day**. About 140 were present including the Belgian residents in the town. Tea was provided at 3.30pm, the tables being presided over by Mesdames B & T Green, A,B, & W Mayes, C Major, J H Haynes, C & F Abbott, C Agutter, S Cunnington, W Underwood, and G Winsor. After tea a splendid programme was gone through, Mr George French being in the chair, and extended a hearty welcome and wished "A Happy New Year" to the guests. Mr G Bass and Miss E Pulpher also briefly addressed the company.

The following items were given: song "Drake Goes West", Mr O D Hall; monologue "Soliloquy of an Old Shoe", Mr A Tebbutt; songs "The Good Old Bassoon" and "Which Switch is the Switch?", Mr O D Hall; recitation "The Bald Headed Man", Master Willis Rands; song "Till the boys come home", Monsieur L Morel; recitation "The Squire's Party", Mr S Head; song "Come Back to Erin", Miss W Pentelow; recitation "The Thinning of the Thatch", Master W Rands; song "Then the Bell of Joy Will Ring", M L Morel ....

Recitations "Snowflake", Maria Deberghes; "6 More Soldiers", C Morel; "5 Little Mice", R Morel; song "Travellers Tales", Belgian children; song "God Bless our Soldier Lads", Mr W Gibbs. Accompanists were Mr J W Hall and Misses Doris Green and Lily Robinson. The very popular event closed with the singing of the hymn "God be with you till we meet again".

The first day of this, a leap year, also saw the "Draw for Comforts for the Gordons and Northamptons". Dr Mackenzie and a committee consisting of Messrs J T Pettitt, Wm Knighton, W Agutter, Thos Pentelow, E Spicer, and G Pollard, brought to a successful conclusion the draw for prizes kindly given by the boot manufacturers and shopkeepers of the town, in order to send comforts to the troops. A net sum of £24 was raised, this being spent on: 8,000 cigarettes, 112 one ounce packs of "Glasgow smoking mixture", clay pipes, 24 dozen boxes of safety matches, 24 dozen Oxo cubes, 24 mouth organs, 15 dozen pairs of leather laces, 24 dozen boxes of dubbin, 6 dozen bars of toilet soap, biscuits in tins, 18 lbs of Brazil and Barcelona nuts, 8 lbs of chocolate, 6 dozen sheets of songs, 6 dozen boxes of vaseline, 2 dozen tins of "Keatings", and 48 dozen candles.

And results of the recent examinations of the Trinity College of Music, held at Wellingborough, were published today and Miss Alice K Whitney, of Butts Road, was successful in passing at the intermediate stage. Miss Whitney was a pupil of Mr W Cyril Groom, ATCL.

A record was set at Thrapston Market on Tuesday, **4 January**, by Mr N Stanton of Scaley Farm, when his very fine tegs fetched the splendid price of 86s-0d each, the highest amount realised in the market this season. The commodity prices this week were butter at 1s-5d per pound, eggs at 3s-6d per score, beef from 9s-9d to 10s-6d, mutton from 7s-4d to 7s-8d, and pork from 10s-0d to 10s-6d.

Details of the work of the local Red Cross Committee, under the leadership of Mrs Milligan of "The Crossways", were reported on Wednesday, **5 January**. Since September last, exactly 1,100 items had been sent to the headquarters at Northampton, in addition to 31 pieces given directly to local men who were in the colours. Articles included 80 night shirts (all but a dozen of which were flannel), 21 pairs of slippers, 48 pairs of mittens (mostly knitted by school children), 14 scarves (one knitted by a child of 10), 10 sheets, 8 Turkish towels, 12 hand towels, 24 handkerchieves, a number of small pillows with cases, and a bundle of old linen. To avoid overlapping, the committee were now working under War Office instructions, whereby all articles would be sent to one distribution centre. And although local men would not in future be directly supplied, their "wants" could be made known to Mrs Milligan or any committee member.

On Thursday, **6 January**, more eggs received from Raunds scholars were acknowledged by the VAD Hospital, Higham Ferrers.

The Brotherhood met in the Wesleyan Church on Sunday, **9 January**, when Mr G Winsor presided over a large attendance. The speaker was the Rev Harry Shaw of Thrapston, whose address on the subject "Modern reasons for unbelief" was listened to with great attention, and was much appreciated. The soloist was Mr J W Jones, who rendered "Land of My Fathers" and "Ebenezer", Mr A W Hazeldine being the accompanist.

10 January was "Plough Monday", and this was observed in Wellingborough by some of the drovers who took a plough round the streets. "Little Bennie" was in charge of the donkey which drew the implement.

Also today was the quarterly meeting of the local Boot & Shoe Operatives Union Branch, held at the Rushden Trades Union Club. The treasurer reported contributions for the quarter of £1,879, sick and funeral pay of £371, war contributions of £180, but no out of work payments.

The assembly heard that the Joint Standing Committee had met and agreed to pay 1s-0d per week in advance, at 23 years and upwards, on the present minimums, viz 31s-0d for the Lasting, Finishing, Clicking, and Pressroom Departments.

The committee had also agreed the following prices for nailing the Italian boot: For one row of ridge nails, round fore-part, per dozen 2s-3d; centre rows in bottom 1s-0d; one row of square nails in heel 1s-3d; total per dozen 4s-6d. If fitters round heel 6d per dozen extra; if pulled on twice 3d per dozen extra; if holed by machine 6d per dozen less. All to be effective as at 13 December 1915.

An interesting pair of cases was brought to Thrapston Police Court on Tuesday, **11 January**. A Raunds shoehand was summoned for being drunk and disorderly on the public highway in the town on Christmas Eve. Sgt Ellingham, giving evidence, said he saw the defendant, very drunk, in Grove Street at 10.20pm, waving his arms about like a madman and using the most filthy, disgusting language. The accused then put himself into a fighting attitude, but two men rushed forward and prevented him from assaulting the Sergeant. The defendant claimed he was sober "bar three pints of beer", and his wife said he was not drunk but had had some drink and was being "a bit obtropulus!" Found guilty and fined 40s-0d, the defendant said he could not pay, but Sgt Ellingham said he earned £4, sometimes £4-5s-0d per week. He was given a fortnight to pay.

His wife was also summoned for using obscene language, to the annoyance of passengers on the public highway, during the same incident. Again giving evidence, Sgt Ellingham said he saw the accused trying to quarrel with a man and when he tried to prevent her from assaulting the man, she "reached over my grasp and serated the man's face until blood ran down and he could hardly see". Her solicitor, however, contended that the County Council byelaws regarding obscene language did not apply in Raunds, as it was an Urban District. The Chairman of the Bench agreed, saying that the case should have been brought under the Town Police Clauses Act of 1847, and dismissed the case.

Private W H Twelftree of the Herts Territorials, the son of Mr and Mrs H H Twelftree of Thorpe Street, was reported on Wednesday, **12 January**, as being at home from France for a week. The soldier had been "out" for about twelve months and previous to enlistment was employed at Hitchin.

"Wanted – Lad about 16 for bakehouse, to live in – Apply to: A Groom, Raunds"

Intriguing acts coming shortly to the Palace, Rushden, were "Harry Hillier", the versatile pierrot, in music and song, and "Roelgin's Performing Parrots", the Acme of Training! While the Royal Variety promised "Moths, Moths, Gigantic Moths!" – From the famous novel by Ouida, the tale that has thrilled the world.

"Lieutenant V Sykes Recalled", read a headline on Friday, **14 January**, and told how the former Raunds resident, who had been seriously wounded in the head and hand some months previously, had been recalled to the forces for home service. During his period of convalescence at home he had given several vivid and interesting addresses on his experiences at the front; and his many friends would be following his future Army career with earnest wishes for his welfare.

"Wanted – Good clickers – Apply to: R Coggins and Sons Ltd, Raunds"

In the Rushden and District Clubs' Billiards League on Saturday, **15 January**, Irthlingborough Working Men's Club entertained Raunds Conservatives and emerged as victors by 545 points to 504.

There was a "startling accident" on the Wellingborough Road, near the "Oakley Arms", Rushden, on Monday afternoon, **17 January**, when a motor 'bus on the Raunds to Wellingborough service lost a rear wheel. As the 'bus bumped along the road the passengers got a considerable shaking up as the driver tried to apply the brakes. The passengers, many from Raunds, were eventually carried to their destination by another 'bus which was coming from Wellingborough but couldn't pass the disabled vehicle and so returned to Ock'ndough.

Today also saw the annual tea and meeting of the Women's Adult School held in the Primitive Methodist Sunday Schoolroom. At the business meeting, officers were elected for the year, with Miss E Pulpher becoming president, Mrs B Green, secretary, and Mrs J H Haynes, treasurer. During the previous year the sum of £7-12s-6d had been distributed for charitable purposes.

The Urban Council met in the evening and letters were read from Miss Gant, thanking the Council for their sympathy in her father's serious illness, and from Sergeant Lee, acknowledging their kind wishes.

The committee appointed to consider the raising of a Volunteer Training Corps in the town reported "that the time was not opportune nor the conditions favourable for further proceeding with the establishment of a Corps". Their recommendation was accepted.

It was decided to apply to the Public Works Loans Board for £178, repayable in 21 years, and £305, repayable in 50 years, for the provision of a cemetery. The interest would be four and three-quarters percent.

The medical officer, Dr Mackenzie, reported a case of enteric fever, the patient having nearly recovered and no fresh cases had occurred. In December 1915, seven deaths and fifteen births were registered in the town. The total number of births registered in 1915 was 78, against 58 in 1914.

Plans for the addition of a toilet at the Coffee Tavern and a toilet and engine house at Owen Smith's factory were reviewed and approved.

The Highways & Lighting Committee recommended the following road works in the town: the channelling of Wellington Road at a cost of £36 and improvements to the road in front of Mr H Beeby's house in Hill Street. Both were accepted.

Finally, the issue of the surveyor's enrolment under Lord Derby's scheme was discussed. The assembly heard that many in his group had already been called up and as his original appointment had been difficult to secure, they decided that an appeal to the Local Appeals Tribunal should be made to retain his services.

The Local Appeals Tribunal met on Tuesday, **18 January**, and Mr John Adams, CC, was appointed chairman and Mr W F Corby, clerk. The claims were not numerous, with most of the men in the groups being badged employees in shoe factories. The case of the Council's surveyor was not presented for consideration.

A former Rushden and Raunds boot operative, Private J Headland, 18953, 1st Northamptons, of Wymington, was reported on Friday, **21 January**, as being in hospital in France suffering from a shell wound in his left foot. He was working at Raunds for a short time before joining the Colours.

Bombadier L Eady, of the Royal Garrison Artillery, was currently at his home in Marshall's Road on a month's leave. Previous to the outbreak of war he had been one of the town's postmen and was called up in August 1914, going out to France the following month. He had been attached to the 1st Indian Contingent up to a few weeks prior to his leave and had seen action at Neuve Chapelle, La Basse, Ypres and Loos. He observed that the present winter was not as near so severe as the first in France, the only things they had to contend with being mud and water. He was wished that his previous good fortune followed him.

On Saturday, **22 January**, Raunds lost a worthy citizen when Mr John Bass died of heart failure at his residence, "Lawson Cottage", just before midnight, aged 67. The deceased had been an ardent Liberal and strong supporter of the Wesleyan Church, being a member of the choir for 40 years. He had played an active part in parish affairs prior to the 1894 Local Government Act and became a member of the first Parish Council and then the Urban Council, twice being chairman. He was also a member of the Thrapston Board of Guardians, establishing and managing the "Scattered Homes" at Raunds ......

At the time of his death he was a Church of England School manager and member of the Old Age Pensions Sub-Committee. A Temperance worker for many years, he was connected with the Temperance Band, treasurer of the Beehive Tent of the Independent Order of Rechabites, and chairman of the Raunds Coffee Tavern Company. He was buried the following Wednesday in the Wesleyan Chapelyard.

The Woodbine Working Men's Club held their annual dinner this evening when 239 sat down "to an excellent spread". The president, Mr E Batchelor, proposed "Success to the Club" and said that about 100 postal orders for 3s-0d each had been sent from the club to Raunds soldiers at Christmas who were stationed in this country, and about 100 5s-0d orders were despatched to the town's soldiers serving abroad. Mr Jesse Shelmerdine responded, after which a concert was held.

At the Wesleyan Church on Sunday, **23 January**, the preacher advertised to conduct the services was the Rev Tasker of Handsworth College. Unfortunately he was unable to come owing to an attack of influenza, and the pulpit was filled by his assistant, the Rev Hugh M Brookes, BSc, who also gave an able address to the Brotherhood meeting in the afternoon.

Monday, 24 January, Conscription introduced with the Military Service Act.

Dr Mackenzie was reported as having received "Major's Thanks for Gifts to Steelbacks" today. Major G A Royston-Pigott of the Northamptonshire Regiment had written thanking him on behalf of the battalion "for the very generous and most acceptable gifts of comforts for the men" adding "please congratulate the organisers on the comprehensive and sensible list of contents of their parcel".

"For Sale" today – "2 strong White Wyandotte Fowls, good strain, hatched last March, fine stock birds, 7s-0d each – Tom Asbery, Spencer Street, Raunds".

And also today, one local newspaper editor thought our lads at the front might be interested to hear that the weather in the district was so mild that already primroses, primulas, violets, wallflowers, and jasmine flowers were in bloom.

The managers of the Church of England Schools met on Tuesday, **25 January**, and passed a vote of condolence with the widow of the late manager, Mr J Bass, who had died suddenly since the last meeting.

In the evening of Wednesday, **26 January**, the Hospital Week Fund committee met at the "Golden Fleece" to hear the 1915 accounts presented by the secretary. Receipts had been £252-4s-4d, and expenditure £175-17s-2d, including £175 sent forward to the County Treasurer, with a balance in hand of £76-7s-2d. It was therefore decided to forward a further cheque of £75, making £250 altogether, exceeding the previous record by £65. Thanks were extended to Mr J G Beach for the free use of the room and to Mr John Ekins for the splendid contribution from his box. It was decided that the 1916 annual demonstration and parade should proceed on the same lines as previous years with the date set as Saturday, 24 June.

Thursday, **27 January**, was the Kaiser's 57th birthday, and no doubt Rance folk joined with the rest of the country in wishing him a very unhappy day!

The Young Helper's League, in aid of Dr Barnardo's Homes, had a successful day on Saturday, **29 January**. The Temperance Band paraded the town, and a collection was made by the Companions of the League and other ladies. A children's tea was held afterwards in the main hall of the Church School, followed by a social with music, recitations, and songs. The children contributing were: Misses E Arnold, K Kirk, M Archer, M Lawrence, S Felce, M Deberghes, A Newberry, and Masters M Spicer, G Newberry, F Sanders, with Miss Dorothy Foster as accompanist. During the evening an interesting address was given on the work of the League and the "Waifs & Strays" savings boxes were opened. All in all, net proceeds amounted to £13.

Also today, the Beehive Tent of the Independent Order of Rechabites held their annual tea and social in the Temperance Hall and Primitive Methodist Schoolroom, when about 180 sat down to a splendid meat tea. The ladies presiding at the trays were: Madames H W Lawrence, J T L Turner, T Pentelow, A Whitney, J T Hall, J T Tebbutt, H Clayton, J Coles, J Harrison, F A Corby, H Twelftree, and Misses H Munns and A Hall. After the tables had been cleared, dancing was indulged in, the music being supplied by Mr W Cyril Groom on piano, interspersed with songs by Mr O D Hall, and Misses Lawrence and W Pentelow, and recitations by Master Willis Rands.

On Monday evening, **31 January**, the juniors connected with the Salvation Army gave a capital entertainment to a crowded audience. The following items were given: recitation, George Brown; duet, Mary Hazeldine and Elsie Lack; recitation, E Brown; hoop drill by the small children; dialogue, "Six little nurses"; recitation, Alderman Pettit; fan song and drill by the children; recitation, Elsie Lack; drill by the children; recitation, Charlie Brown. At the end of the programme, the prizes for attendance were presented to the scholars by Mr George Bayes, of Rushden, who expressed his pleasure at being there to give so many prizes away, and urged all of the children to attend the Sunday School even more regularly in the future. He then wished the workers at Raunds "God speed".

Mr T Pentelow presided over a limited attendance at the 48th half yearly meeting of the Raunds Distributive Co-Operative Society, held in the Temperance Hall this evening. Before the business was commenced, the chairman briefly referred to the death of their late president, Mr Charles Groom, and to the loss that the district had sustained, as well as the local society. The treasurer reported that total sales for the period amounted to £19,301-0-6d and exceeded the total for the corresponding period by £5,391-5s-11d. Seventy-five new members had joined the society during the half year, making a present membership of 1,220. It was proposed to divide the dividend as follows: General dividend, 2s-0d in the £; coal, 1s-10d in the £; and non-members, 1s-0d in the £.

FEBRUARY – The Vicar, returned from his chaplaincy duties at the front, was in a campaigning mood in his Parish Notes for the month: "This war and all that comes with it has emphasised our great need of God's help and strength. Many are now realising, away from home, their need of God's help. Is this same awakening of conscience taking place at home? Or is it one of the many things which are going to happen after the war? Do we realise that for many 'After the war' has already begun? Many must be coming back even now, can they see a change at home, and are we taking care that for our part we are a better nation?"

All the Sunday School teachers were asked to note that the Rev E Leonard Urch, of the Church of England Sunday School Institute, would be giving a lecture in the Schools at 8.30pm on Friday, 11 February. He would be dealing with the preparation and delivery of a lesson and all were urged to be present.

The next dancing classes in the Institute would be on 14 and 28 February.

And included in the list of baptisms carried out in January was one **Walter Edward Hall (153).**

On Tuesday, **1 February**, at the monthly meeting of the Thrapston Board of Guardians, and before commencement of the business of the day, the chairman said it was his painful duty to refer to the great loss which the Board had sustained in the death of Mr John Bass. He added that "he was a very useful member of the Board who did his duty most faithfully, and who took a great interest in the responsibilities of the Board, especially the work of the Cottage Homes".

Friday, **4 February** – "For Sale, Grey Cob, 14-2, Apply: W M Gambrell, Raunds"

Today, it was reported that news had been received of the distant marriage of Raunds born Miss Florence Driver to Private M Gardner, at Yarram, Australia.

The Northamptonshire Union Bank Ltd, Raunds branch open daily, in its 79th annual report of the directors, announced a net profit of £69,636-19s-10d for 1915.

Distressing news came out of Burton Latimer though, as it was disclosed that 20 cases of diptheria had been notified during January, two of which had proved fatal.

Saturday, **5 February** – "For Sale: Front Shop, Factory, Yard, newly-built Dwelling-house and 2 Cottages, in the main street in the centre of Raunds, excellent business position. Apply: W F Corby, Raunds".

Rushden Conservatives took on the Raunds Woodbine Club in the Rushden & District Clubs' Billiards League today, winning convincingly by 600 points to 246.

At the choir festival service in the Wesleyan Church on Sunday, **6 February**, the Rev C J Keller, of Rushden, preached the sermon and addressed a great open meeting of the Brotherhood on "The spirit of Germany" in the afternoon. The choir also sang anthems accompanied by the Brotherhood String Band. It proved to be one of the most successful choir anniversaries held and £10-7s-5d was raised.

The local Boot & Shoe Operatives Union met at the Trades Union Club, Rushden, on Monday, **7 February**, and considered a circular from Head Office in respect to the Union purchasing a motor ambulance for the Red Cross Society at a cost of £500 to £600. After discussion a resolution was passed in favour of the purchase.

Also raised was that some firms were not paying the 10% bonus on the 30s-0d minimum. Members affected were instructed to make a claim and report the result.

On Tuesday, **8 February**, it was reported that Dr Mackenzie, of Aberlour House, had received the following letter from the Commanding Officer of the 6th Gordon Highlanders acknowledging safe receipt of a New Year's parcel contributed by the inhabitants of Raunds: "Dear Sir, a case of goods has arrived from the Editor of "The People's Journal" and it was accompanied by a letter which stated that it was due to your energies that money for the articles was obtained. An excellent choice has been made, and the men thoroughly enjoyed the good things contained in the box. I wish to thank you for your interest in the battalion and for your kindness and trouble in this matter. I presume from the name of your residence that you have a territorial connection with the regiment, James Dawson, Lt-Col Commanding 6th Gordon Highlanders, Le Havre, 1 Jan 1916."

That afternoon at the Thrapston Police Court, the licensing justices objected to the renewal of the license of the "Golden Fleece" as there were 65 other licensed premises in the district, which included Raunds, for a total population of 12,958. This was one less than 1915 since the closure of the "Bakers Arms" on 7 August.

The same sessions saw a "music hall artiste", of no fixed abode, summoned for keeping a dog without a licence at Raunds on 7 March 1914. She had left the neighbourhood before the summons could be served but had turned up again just last week. Found guilty, she was fined £1 or ordered to be detained for 14 days.

Also "on the bill" were three young Hargrave shoehands, summoned for a game trespass in the village on 23 January. The defendants did not appear as their employer in Raunds wrote asking that their attendance be excused as they were all employed on Army work. In their defence their parents said they had repeatedly warned their sons about rabbiting, but they were always "at it". Fining them each £1 for this first offence, the chairman of the Bench remarked that he hoped it would be a lesson to them all.

Wednesday, 9 February, the Military Service Act becomes law.

"Wanted, 2 or 3 Unfurnished rooms, Good house in Raunds. Write stating particulars and terms, to Box 700, "Evening Telegraph" Office, Kettering."

In the evening, a dance arranged by Mrs Lawrence of "The Hall" and Mrs Camozzi of the "Manor House" in the Church of England School raised £6-10s-0d for the Temperance Band funds.

There was also a special meeting of the Urban Council today when a packed agenda of militarily related matters were discussed. First they considered a circular from the Local Government Board asking them to appoint a tribunal for the new Military Service Act 1916. After some discussion it was proposed that the same gentlemen be appointed as in the case of the Derby scheme. However, Mr G E Smith said he did not wish to serve again so Mr Batchelor was appointed in his place and Mr Asberry was also added.

Owing to the possibility of attacks by hostile aircraft, the lighting arrangements were also considered and it was resolved to cease lighting the lamps for the remainder of the season and have them taken down as soon as possible. It was also decided to ask the Raunds Gas Company to immediately turn off the gas at the works upon warning being given of the approach of hostile aircraft, and not to turn it on again before 7 o'clock the following morning.

Additionally, it was decided to issue a circular requesting all tradesmen and private residents to darken their windows with blinds. The same would apply to factories, who would be asked to close as early as possible. Furthermore, the councillors resolved to approach the Education Committee with respect to closing down the Evening Schools, or otherwise hide the lights. As regards the places of worship, it was decided to ask those in charge to so arrange matters that all lights should be out by 7 o'clock.

Finally, attention was called to the alleged improper conduct of the military representatives who distributed the armlets to those enrolled under Lord Derby's scheme on Monday evening. It was decided to report the matter to Col Fawcett.

It was announced on Thursday, **10 February**, that the Raunds Wesleyan Methodist Circuit had raised £77-15s-2d for Foreign Missions in 1915, an increase of £4 on that raised in 1914.

Also today, it was reported that the net amount of the corresponding number competition in aid of the funds of the Raunds Red Cross Committee resulted in the splendid sum of £20 being handed over to the county committee. For this excellent contribution, the committee were "very much indebted to those who generously gave the prizes for the competition".

And latest edition of the "Raunds Circuit Wesleyan Methodist Church Recorder" paid tribute to the late Mr John Bass, observing that "the one man we could least of all afford to lose, was the one to be taken, and nobody would feel the influence of his smiling face again!"

Friday, **11 February** – "For Sale, 1 or 2 well built and commodious Dwelling-houses in Harcourt Street – Apply: W F Corby, Raunds".

A Raunds factory owner defended an action against him today in the High Court, before Justice Bailhache. The plaintiff, a civil engineer from Kent, claimed £500 on a draft, with interest, less three payments made since 28 October 1905, when the draft was made. The transaction had been carried out in Buenos Aries. The defendant did not admit to the signature, and said the draft was for the accommodation of the plaintiff, denying that the three payments were made on account. He also set up the Statute of Limitations, and countersigned for a sum he alleged was due to him. His Lordship held that the plaintiff had failed to make out his case, giving judgement in favour of the defendant.

The 21st gathering of the Lilac Lodge of Free Gardeners was held on Saturday, **12 February**, in the clubroom of the "Golden Fleece" when about 180 members and friends sat down at 4.30pm to tea, the catering being admirably carried out by the Raunds Distributive Co-Operative Society. Dr Mackenzie then presided over the social at which Mr J T Pettitt, District Master, was presented with a pocket book and case and a gold watch, and Mr J Walker, with an emblem of the Order for services rendered as Lodge Master.

Also on this day, a Raunds factory owner was summoned at Huntingdon for showing electric headlights on his car at Spaldwick on 30 January. Sergeant Dighton said he stopped the defendant, who thereupon put out the lights. Special Constable Nichols said that the defendant afterwards put on the lights again. His plea that he only put the lights on again when he reached Northamptonshire, where lights were allowed, was rejected. The Bench advised the defendant that the offence carried a maximum fine of £100, but as this was his first offence he would be fined £6, "principally for disobeying the advice of the police sergeant!"

Raunds Wesleyan Prize Choir, under the talented conductor, Mr Walter W Hall, gave a delightful concert in the Park Road Wesleyan Schoolrooms, Rushden, on Monday, **14 February**. To a crowded attendance they rendered "Behold, God the Lord" (Mendelssohn), "Holiest, Breathe an Evening Blessing" (Martin), and the ever popular part song "My Bonnie Lass she Smileth" with which the choir won the Lady Lilford Cup in the North Northamptonshire Musical Competition. Mrs Jethro Hall (Miss Irene Lyne) gave a superb rendition of "Bantry Bay", Miss Grace Lawrence charmed the audience with "Waltz Song" and two of the younger members, Misses Miriam Sanders and Winnie Pentelow, sang "The Old Conntree" and "My Dear Soul". A humorous sketch featuring "Mr & Mrs Orfley Trampledon" evoked considerable amusement. Though of necessity changing in personnel from time to time, the choir still bears the "Hall"-mark of excellence!

At the meeting of the Thrapston Board of Guardians on Tuesday, **15 February**, a letter written on behalf of Mrs Bass was read, thanking the Board for their note of condolence on the death of her husband, the late Mr John Bass, and for the expression of their appreciation of his services as a Guardian. The Board then resolved to ask the Raunds Urban Council to submit names for his successor.

The annual gathering of employees of the Raunds Distributive Co-Operative Society took place in the Wesleyan Schoolrooms on Thursday evening, **17 February**. Tea was provided at six o'clock when about 100 sat down, including the employees, the committee, their wives, and other friends, the tables being presided over by Madames G Matthews, S Wright, A Hanger, E Coles, S Townsend, and Misses A Pentelow, D Draper, E Sanders, M Dix and W Betts. Afterwards the following programme was contributed: song, "When the Boys Come Home", Miss M Dix; violin solo, "Capprices", Mr Frank Groom; song, "Wee Hoose 'mang the Heather", Mr S Wright; song, "When Love is Kind", Miss C Lawrence; recitation, "The Old Song", Mrs F Lawrence; action song, "Lady Barbers", 12 employees; song, "The Rose Garden", Miss M Sanders; comic song, "And Then", Mr S Wright; song, "Until", Miss M Dix; comic song, "Hot Meat Pies, Saveloys and Trotters", Mr S Wright. Mr W Cyril Groom was the accompanist, and the above items were interspersed with dancing and games.

On Saturday, **19 February**, the Wesleyan Church announced that the services on Sunday evenings would, until further notice, commence at five o'clock, instead of six o'clock, owing to the stricter lighting regulations.

And today, the Raunds Conservatives travelled to the Rushden Athletic Club in the Rushden & District Billiards League but were beaten by 564 points to 471.

Also in Rushden, at the Windmill football ground, a charity match in aid of the Higham Ferrers VAD Hospital between Rushden Windmill and Raunds came to a very early and unfortunate termination after just 10 minutes play when an accident happened to Mr Smith, a Higham Ferrers player who was assisting the Windmill team, and who had just scored the opening goal of the game. He fell in a melee near the goal mouth and was badly injured. Mr Coles, a local ambulance man, with a member of the RAMC who was present, gave prompt and skilful first aid and got the injured man to Dr Baker's surgery. It was a disappointing finish to a game which promised to be a success. The match had been well organised and many tickets sold in advance. Representing Raunds were: Cooch (the old Cobbler), Sykes (Peterborough City), **J Haxley (60)**, Hall, **G Webb (122)**, Coles, Nunley, Maddocks, Lack, Chambers, Upton (Portsmouth).

Mr W F Corby presided at the Brotherhood meeting on Sunday afternoon, **20 February**, when Mr F Sharwood spoke on "Peter's fall and restoration", and Mrs S C Brightwell sang "How lovely are Thy dwellings" and "Nearer my God to Thee", accompanied by Miss Corley, all of Rushden.

In the evening, the preacher at the Wesleyan Church was Sgt L G H Lee, home from France on leave. Collections were taken for the Home Missions.

Meanwhile at the Primitive Methodist Church, Missionary anniversary services were held and the Rev H W Hart, of Wellingborough, was the preacher for the day.

Monday, 21 February, the Battle of Verdun begins.

A packed agenda awaited the Urban Councillors at their meeting tonight when their number was unexpectedly swelled by the appearance of Sergeant (and Councillor) L G H Lee, home on leave from the front.

The committee appointed to consider the question of a Volunteer Training Corps for the town reported that, in view of the fact that the Volunteer movement would shortly receive Government recognition and control, they thought it polite to defer further proceedings until the Government's intentions were announced.

Several councillors expressed the opinion that the latest Local Appeals Tribunal committee, appointed under the new Military Service Act 1916, should be enlarged, so the names of Messrs G E Smith and Walter Gates were added.

A letter was read from Colonel Fawcett regarding the alleged improper conduct of the military representative at a recent recruiting meeting. He apologised for any friction that had arisen between the townsfolk and the officer who went to distribute the armlets to the enrolled men. The officer, Lieutenant Franklyn Smith, claimed that he had been pushed and sworn at when the men became unruly but admitted losing his temper, under provocation and using hasty language. The Colonel advised that he had rebuked the officer for his reprehensible conduct and had since withdrawn him from recruiting duties and returned him to his regiment.

The medical officer, Dr Mackenzie, reported 8 births and one death in the town during January but otherwise nothing special with respect to the district's health.

The Highways and Lighting Committee reported that in view of the demand of the War Office, the contractors for the supply of slag were unable to give any undertaking as to the date they would be able to fulfill their contract, and in order that the Station Road repair might not be longer delayed, recommended the purchase of 150 tons of granite – to this the Council agreed.

Considerable discussion then took place with respect to the Cemetery Committee's report that the whole of the fence contemplated at the proposed new cemetery be carried out at once, and that the making of paths and laying out be reduced to a minimum. It was therefore proposed to write to the Local Government Board asking to modify the conditions of the loan so that the whole of the land be retained for the present.

Next, the seal of the Council was ordered to be affixed to a series of bye-laws with respect to motor omnibuses on the lines of which the Local Government Board would be prepared to give their approval.

Finally, the need to identify representatives to fill the various vacancies caused by the death of Mr John Bass was undertaken. As a result, Mr W F Corby was appointed Council representative on the Church of England School board of managers, Mr Enos Smith, JP, would join the Raunds District Sub-Committee of the County Old Age Pensions Committee, and Mrs G E Smith would be nominated to become a member of the Thrapston Board of Guardians, as Miss Pulpher had been constrained to withdraw her offer to serve.

At Thrapston Petty Sessions on Tuesday, **22 February**, a number of license renewals were referred to the County Compensation Authority, including the "Golden Fleece" of Raunds. Mr A J Darnell appeared for the owners (Messrs Praed & Co, Wellingborough) and Mr Robinson for the tenant (Mr J G Beach, a bricklayer). The objection was based on the testimony of Superintendant Tebbey, who spoke of several other licensed premises within 400 yards of the hostelry, and consequently the Bench held that there was a redundancy of licenses at Raunds.

Also at the hearing, a shoehand, who did not appear when summoned, was fined 7s-6d for keeping a dog without a licence on 7 February. In his defence he wrote to say that he took out a licence the next day and had had five licences previously.

In the evening, the Primitive Methodists held their annual Missionary meeting when Mr J Tanner presided. Addresses were given by the Rev E T J Bagnall, of London, and the Rev H W Hart. A solo was given by Mrs Hart, and a collection was taken in aid of mission funds.

And also this evening, a Whist Drive, arranged by Mrs A Camozzi and Mrs A Lawrence, in aid of the Church Institute, was held in the Central Hall of the Council Schools. Upwards of 100 took part, the winning lady being Miss E James, the winning gentleman, Mr W Young, with the prize for the hidden number going to Mrs J W Pentelow. Mr A Camozzi carried out the duties of MC, and refreshments were provided, being handed round by a number of young ladies.

The first Raunds Local Appeals Tribunal as constituted under the new Military Service Act met in the Town Clerk's office on Wednesday, **23 February**. Mr John Adams was elected chairman and 15 claims were considered, several of which were granted exemption, as being under certified occupations, while others were postponed for periods extending from one to three months.

That same evening, the annual meeting of the members of the Conservative Club Co Ltd was held at the club. Mr J Shelmerdine, JP, chairman of the directors, presided, supported by all the directors and Mr H Varah, Conservative agent. A vote of thanks was accorded to the auditor, Mr T W Johnson, of Ringstead, who was unable to be present owing to the unfavourable weather. Mr Varah, in a very eulogistic speech, congratulated Mr Shelmerdine on being appointed a magistrate, to which Mr Shelmerdine responded.

The annual meeting of shareholders in the Raunds Gas Company Ltd was held at the Coffee Tavern on Thursday evening, **24 February**. The unavoidable absence of the Chairman, Mr J Gant, JP, resulted in Mr G E Smith being elected to preside over the reading of the annual financial report.

It was reported that the sale of gas for 1915 showed an increase of one and a half million cubic feet. On the renewal of coal contracts last June, the directors had been compelled to pay as much as 6s-2d per ton in excess of the previous year making it necessary for them to advance the price of gas by 4d per 1000 cubic feet.

During the latter part of the year the process of purification by oxide of iron in place of lime had been installed and it was hoped that this new method would effect a saving. And at the insistence of the Ministry of Munitions, a plant had been installed for the washing of the gas through tar for the purpose of increasing the output of toluol, this was working satisfactorily.

The directors recommended a dividend of 10% subject to income tax, an amount to be set aside for income tax on excess profits, and a provision for an amount of undivided profits. However, in view of these facts, Mr John Adams asked if it had been necessary for the directors to raise the price of gas. The Chairman explained that a significant amount in reserve was due to sale of a large stock of coke at an increased price, not through the production of gas during the year. Also, a contingency had been set up for the possible replacement of the main at the upper part of the town, but this had been delayed by the great scarcity of labour.

The meeting closed with the passing of a vote of sympathy with respect to the serious illness of Mr Gant.

In the recent Trienniel Competition of the Madrigal Society, the judges unanimously awarded the "Molineux" (or first) prize of £10, with the society's medal, to "MS.No.21" and when the sealed envelopes were opened this composition proved to be by Dr C H Merrill, FRCO, who gained the only prize awarded by the judges in 1912. It was understood that the prize madrigal would shortly be performed at the society's meeting in London. Dr Merrill was the eldest son of Mr J Merrill, High Street, Raunds.

"Snow Clad Britain" announced the newspapers on Friday, **25 February**. Up to 8 inches was recorded in Northamptonshire, with drifts in places of up to 6 or 7 feet.

"Golden Wedding at Raunds" heralded the celebration today of Mr and Mrs George Lee's 50 years of married life. The date of the anniversary had actually been the 7th August 1915, but the festivities were delayed in order that their two soldier sons, Sergeant L G H Lee and Lance Corporal J W Lee, might be present.

At a gathering of about 120 relatives and friends in the Wesleyan Schoolroom, Mr John Adams, CC, presented to Mr Lee, a life sized photograph of himself to be hung in the schoolroom as a companion picture to that of Mrs G Bass. He said that there was no one in Raunds who had been a greater influence for good than Mr Lee, Day School headmaster for over 45 years and Sunday School superintendent for 54 years. The Rev J Burrows then asked the happy couple's acceptance of 6 volumes of the standard edition of "Wesley's Journal" on behalf of the society classes led by Mr and Mrs Lee for so many years. Sergeant Lee expressed the thanks of the family. A musical programme followed, Misses Louie Smith, Grace Lawrence, and Edith Adams, Mr O D Hall, and Mr and Mrs Jethro Hall taking parts. Sgt Lee also gave a short sketch of his life and work at the front.

The following day, the scholars at the Sunday School presented Mr Lee with a revolving bookcase.

A serious accident befell Mrs Price, wife of Mr James Price and mother of **Henry Price (93)**, one evening earlier this week. She had suffered for some years from partial paralysis, and had the misfortune to fall on the fire and was unable to get off. Her daughter found her terribly burned and Doctors Mackenzie and McInnes both attended her. She was later described as being as well as could be expected.

On Monday, **28 February**, the motor omnibus service, which had been held up for four days because of the inclement weather, was partially resumed in the district.

In the Wesleyan Schoolroom, the Wesleyan Choir, with friends and sweethearts, were entertained to tea by Mr and Mrs W F Corby. The catering was by the Raunds Distributive Co-Operative Society who provided an excellent repast. After the tables had been cleared, games and amusements were heartily entered into and an enjoyable time was spent until the host separated at about 11 o'clock.

Also that evening, the annual meeting of the British Women's Temperance Association was held in the Temperance Hall. The election of officers for the coming year resulted in Miss Pulpher remaining as president, with Madames G Bass, Burrows and Lee as vice-presidents. Mrs W Wagstaff would continue as honorary secretary as would Mrs Matson as treasurer. Additional appointments included Madames C Yorke and C Abbott as "Tiny Tot" secretaries. After a short discussion on the work of the Association, a cup of tea was handed round, the provisions for which were kindly given by members of the committee.

At the Thrapston Police Court on Tuesday afternoon, **29 February**, a 16 year old Raunds shoehand was accused of embezzling 2s-3d, the money of his employers, Messrs Adams Bros, shoe manufacturers, on 17 February. He appeared alongside an Irchester man charged with obtaining by false pretences, 11cwt of rope, valued at 33s-0d, from the firm. Both were remanded until the following Tuesday.

At their latest meeting, the Church of England School managers decided to apply to the Local Education Authority for salary increases for: Mr F A Potter, Head of the Mixed Department, Miss W Gooding, Head of the Infants Department, Miss G Lodder, certificated assistant, and Misses M Yorke and F Hall, uncertificated assistants, in accordance with the published scales.

And also today at the meeting of the Thrapston Board of Guardians, the clerk read a letter from the Raunds Urban Council nominating Mrs G E Smith, of Thorpe Street, to fill the vacancy left owing to the death of Mr John Bass. She was said to be "a most useful member of the Raunds & Stanwick Belgian Committee and who, for a long time, had taken a very great interest in all the affairs of Raunds". Her nomination was duly carried unanimously, as was her appointment to the Cottage Homes Committee.

MARCH – This month's Parish Magazine included a range of notices and appeals from the Vicar. Gratefully acknowledged was the sum of £3-10s-0d for the Institute Funds raised by Mrs Camozzi's Whist Drive.

Members of the Vestry Class were asked to bring eggs and cigarettes to the service on Sunday, 5 March, for distribution to their "comrades in khaki". The message was "last time we got 400 cigarettes, can we beat this?"

Owing to the need for precautions against possible air raids, it was announced that future Sunday evening services would begin at 5 o'clock and that the mid-week services would be held in the Institute, which had been fitted up as a chapel.

Concerns that this year's "Freewill Offering Scheme" was falling behind last year's total prompted a plea for all subscribers to take care that their payments were made regularly!

Members of the Mother's Union were asked to note that there would be an address on the "Vigil of the Annunciation" at 8pm when the annual Corporate Communion was held on Saturday, 25 March.

Finally, members of the congregation who were responsible for cleaning church furniture etc were "kindly" asked to do their work regularly and were reminded that "one person's neglect may spoil the labours of all the others!"

Raunds lost a second prominent citizen in less than two months when the death occurred of Mr Joseph Gant, JP, at his residence, "Haywood", Stanwick, during the early hours of Wednesday, **1 March**. He had suffered failing health over a number of months and his last public appearance was at the recent dinner given to members of the fire brigade by Mr John Adams, CC.

A native of Spilsby in Lincolnshire, Mr Gant came to Raunds in 1880 and took over the chemist business from Mr Swift, *and nearly one hundred years later, older locals still refer to the corner off The Square near the zebra crossing as "Gant's Corner"*. He became a JP in 1912, was a member of the Urban Council, a manager of the Council School, treasurer of the Raunds Hospital Week Committee, and Chairman of the Raunds Gas Co. A Wesleyan local preacher, and a strong Liberal, he left a widow and three children.

In the evening, at a meeting of the Council School managers, the Chairman, Mr John Adams, JP, CC, referred in sympathetic terms to the loss they had sustained by the death of their old friend and colleague, Mr J Shelmerdine seconded the vote of sympathy.

"Wanted, Good Sorter for Rough Stuff Room, Apply: R Coggins & Son, Raunds"

On Thursday, **2 March**, the Hospital Week Committee announced that the Rt Hon Arthur Henderson, MP, had consented to attend the next annual demonstration which would be held on 24 June. The committee considered themselves most fortunate in having secured the promise from the right honourable gentleman to pay a visit and opinioned that most likely the day would prove to be a record one.

At today's meeting of the Raunds District Old Age Pensions Sub-Committee, seven claims came up for consideration. Six were allowed at the full rate of 5s-0d, and the other at 1s-0d. Two claims for dependancy allowances were also dealt with. A letter was read from the Supervisor of Customs and Excise, stating that the complaint made at the last meeting with respect to the alleged delay of the pensions officer in dealing with Raunds Claims was being investigated.

Another letter was read from Mrs John Bass thanking the committee for the sympathy letter sent to her by the last meeting upon the death of her husband. The Chairman also referred to the further loss sustained by the committee in the death of Mr J Gant, JP and asked their sympathy to be expressed to the friends of the deceased gentleman.

In the evening, Mr O D Hall took a party of performers from Raunds over to the Harmonic Hall in Irthlingborough, to give an excellent concert in aid of local efforts to provide comforts for soldiers and sailors. Not only was the event a musical treat, but a great financial success too, clearing £15. The programme included both serious and humorous songs, many of which drew encores.

The Raunds Red Cross Committee confirmed on Friday, **3 March**, that they had sent over 100 items to the Northampton Depot during February. These included: 39 pairs of mittens, 16 scarves, 12 pairs of slippers, 15 pairs of day socks, 7 bed jackets, 5 dressing gowns, 4 pairs of operation stockings, 3 flannel night shirts, 1 body belt, and 8 pairs of knee caps! The dressing gowns were gratuitously made by Misses Atkins, Clayton, Hall and Thompson, while 24 pairs of the mittens were made by school children.

Saturday, **4 March** – "For Sale, Large Stock of New Cycles, 3 speed gears, Second hand cycles from 30s-0d to £5, Rear Lamps, Tyres, Accessories, Any make of cycle repaired – H Gaunt, Raunds".

Sadly, 71 year old Mrs Mary Ann Jane Price died today from the burns she sustained through falling on the fire a few days earlier. An inquest was arranged for Wednesday morning at the "Globe Inn".

The afternoon saw the impressive funeral of the late Mr Joseph Gant, JP. The service was held in the Wesleyan Church, followed by the internment in the adjacent burial ground, both conducted by the Rev J Burrows. The organist played the "Dead March" and the air "O rest in the Lord". The committal at the graveside was performed during a fall of snow.

Later in the afternoon, the members of the Temperance Band held their annual tea and social. At 4.30pm a substantial meat tea was provided in the Temperance Hall and Primitive Methodist schoolroom when about 180 sat down, the catering for which was admirably carried out by the Raunds Distributive Co-Operative Society.

Before the tables were removed a short meeting was held and the secretary presented the report and balance sheet for the year showing a balance in hand of £45-7s-9d, an increase on the year of £31-3s-10d. The Rev W S Bethway then moved "Success to the Band".

A quartette contest for Band members followed in which five parties competed. Mr J W Hall acted as judge, his decision as follows giving general satisfaction: 1st – **F Bailey (17)**, W Bugby, W Groom, E Vickers; 2nd – H Hide, E Hide, R Annies, F Jeffkins; 3rd – W Groom, R Dickerson, W Wright, J H Haynes; 4th – A Higby, A Turney, S Hodson, W Wood; 5th – H Bailey, A Harvey, **H Bugby (29)**, J Vorley. The evening was spent in dancing to music played by band members.

In the evening, a concert was held in the large room at the Woodbine Working Men's Club when Mr E Batchelor presided over a crowded attendance. The Rushden Athletic Club Choir had been engaged and contributed some splendid selections, duets and solos being given by various members of the choir. Mrs J Stratford (Rushden) and Mr C W Knighton were the accompanists. During the evening Mr J Shelmerdine, JP, was called upon to make a presentation on behalf of the members of a gold hunter watch to Mr W F Lawrence, who was retiring as secretary after more than 13 years service. Mr Batchelor, on behalf of the committee, also presented Mr Lawrence with a silver mounted walking stick.

At the Wesleyan Church on Sunday, **5 March**, the Rev Harry Shaw, of Thrapston, manned the pulpit for both morning and evening services. At the latter, special hymns were sung in memory of the passing away of Mr Gant, JP, and the choir rendered the anthem "What are these arrayed in white?"

The question of old age pensions was raised at the monthly meeting of the local Boot & Shoe Operatives Union held at the Rushden Trades Union Club on Monday, **6 March**. It was decided to support the Council of the Union in their efforts to raise the current full rate old age pension from 5s-0d to 7s-6d per week. On a recommendation of the executive it was also decided to invest £300 of the branch funds in Government Exchequer Bonds. The chairman then gave a report of the Arbitration Board meeting held earlier that day at Raunds, in respect to the claims for another 10% increase to day workers on Government contracts and increased rates and percentages to Government piece workers.

More heavy snow fell in the district during the early hours of Tuesday, **7 March**.

At the request of the Evening School committee, Mr Arthur Hazeldine consented to fill the position of secretary, rendered vacant by the death of the late Mr John Bass, for the remainder of the present season.

The two prisoners on remand from the previous week re-appeared at Thrapston Police Court today. The Irchester man charged with obtaining by false pretences 11cwt of rope, value 33s-0d, property of Messrs Adams Bros, was found guilty and sentenced to three months hard labour ......

The 16 year old Raunds shoehand, charged with embezzling the sum of 2s-3d, the money of the firm, pleaded guilty and was bound over in £10 for twelve months. In a statement, the firm stated that they had felt bound to bring the boy's case forward, but did not wish to press it seriously as it appeared that the Irchester man had deceived the lad.

Three other Raunds cases were also presented at today's session: a shoehand from the town, who did not appear, was fined £1 for being drunk and disorderly on February 19; a 19 year old domestic servant was charged with obtaining by false pretences, a pair of shoes, value 9s-6d, property of Frederick Abbott, boot and shoe dealer. She was fined £2 and allowed six weeks to pay; and a 12 year old schoolboy was charged with breaking and entering a dwelling house at Raunds on February 16 and stealing 1s-0d in coppers and one pocket lamp, property of a widow in Park Road. In his defence, the lad's father said that he and his wife had been laid up and if they hadn't been he did not think this would have happened. A fine of £1 was imposed, with one month to pay.

At the conclusion of the business, the Chairman, Mr Enos Smith, made a brief but feeling reference to the late Mr Joseph Gant, JP.

A dance was held on this Shrove Tuesday evening in the Central Hall of the Church of England Schools, arranged by Mrs Camozzi, of the "Manor House", in aid of the school funds. Music was supplied by Messrs Bert Clark (violin), and W Cyril Groom (piano), Messrs H Betts and D Bamford were the MCs.

Also this evening, a lecture was given in the Wesleyan Schoolroom by the Rev J C Adlard, of London, entitled "Prussia and Prussianism, or Who is the Kaiser?" In the afternoon a sermon was preached by Mr Adlard, which was much appreciated and collections were taken for the school funds.

Wednesday, **8 March** – "Wanted, good Man for Shoe Room, able to pack goods and do necessary bookings, Apply to: Adams Bros, Raunds"

The inquest into the death of Mrs Mary Ann Jane Price was held today at the "Globe Inn". The hearing was told how the deceased was in feeble health and suffered paralysis. She had been left alone in a room for a short time when a neighbour heard moans. Her daughter was called and discovered her mother lying in front of the fire with her clothes burning. Dr Mackenzie was called and she died later from the effects. A verdict of "accidental death" was returned.

News of a former Raunds resident appeared today when it was reported that Ernest Archer had successfully passed his examination for American citizenship, held on February 16, at the Circuit Court Kalamazoo, Michigan, USA.

The desperate need for more men to join the military raised its head on Thursday, **9 March**, when it was disclosed that married men up to the age of 35 would be called up on or about 17 April and that a special Cabinet Committee had been formed to revise the list of reserved occupations.

Monday, 13 March, Arnold Hayes Burrows (30), killed in action.

On the day that Raunds suffered its first war casualty for nearly six months, a clerk from the town appeared at Higham Ferrers Police Court charged with "riding a cycle without a red rear light" on 12 February. The defendant claimed that he had tried at Raunds to get a red rear light, and also at other places, but failed. However, Superintendent MacLeod said that the defendant could have covered the lens of an ordinary lamp with red paper and that would have answered the purpose. The Bench agreed and fined him 10s-0d.

"Wanted – Home for two or three vermin killing cats, R Ward, Stanwick"

The Rev J Burrows, superintendant Wesleyan minister, received a telegram from the War Office on Thursday morning, **16 March**, notifying him that his son, Captain **A H Burrows (30)**, 6th Northants, had been killed in action three days earlier. The former Mercer's Company schoolmaster was described as "a great favourite with his fellow officers and men".

"Eat Less Meat" was another appeal issued today by the Board of Trade on account of the increasing requirements of the British and Allied Forces, stressing the urgent importance of greater meat economy by the general public, thus diminishing the demands upon shipping, and avoiding a further advance of price.

This afternoon in the Parish Church, the Right Rev Bishop Clayton administered the sacrament of confirmation upon 30 candidates; 10 boys and 13 girls from Raunds and 3 boys and 4 girls from Denford.

Changes to Post Office opening hours at Raunds were announced on Friday, **17 March**. From Monday, 20 March, the office would open from 9am to 1pm and 2pm to 7pm, except Thursdays, when it would close at 1pm, but open from 6.30pm to 7pm for the sale of stamps only. Telegrams could be handed in at the side door between 8 & 9am, 1 & 2pm, and 7 & 8pm.

Today it was reported that Mr E Batchelor had been elected as secretary to the Woodbine Club succeeding Mr W Lawrence, who was shortly leaving the town.

On Saturday, **18 March**, at the quarterly meeting of the Wesleyan Methodist Circuit, Mr W Askew moved, and Mr J Adams seconded, a resolution of deep sympathy with the Rev & Mrs Burrows in the loss of their son. This was carried unanimously by a silent standing vote. Mr Burrows replied "under deep emotion" thanking all present for their sympathy. The meeting also placed on record its deep sense of loss the circuit had sustained during the past quarter by the deaths of Brothers Warren, Bass, and Gant, and Harry Gray of Tichmarsh. The numerical statement showed a decrease on the year of 30 members, leaving a present membership of 406. The financial accounts were again of a satisfactory nature, showing a balance in hand. Subsequent to the meeting those present were entertained to an excellent meat tea by Mr and Mrs George Bass.

Mr Jabez Woolston, of Hill Street, an old and well known inhabitant of the town, died somewhat suddenly on Monday evening, **20 March**. The deceased had been ailing for the past two months, but had only been confined to the house for the last few days. He would have been 80 had he survived until May of this year.

During that evening, the Urban Council met and Dr Mackenzie presented his annual report. He estimated the population to be 4,081. There had been 80 births registered in the town in 1915, being an increase of 22 on the previous year, with an increase from 14.9 per 1,000 of the population to 19.7. The number of deaths was 51, being 12.5 per 1,000. The infantile death rate was 112.5 per 1,000, against 106.3 for 1914, and was the highest for seven years. Taken altogether, the health and sanitary conditions of the district were very good, and the water supply was judged as the very best both as regards quality and quantity.

Mr Shelmerdine called attention to the fact that the Government had now recognised the Volunteer Training Corps and moved that under the revised conditions the committee which had been appointed to consider the creation of a VTC for Raunds, should be discharged. This was agreed.

The retiring overseers, Messrs James Adams, James Hodson, J Shelmerdine, and G E Smith, were unanimously re-elected for the ensuing year.

At the close of business, the chairman referred in sympathetic terms to the death of Mr Gant, a "very able member of the council", and read a letter from Miss Alice Gant thanking the Council for their personal attendance at the funeral and their fine floral tribute. To fill the various vacancies caused by his death, Mr Arthur Hazeldine was elected to the council, Mr Shelmerdine joined the Pensions Sub-Committee, and Mr Camozzi, the Council School's board of managers.

Tuesday, **21 March**, and the first day of spring began with 10 hours of continuous rainfall!

The first Raunds summonses for breaches of the Lighting Order under the Defence of the Realm Act in regard to houses came before the Thrapston Bench this afternoon. A foreman was accused of disregarding the warnings of Special Constables on two occasions during the evening of 14 March that a light was showing. In his defence he said that he didn't think the light was very bright, that he was moving some furniture, and that he was very sorry. He was fined 20s-0d.

Similarly, a clicker was charged with showing a light at his house on 7 March. Prosecution testimony again came from two Special Constables who said that despite their warnings, the defendant took no notice and slammed the door in their faces. He too was fined 20s-0d.

The final case concerned a grocer, summoned in respect to having a light, not subdued, in the Primitive Methodist Schoolroom on 4 March. Sergeant Ellingham said that he found several gas lights in the schoolroom with incandescant burners. There were three large windows in the room and they had no blinds drawn at all.

The defendant claimed that he was not in charge or responsible. Superintendent Tebbey said that this case was different as it was his first offence. In view of this, the Bench imposed no fine but ordered the defendant to pay 4s-0d costs.

In the evening, the Church of England School managers considered an application for the post of Certified Assistant in the Mixed Department. After discussion, it was decided that "the present staff being satisfactory, no appointment should be made and the staff be allowed to remain unaltered for the present time".

"Chaplain with the troops explains why the lady disliked melons!" was the curious headline appearing today in the Rushden Echo. The Rev E E Law, Vicar of St Mary's, Peterborough, and former Vicar of Raunds, who was currently a chaplain with the troops in the eastern counties had written: "There is no change here, just the same old round, the men who were in training during the winter are getting fed up wondering when they will be used, we have to drink our tea out of basins big enough to wash in. They always remind me of the old lady who said that she didn't like eating melons because they made her ears so wet!"

At the Local Appeals Tribunal on Wednesday, **22 March**, a factory clerk was given 3 months exemption as indispensable owing to his technical knowledge, a pork-butcher was also allowed 3 months, as were a baker and a hairdresser, but several other appeals were refused.

At Wellingborough Police Court on Friday, **24 March**, a Raunds chauffeur was fined 6s-0d for not having a light attached to a motor car at Rushden on 10 March, and a Newtown Road resident was fined 10s-0d for carrying a gun without a licence at Stanwick on 27 December.

Also today, an inquest into the death of Raunds shoeworker, Mr Alfred Walker, aged 63, was held by the Borough Coroner at Northampton. The deceased had been a handsewn boot maker and foreman of the finishing room at Messrs Stanley's factory. A shoe laster of Clare Street, giving evidence, said that Mr Walker had run an awl into his right index finger while stabbing a boot. After a few days it had turned blue so he had advised him to go to Northampton Hospital.

Dr Grace Sherwood, house surgeon at the hospital, said the finger was very inflamed and swollen, and amputated it that same day. She gave a certificate to the effect that death was primarily due to bronchitis. When she said she had forgotten to send the certificate to the Coroner, he replied "I hope that doctors will not forget in future, or it may lead to trouble!" Dr H Cropley, who performed a post-mortem, said one of the deceased's lungs was disorganised and he had a diseased heart. He was surprised a man in that condition should have been able to go on working. A verdict of "death from heart disease" was returned.

Monday, **27 March** – "Wanted, Man for Pounding-Up Machine, B.U. Solely on Government work, Apply: Tebbutt and Hall Bros, Raunds"

The Raunds Gas Company held an extraordinary shareholders meeting in the evening when Mr John Adams, CC, was appointed to fill the vacancy on the board of directors caused by the death of the late managing director, Mr J Gant, JP.

Also that evening, the Local Appeals Tribunal met in the clerk's office to consider 8 appeals. One was held over until the appellant's group was called up. In all of the other cases, the employers put in a strong appeal that the men were indispensible to them if they were to fulfil the Government orders they had on hand. Exemption was granted in each case varying from two to three months.

"The Great Blizzard" – the night of 27 March saw the arrival in the district of the most appalling snowstorm for forty years, since Good Friday 1876 to be precise. At Raunds, the blizzard began on Monday night and continued throughout Tuesday lasting for a period of 24 hours, the snow, sleet and rain causing great loss. Several conveyances were snowbound, and had to be left until the following day, when ways and means were instituted for their removal. Traffic was at a standstill and no mail was received for two days. Only a few phones worked within the town as most of the wires had been dislocated. In several instances chimney pots were blown off and damage to the roofs resulted.

Railway chaos ensued and both its telegraphic and telephone services were greatly interferred with. On Tuesday, **28 March**, the 2.35pm Midland Railway train out of Kettering for Cambridge reached Thrapston four hours late, and then got snowed up at Raunds. An engine and brake were sent to pull it out and bring it back to Thrapston, where the passengers were put up for the night. On Wednesday, 29 March, up to 1pm, the only passenger train was the 8.15am from Kettering, which got snowed up between Raunds and Kimbolton. The Wellingborough to Raunds omnibus services were stopped and 200 members of the Royal Engineers were brought in to help reinstate telegraphic communication in the locality.

Despite the attrocious weather, a meeting of the Thrapston Board of Guardians still took place on the Tuesday when Mrs G Ernest Smith, of Raunds, was appointed to the vice-chair of the Children's Home committee. Service arrangements relating to two or three of the children was also reviewed and agreed.

At the County Appeals Tribunal, a Raunds hotel proprietor appealed against the Local Tribunal's rejection of her son's case. She claimed his assistance was vital to the running of her business. Her plea, however, was disallowed.

At Denford's Wesleyan Sunday School on Thursday, **30 March**, the Ladies' Working Class held a sale of work in aid of the chapel debt. Mrs C Horrell, of Raunds, performed the opening ceremony and made "an appropriate little speech".

Finally, meeting a number of men and women dragging home branches of fallen trees brought down by the snow, a local wag remarked "it's an ill wind that blows nobody any wood!"

10 – April to June 1916

The first cuckoo of spring is heard but three lads fall in a week.

APRIL – In his Parish Magazine notes, the Vicar acknowledged Mrs A Camozzi who had raised £3-8s-1d for the School Building Fund as a result of the Shrove Tuesday Dance. Also thanked were the St Mary's Guild and the St George's Guild, who had given £5-5s-0d and £1-11s-6d respectively towards the new piano.

And speaking of the Piano Fund, he was delighted to announce that "at last the old wooden box, which did duty as a piano in the Institute, has been pensioned off, and a new instrument installed". He added that a good many of the congregation had already sampled the new piano, having been bold enough to buy it before they had the money. But now it was paid for, which was why it sounded so well!

Some may have considered it suspicious in view of the date, but on Saturday, **1 April**, the headline "Bells Banned" would have caught the reader's eye. For in an amendment to the Defence of the Realm Act, the ringing and chiming of bells and the striking of clocks audible in any street, was now prohibited during the hours of reduced lighting.

This would not, however, have concerned the members of the Wesleyan Choir and the Temperance Band who today, together with their wives and sweethearts, numbering in all over a hundred, were entertained to an excellent tea in the Wesleyan Schoolroom by Mr W W Hall (conductor of the choir) and Mr W F Corby (president of the band). The catering was splendidly carried out by the Raunds Distributive Co-Operative Society. After the tables had been cleared an entertaining programme of music was gone through in which Messrs O D Hall, F D Brazier, and W Groom, Mrs J W Hall, Misses Grace Lawrence, M Sanders, and Winnie Pentelow, the choir and the Band Quartette Party took part.

There was an open Brotherhood meeting in the afternoon of Sunday, **2 April**, when, not withstanding the very fine weather, there was a large congregation of both sexes. An excellent address on "The Great Illusion" was given by Mr Bernard Campion, barrister-at-law, of Northampton. The Wesleyan Prize Choir was in attendance and rendered a selection, and the Temperance Band paraded the town previous to the meeting. Corporal **G H Hall (59)**, RFC, who was home on leave, read the lesson. The total proceeds of the event amounted to nearly £40.

A special meeting of the Urban Council was held on Monday evening, **3 April**, to consider the estimates for the coming year. The clerk advised that £3,642-10s-0d would be required, estimated receipts were £1,059-10s-0d, and an excess bank balance of £417, due to the inability to carry out works decided upon, left £2,166 to be raised by a general district rate.

Mr Shelmerdine proposed that this should be raised by a rate of 4s-6d in the £, to be collected in two equal half year instalments of 2s-3d in the £, a reduction of 3d in the £ on the previous year.

Also at the meeting, the seal of the Council was ordered to be affixed to the water rate, and attention was called to the announced alterations of the town's postal facilities. It was resolved to request the authorities, if possible, for the Post Office to be open between 1pm and 1.30pm for dinnertime convenience.

The latest Local Appeals Tribunal was held in the clerk's office on Tuesday, **4 April**, when five cases were presented for consideration. In four cases, exemption was granted for a fortnight, month, two months and three months respectively, the fifth case was adjourned awaiting further particulars.

Mr W Denton, of Raunds, attended the annual meeting of the Thrapston & District Shire Horse Society held at the "White Hart Hotel", Thrapston in the afternoon. He proposed that long-serving secretary, Mr Arthur G Brown, should continue in his position. This was carried unanimously.

Meanwhile in his Budget speech in Parliament today, Mr McKenna, Chancellor of the Exchequer, announced new taxes on "amusements", matches or lucifers, and most unpopular of all, railway tickets. He also increased the basic rate of income tax to 2s-3d in the £ (or 11.25%) and the higher rate to 5s-0d in the £ (or 25%)!

Wednesday evening, **5 April**, saw an entertainment given in the schoolroom in connection with the Wesleyan Sunday School. The Rev J Burrows was in the chair and the spacious premises were crowded. In addition to items by the scholars, who had been admirably trained by Misses M E & G Lawrence and E Adams, the following also kindly contributed to the programme: Miss E Adams (elecutionist), Misses F L & W Wooding (Rushden), and Mr Wm & Mrs G White (Irthlingborough). A sketch was also given in which the following took part: Mrs F Collins, Misses E & L Adams, and Mr R Sanders. Misses G Lawrence, E Sanders, and L Featherstonehaugh were the accompanists. The proceeds, which were in aid of Sunday School funds, amounted to nearly £8.

An accident befell Mr John Matson, 63, on Friday, **7 April**. Employed by Mr Wm Pettit, farmer, he fell from a load of straw, injuring his ribs and shoulder. A rope had been thrown over the straw and the victim thought it had been fastened and was sliding down, a practice witnesses said he often did, when he fell heavily to the ground.

The Boot & Shoe Operatives Union local branch reported that the "out of work benefit" paid out during the past quarter amounted to only 10s-0d.

And the final positions in the Rushden & District Clubs' Billiards League were published today. Raunds Conservatives finished fourth with a balanced return of 7 wins and 7 defeats, whilst the Raunds Woodbine emerged the strongest team of all (holding the rest up!) with only 2 triumphs, finishing eighth and bottom.

"Wanted, good Clicker on Army and Navy work, Apply: Adams Bros, Raunds"

The employees of the Raunds Distributive Co-Operative Society assembled together on Saturday evening, **8 April**, to bid farewell to Mr S Townsend, who after 23 years service at Raunds, had accepted a position with the Barnsley Co-Operative Society. Mr Townsend was presented with a beautiful oak overmantel, as a token of esteem, and the best wishes of the employees for him in his new sphere of labour were expressed.

Two days after her son's accident, Mrs Mary Ann Matson, of Newtown Road, was also involved in an "incident", on Sunday, **9 April**. The 84 year old struck a match which set fire to the bed; her grandson asleep in the adjoining room, heard her shout, and the fire was soon put out. Had the fire got well hold, the row of twelve houses might easily have been burnt down.

Monday, **10 April** – "For Sale, Freehold Dwelling House in Midland Road, 6 rooms and premises, detached. W F Corby, Raunds"

An aged Raunds man met a sad end today. A shoehand was going to work in the morning at Messrs R Coggins & Son's factory in Marshall's Road when he was startled to see the head of a man protruding from one of the water butts on the premises. It was that of a 69 year old who occupied one of the houses nearby and was also an employee of the factory. It emerged that he had had a cup of tea at his daughter's, who lived nearby, and had said that he felt miserable. She had told him to stay and not to go to work but he said no. He was found dead soon after. The deceased's son said that his father had been in poor health lately and had continually worried over his other son who was killed in France in 1914. At the subsequent inquest, the jury returned a verdict of "Suicide by drowning himself in a soft-water butt whilst temporarily insane".

On Tuesday, **11 April**, Quartermaster Sergeant E Medlock, of the RAMC, was reported as being home on leave after ten months service in France.

And housewives would have been glad to read today that the Royal Commission on Sugar Supply had threatened to take drastic action against any grocer who was refusing to sell sugar unless tea was bought at the same time.

Sir George Askwith, Chief Industrial Commissioner, the umpire for payment and price claims referred to him by the Joint Standing Committee in connection with the Government Boot & Shoe Contractors, announced on Wednesday, **12 April**, his decisions regarding five recent shoe worker's claims. Of the five, two were rejected. Those allowed were: 1) 1s-6d per dozen pairs for cutting uppers of British Army boots B5; 2) 1s-9d per dozen pairs for cutting uppers of half-boots for seamen of the Fleet; and 3) 5s-6d per dozen pairs for cutting uppers of field service boots, cut throughout. Applicable to Northants County contracts only.

"Lost – On Saturday, 8 April, between Lowick and Raunds, a Prismatic Compass, Mark 7, in a leather case. If returned to the Police Station, Thrapston, a reward will be given."

At Wellingborough Police Court on Friday, **14 April**, four Raunds boys and one from Stanwick were charged with malicious damage to telegraph insulators at Stanwick between 21 December 1915 and 9 March. Also summoned were four shoehands from Stanwick and four other Raunds scholars, charged with attempting to injure certain telegraph insulators at the same time and place. Giving evidence, an engineer said that considerable damage had been done to the property of His Majesty's Postmaster-General along this particular road and 69 insulators had been broken in recent months. The Bench said they would deal leniently with the defendants but warn them as to their future conduct. The three eldest boys were each ordered to pay 5s-6d costs and the two youngest were dismissed, the other eight were each ordered to pay 4s-0d costs.

In the evening, the Raunds District Education Sub-Committee met in the Council Schools. The attendance report showed for the last quarter an average attendance of 919 against 953 for the corresponding period in 1915. This was chiefly due to chickenpox at the Church of England School, whooping cough at the Council Infants School and much general illness at Hargrave. A number of permits for employment were granted under the relaxed byelaws. Several cases of irregular attendance were brought before the committee and dealt with, and in one case proceedings were authorised as no satisfactory explanation had been given.

The speaker at the Brotherhood meeting on Sunday, **16 April**, was Mr Brown, of Wellingborough, who gave an address on "The Value of Man". Mr W Gibbs rendered two solos "The Silver Lining" and "The Storm King", in fine style, ably accompanied by Mrs Gibbs at the piano.

The Urban Council held their annual meeting on Monday, **17 April**, and Mr J Shelmerdine heartily thanked Mr John Adams for being chairman during a very strenuous year. Mr Adams responded and remarked on the loss to the town of four prominent citizens during the past year, Messrs Amos Fisher, Charles Groom, John Bass and Joseph Gant. Mr James Adams was then proposed as chairman for the coming year but declined to take office. As a result, his brother Mr John Adams, CC, was thereupon re-elected to serve a further term. Mr A Camozzi was elected vice-chairman, an amendment in favour of Mr Batchelor being defeated.

The balance sheets of Peaps' and Blaise's Charities were presented and accepted. It was noted that from the balance sheet of Peaps' Charity, the proceeds, instead of being equally divided between the schools as in previous years, had been distributed to the parents of children holding scholarships, to assist in their educational expenditure. To this the Council expressed their agreement.

The Cemetery Committee recommended that the laying out of the proposed cemetery be proceeded with, and it was decided to do the minimum work considered necessary at the present time at an estimated cost for fencing, paths and drainage, of £300. Finally, the medical officer, Dr Mackenzie, reported 3 deaths and 7 births registered in the town during March.

Sir George Askwith was called into action again on Wednesday, **19 April**, to give judgement on a claim, brought to him by the Arbitration Board, for a price to be fixed for cutting uppers of the new Russian Ankle boot. He awarded, per dozen pairs in each case: cutting vamps, 7d; backs, 9d; counters, 4d; whole tongues, 4d; and half or joined tongues, 5d. The prices would be effective from today.

On Thursday, **20 April**, the Brotherhood announced that the sum raised by their collection from local businesses on behalf of the YMCA War Emergency Fund was £37-14s-0d. The money had been remitted to the treasurer and a letter of thanks in acknowledgement received.

On the same day it was also reported that a recent collection had been made in the factories for the benefit of Mr Fred Hall, of Park Street, who had been suffering from a diseased foot for the past two years, and had recently had the limb amputated. This was initiated by Dr Mackenzie, Messrs E Batchelor and G Underwood, for the purpose of providing the poor man with an artificial foot and leg. Both employers and employees had generously subscribed to the fund, with the result that the splendid sum of £27-1s-8d had been raised. The balance, after providing for the artificial limb, would be paid to him at the weekly rate of 10s-0d.

At the quarterly meeting of the Hospital Week Committee this evening, the treasurer reported receipts of £33-6s-9d, expenditure of 17s-6d, leaving a balance in hand of £32-9s-3d. From this, the sum of £25 was voted to go to the county treasurer. A sub-committee had been appointed to arrange for the annual demonstration and they decided to seek permission for use of the "Greenhouse Field", to invite the Distributive Co-Operative Society to undertake the provision of refreshments, and to ask the head teachers of the two schools to arrange for a representation by the scholars of some phase of hospital work in the procession.

Good Friday, **21 April**, and Dr Mackenzie reported the first hearing of a cuckoo this spring, meanwhile, the receipt of yet more eggs collected by the town's scholars was acknowledged by the VAD Hospital at Higham Ferrers.

In the afternoon, the funeral of Mrs Ann Barnett Hazeldine, the 79 year old widow of the late Mr Owen Hazeldine, took place at the Parish Burial Ground, the Rev W S Bethway, Curate-in-charge, officiating. The deceased had died on Monday, 17 April, after an illness lasting about six months.

The annual tea was given by the British Women's Temperance Association today, to the old people over 65 and widows of the parish, in the Temperance Hall. At 3.30pm, about 120 sat down at the tables, after which a hymn was sung and prayer was lead by the Rev J Burrows. Addresses were then given by Mr G Lee and Mr Enos Smith, and a social followed which included contributions from: Mr Athol Tebbutt, Mrs F Pentelow, and Mr Janes (songs); Mrs Pentelow and Mrs F Lawrence (duet); Mrs Lawrence, Mr Tebbutt, and Master Willis Rands (recitations); and Miss Pettit (violin solo).

On Easter Sunday, **23 April**, a concert was given at 2.30pm on "The Hill" by the Temperance Silver Prize Band, conducted by Mr Owen Pentelow, a collection being taken in aid of band funds.

Also that afternoon, an open meeting in connection with the Men's Adult School was held in the Temperance Hall when a good number of both sexes were present to hear an address on "Citizenship" by Councillor J Haynes, of Kettering. Miss E Pulpher presided and a collection was taken in aid of the War Victims Fund.

Monday, 24 April, the Easter Rising in Ireland begins. Raymond William Vallance (116), killed in action.

The Parish Church, Ringstead, was the scene of an interesting event today, the union of two Ringstead and Raunds families. The bride was Miss Gertrude Manning, second daughter of Mr and Mrs J Manning, of Ringstead, and the bridegroom Mr Charles William Pettitt, youngest son of Mrs J Pettitt, of Raunds. Mr Arthur Pettitt attended as best man. The Rev C Page Wood conducted the service and Mr J P Archer, of Raunds, at the organ, played the "Wedding March" and other selections. A reception was afterwards held in the Church School, the happy pair being the recipients of numerous handsome and useful presents.

Denford Wesleyan Church held an anniversary congregational meeting this afternoon at which Mr W F Corby presided and Mr Warner Pond, of Peterborough, gave a most interesting lecture, entitled "A dog's opinion of the world".

The 58th anniversary of the Temperance Society was celebrated in glorious weather on Easter Tuesday, **25 April**. A procession was formed at the Temperance Hall, consisting of the Band of Hope, Temperance Society, and Salvation Army, and headed by the Temperance Band, it paraded the town, halting at intervals to sing temperance melodies. The children were conducted by Mr A Tebbutt. The Band of Hope then marched to the Temperance Hall where about 200 sat down to tea, followed by a public tea when about 100 sat down.

After tea, the company adjourned to Carter Hill field, lent by Mr W Denton, where some interesting and exciting sporting events took place and the Temperance Band played selections, and for dancing. At 7.30pm a meeting was held in the Temperance Hall, the speaker being the Rev C L Atkins, BA, of Rothwell. Two much appreciated solos were rendered by Miss M Sanders entitled "Rose Garden" and "The Old Country", and Miss E Sanders accompanied.

"War Prophecy of a Raunds man now in Tasmania" was a startling headline on Wednesday, **26 April**, and told of the remarkable predictions made by Mr Charles Lucas, of Derby, Tasmania, formerly of Raunds, in 1910. Mr Lucas, the brother of Mrs E J Whitney, still a resident of our fair town, had apparently written six years earlier, "One of the greatest dangers is the position of Germany and Austria, those two nations practically dominate Europe today, and when they make the next move in the game of chess that is going on, something big will happen!"

Also today, a wedding of considerable local interest took place at the Registry Office, Bedford, when Miss Evelyn Ursula Lawrence, eldest daughter of Mr and Mrs Amos Lawrence, of "The Hall", Raunds, was united to Mr Charles Fenton, farmer, of Yelden, Beds. The wedding breakfast was served at the "Embankment Hotel", after which the happy couple left by motor for Bournemouth, where the honeymoon was spent. The wedding presents were both numerous and costly. On returning home, Mr and Mrs Fenton planned to take up residence at Yelden.

The Easter Vestry meeting was held on Thursday, **27 April**, the Rev W S Bethway presiding. The Vicar, who was away on military service, re-appointed Mr A Camozzi as his warden and Mr J Shelmerdine, JP, as people's warden. The accounts of the Ecclesiastical Charities were accepted and the Vicar's warden announced that the Easter offering to the Vicar amounted to £10.

A congregational meeting followed to consider the most convenient hour for Sunday evening services during the summer months. It was decided to begin Evensong at 5.30pm on and after 7 May until further notice. It was thought that the new time would give ample opportunity for a walk in the afternoon and also for another after service, so the message from the Curate was "Please buck up!"

Today, the Raunds Red Cross Committee announced that they had sent to headquarters at Northampton during March, 3 dressing gowns (gratuitously made by Misses Eady, Morris, and Black), 26 bed jackets, 12 pairs of mittens, 6 pairs of operation stockings, 6 pairs of bed socks, and 3 pairs of day socks. The April contribution had been 12 pairs of slippers, 12 huckaback towels, 4 pairs of mittens (3 knitted by Church School children), 1 pair of day socks and 2 body belts.

Saturday, 29 April, the surrender of Kut, General Townshend capitulates.

While our boys out in the Middle East were suffering in the extreme, there was success for two Raunds children at the North Northants Musical Competition, held in the Great Hall of Oundle School. Taking first prize for Class 3, Pianoforte solo, (under 16), 2nd movement Andante from Sonata, op 14, No.2, (Beethoven), was Dorothy Foster. Kenneth Spicer took second place, and was also placed second in Class 5, Solo for Boys under 16, "The Harper's Song", (Schubert). Both were pupils of Mr J P Archer, organist of the Parish Church.

The 9th anniversary of the Brotherhood was marked on Sunday, **30 April**, in the Wesleyan Church. The Rev Richard E Brown, a former resident of Raunds, preached to good congregations, the subject of both services being "The eternal issues of sin". At the morning service, the anthem "All Thy works praise Thee" was rendered by the choir, and at the evening service, solos, entitled "Nearer, my God to Thee" and "Lead, Kindly Light", were sung by Madame Ella Barlow. At the afternoon meeting for men, Mr Brown gave an excellent address on "The Evolution of Democracy", vocal duets being contributed by Misses Louie Smith and Letha Spicer, with Mrs H Ruff accompanying at the piano.

MAY – The Curate's notes this month included thanks to all those who had helped in decorating and cleaning the Church in preparation for the well attended Easter services.

He also made the following advance plea regarding the forthcoming Ascension Day on 1 June: "Will those who are able try and keep this great festival in the proper way? – It is the Coronation Day of our Triumphant King!"

And for the subsequent Sunday School Festival on 4 June, when the collection would be for the work of the Sunday School, his message was: "We are trying to do more this year for our children by giving the younger ones picture stamps and encouraging the scholars in other ways. This means greater expense, so in order to keep out of debt we need something like £10 on 4 June as these collections are practically our only source of income".

Included in the list of burials in the churchyard in April was Louisa Brayfield, the mother of **Sam Brayfield (27)**.

There was a busy agenda for discussion at the monthly meeting of the local Boot & Shoe Operatives Union branch, on Monday, **1 May**. The question was raised regarding the Increase of Rent & Mortgage Interest Restrictions Act. Although tenants were being treated fairly to a large extent, many had had their rents raised. The secretary wished it to be known that tenants had the power to recover extra rent paid. If the landlord declined to put the rent back to the 3 August 1914 level, the tenant should offer the amount paid before that date, less the sum charged extra since 25 November 1915.

The monthly report showed trade to be still good, but there was a great shortage of skilled labour to run the work through the factories. The introduction of unskilled, untrained labour for the manufacture of boots to satisfy the Government departments' standard of quality and workmanship had been a failure, whether male or female, this equally applied to the civil trade.

Appearing this week at the Palace Theatre, Rushden – "Daisy & Her Eight Stars", Nine Charming Young Ladies who Twinkle Nightly!

For breaches of the Lighting Order, twenty-one Raunds residents were summoned to appear at Thrapston Police Court on Tuesday, **2 May**. The pontoon of eight shoehands, five housewives, club steward, fishmonger, baker, butcher, labourer, traveller, dressmaker and currier received fines ranging from 2s-6d to 15s-0d.

Wednesday, **3 May**, saw the funeral of a well known and highly respected former Raunds resident, Mr Alfred Bailey, aged 62. He had died on the previous Sunday at the residence of his daughter, Mrs Jervis, of Raynes Park. The deceased, an ardent Welseyan, had endured a long and painful illness. He was the father of Mrs John Adams, of "Darsdale", to whose residency the body was brought prior to the funeral. The service at the Wesleyan graveyard was conducted by the Rev Harry Shaw, of Thrapston.

On Friday, **5 May**, Miss Doris Warth, of "The Grange", collector of eggs for Raunds in connection with the National Egg Collection for Wounded Soldiers & Sailors, was reported to have sent to the head office at London, for the month of April, the sum of £2 and 106 eggs.

Nearly 12 months after being listed as "missing", official news was received on Saturday, **6 May**, to the effect that Private **William Webb Chambers (33)** was now considered to have been "killed in action" at Aubers Ridge on 9 May 1915. However, friends were still seeking any information on the manner of his death.

"Wanted – strong Youth or Man (ineligible), to help in stables and deliver goods, Palmer's Stores, Raunds"

The Rev Dr J G Tasker, of Birmingham, president-elect of the Methodist Conference, preached at the Wesleyan Church on Sunday, **7 May**. At the evening service, the choir sang the anthem "Harken unto me, My people", with Mr J W Hall at the organ.

Advance word on the new Wesleyan Methodist minister appeared on Tuesday, **9 May**, when it was revealed that "Rev E Percy and Mrs Blackburn celebrated their silver wedding last Thursday. Mr Blackburn's ministry in Kent has been marked by much success as shown by the fact that membership and class contributions have been nearly doubled, and missionary income showed increases in both 1914 and 1915, in spite of air raids!"

The monthly and annual meeting of the Thrapston Board of Guardians was held today at the Thrapston Workhouse and Mrs G Ernest Smith gave the report of the Children's Home Committee. Five of the children in the Home had been vaccinated. One boarded-out boy who had been described as incorrigible had been received into the Home, and was found quite manageable. The eldest girl in the Home had gone into service, and had proved quite satisfactory. The committee also applied for £4 to purchase an outfit, which was granted.

At the Wesleyan Church anniversary service at Higham Ferrers on Sunday evening, **14 May**, Miss Grace Lawrence, of Raunds, made a guest appearance, singing a solo "in delightful style".

The Urban Council met on Monday, **15 May**, and the medical officer, Dr Mackenzie, reported that in April, 4 deaths and 10 births were registered and that the district was "quite free from notifiable infectious diseases", and the seal of the council was affixed to the loan of £453 with the Public Works Loans Commission for a cemetery.

Councillors agreed to apply to the Local Appeals Tribunal for the man at the pumping station to be exempted from military service on the grounds that he was engaged in a certified occupation. They also decided to apply for an extension to the exemptions granted to the surveyor and inspector of nuisances.

Finally, councillor's attendances for the past year were disclosed: A Camozzi, 54 out of a possible 54; W Asbery, 48 out of 48; J Hodson, 47 out of 47; W Agutter, 45 out of 47; G E Smith, 41 out of 43; James Adams, 42 out of 48; John Adams, CC, 40 out of 47; W Gates, 39 out of 43; E Batchelor, 36 out of 43; J Shelmerdine, JP, 33 out of 42; J Gant, deceased, 20; and L G H Lee, on active service, 1.

The County Licensing Committee today confirmed the refusal to renew the license of the "Golden Fleece" on the grounds that there were six licensed houses in a radius of just 400 yards, and also today, Messrs Adams Bros announced that their tender for the supply of 300 pairs of firemen's boots had been accepted by the London County Council.

The Wesleyan District Synod, Bedford & Northampton District, was held at Northampton from Monday 15 until Thursday, 18 May, and local ministers present included the town's Reverends J Burrows and H Shaw. The only lady representative attending was Mrs J Cecil Horrell, of Raunds. Delegates heard that the total circuit membership in Raunds was 407, a decrease of 30, with 125 juniors, and 39 "on trial". Foreign Missions income for the period just completed was £77-15s-2d, an increase of £4-3s-0d.

"For Sale – Broadwood piano, nearly new, £35, Archer, Organist, Raunds"

At the Church of England School manager's meeting on Tuesday, **16 May**, consideration was given to the application from Miss Florence Adams for the post of Certified Assistant in the Mixed Department. However, again the board decided that no recommendation be made "as the present staff were working well and satisfactorily, and should not be altered merely for the sake of greater theoretical efficiency".

Royal assent was given on Wednesday, **17 May**, to the Summer Time Bill and daylight saving thus became the law of the land. Residents were advised that it would come into force on Saturday night, 20 May, "when you must put your clock forward an hour just before going to bed. Then on Sunday you will do everything as usual at the usual time by the clock". Confusingly, it was also stated that the minute hand on Big Ben's four clockfaces would need to be advanced by 60 feet!

"Wanted – Governess for lad of six years, daily, four miles from Thrapston and Raunds – Letters to Box 627, "Evening Telegraph, Kettering"

Northamptonshire County Council met on Thursday, **18 May**, and representing Raunds was Mr John Adams. The assembly heard that the blizzard of 28 March had resulted in additional expenditure for the council of £180-9s-11d for extra labour to clear snowdrifts and £15-15s-10d to remove fallen trees from the roads.

And among those elected to the committee under the Naval & Military War Pensions Act was Mr J T Pettitt, of Raunds, nominated by the National United Order of Free Gardeners.

The first conscientious objector to be arrested in Northamptonshire, was charged and fined £3 on Saturday, **20 May**, and handed over to a military escort.

The Primitive Methodist Sunday School anniversary services were held on Sunday, **21 May**, when the Rev W Bache, of St Neots, preached. In the afternoon, a cantata, "The Adorning of the Cross", was given by the scholars. At the evening service, solos were rendered by Mr Freeman, Misses Nellie Adams and Emmie Butler, and recitations were given by Misses Mabel Reynolds, Edna Roughton, and Kate Shrives. On Monday, **22 May**, an entertainment took place in the schools, consisting of a sketch entitled "A Bow with Two Strings" and a cantata, "The Little Gipsy Girl", by the scholars and young people.

The town's experiences of the coming of the new "Summer Time" were told on Tuesday, **23 May**. The clocks in the various factories had been altered on Saturday, before closing for the half day, so that they were ready for "summer time" attendance on Monday morning. The public clocks were altered late on Saturday evening, including the clock on the Post Office. There were not such large congregations at the various places of worship on Sunday, but the splendid weather was probably more the cause of this than the alteration of the time, as large numbers of the townspeople were noticed in the fields and walks frequented by the parishioners. It had been quite the talk on Saturday evening asking "Have you?" or "When are you going to put your watch on?" However, the question now was "Willett be a success?" – We should have to "Wait and See".

Wednesday, 24 May, Francis William Warner (118), dies.

Today, Private F W Warner, the son of Mr and Mrs John Warner, of Brook Street, died at about 6.30am, aged just 18. Soon after returning to camp at Colchester from home leave in January, he was taken ill and became a patient at the Military Hospital there until he was removed to Raunds on 22 April. Since Easter he had been wheeled about in a bath chair and was seen out as recently as Sunday last. He was taken worse in the early hours of Wednesday morning and died three hours later from valvular disease of the heart.

His funeral took place on Saturday, 27 May, the coffin being draped with the Union Jack, and the deceased soldier's coat and cap were placed on it. The coffin bearers were six Royal Welsh Fusiliers, who were billeted in the town, and the mourners included Sergeant F Draper, of Higham Ferrers, and Mr J Shelmerdine, JP, the local military representative.

The flags were flying today as Empire Day celebrations took place at both schools. At the Church of England School, national songs were sung, and at the Council School, both the infant and older scholars assembled in the central hall as the latter portion of the morning was devoted to the celebrations. The Rev J Burrows gave an address on "Our Empire" and a representation of "Britannia and her children" was given by some of the smaller scholars, dressed in national costume.

Recitations and songs given by the scholars included: "The daisy & its story", Pauline Smith; "What a little chap can do", Jack Hall; "England's Dead", Louie Pettit; "Our Flag", Fred Cripps; "We'll never let the old Flag fall", George Newberry; "There is a Land", Winnie Lansom; and "Shakespeare on his country", George Finding.

"Wanted – Good Machinist for Closing Room, Apply: Adams Bros, Raunds"

Another of Sergeant L G H Lee's letters appeared in print on Thursday, **25 May**, with the eye-catching title of "Shares Lodgings With Rats"! Writing to friends at Ringstead from "somewhere in France", he first congratulated them in having had conferred on them the benefits of daylight saving. With tongue in cheek he observed "When you push on the hands of your clocks and watches please remember that eight years ago when the idea was merely ridiculed, I did my 'bit' by giving evidence as to the advantages of the plan before a Select Committee of the House of Commons. Truly, great men live before their time!"

Describing his current situation and rodent friends, he confided that: "I occupy an empty cottage with my assistant, I say empty, but we are obliged to share it with sundry rats and mice. The rats, I am thankful to say, remain upstairs, which we do not use. The mice keep us company in the lower quarters, and have a decided liking for the warmth of my bed from which I have to pluck them when they get too numerous for sleep".

He closed with this amusing ditty: "When you tread the floor with baby, In an all-night crooning song, Thank your stars you're not in Greenland, Where the nights are six months long!"

At St Neots Petty Sessions this afternoon, a Raunds resident of Newtown Road, who was now serving in the Army Service Corps in south east London, was charged with not using two electric headlights on a motor car at Kimbolton, at about 8.30pm on 26 April. Pleading guilty by letter, he said that he did not understand the law. The unsympathetic Bench fined him 5s-0d, the Chairman observing that "it is possible that many people do not understand the regulations, but they cannot be let off for that sort of thing, they ought to understand!"

"OHMS – Royal Engineers & Army Ordnance Corps – Shoemakers Section: The above branches are open to men who are medically unfit or between the age of 41 and 47. An Inspector will be at the Library, Kettering, on Saturday, 27 May, at 2pm. All men desirous of joining should bring a letter from their employer to the effect that, if accepted, he can be released. Rate of pay: 1s-2d per day & 6d extra working pay if at home; 1s-2d per day & 1s-0d extra if working in the Field."

Members of the bands associated with the Northamptonshire Brass Band Association had a rehearsal on the lawn of the Irthlingborough Band Club on Saturday, **27 May**, Mr Owen Pentelow, of Raunds, conducting. At the close they played the "Dead March" (Handel) in memory of the late Mr H B Harris.

Today saw the death of an old and respected inhabitant of the town. Mr John Sinfield, of Midland Road, who had been in failing health for some time, but had not been confined to bed, was getting up in the morning when he expired. The deceased, aged 88, was a retired dairyman.

On Monday evening, **29 May**, Mr A G Brown, auctioneer of Thrapston & Raunds, offered for sale by auction at the Coffee Tavern, the following properties, by instructions from the trustees of the late Mr Owen Nunley: Lot 1, two freehold houses with shops etc in Grove Street, occupied by Mr H Turnill, butcher and Mrs Corby, newsagent; Lot 2, stable, coachhouse, barn and yard in the occupation of Mrs Corby; Lot 3, garden or building site, adjoining lot 2, containing 576 square yards; Lot 4, two houses in Grove Place, with gardens and outbuildings, occupied by Messrs Mayes & Sanders. The whole were put up as one lot. Bidding commenced at £500, and advanced to £695, at which they were knocked down to Mr A Camozzi. A plot of freehold building land in Spencer Street, about 1,000 square yards, belonging to Miss S J White, was sold at £49. Several freehold building plots, belonging to Mr Enos Smith, JP, were offered, but not sold.

At the Thrapston Petty Sessions on Tuesday, **30 May**, a Raunds jobmaster was summoned for a breach of the Lighting Order by leaving a motor car on the highway at Ringstead from 8.15pm to 9.45pm and failing to shade the lights. He was fined £1 with 9s-0d costs.

In another unusual case, a single woman from Ringstead was summoned by an army boot cutter from the village for "calling him a German in a public place". The chairman said it was a great outrage to accuse an honest Englishman doing his duty in an English factory as being a German. She was fined 10s-0d and bound over for twelve months. Two or three minutes later, the complainant returned protesting that the defendant's mother had just insulted his wife outside the court. He added that she was also subjected to continued insults from morning til evening. In response, the angry chairman said "You people at Ringstead must learn your manners and not behave in this disgraceful way to your neighbours!"

Wednesday, 31 May, the Battle of Jutland.

The Council School managers met this evening and tensions between the different religious factions in the town reared their head when Mr Hodson said that he was surprised to have read in the paper that the children had been addressed on Empire Day by the Rev J Burrows, and that the minister had been invited to give the address without the knowledge and consent of the managers. Obviously in a parochial mood, he also asked if children of the town might not be prepared for Secondary education in the county, instead of at Kimbolton. It was decided to invite the headmaster to the next meeting for consultation and discussion.

JUNE – This month the Curate gave advanced notice that a "Children's Service" would be held at 2pm on Whit Sunday and asked for all to bring eggs for the wounded soldiers. Likewise eggs would also be on the wanted agenda at the Feast Sunday service on Sunday, 2 July.

Also in this issue of the Parish Magazine was a report on a meeting held on Monday, 8 May, to discuss ways of raising money to help clear the School Debt. Strong opinion was voiced in favour of voluntary subscriptions, and as several ladies and gentlemen volunteered to help organise the project, it was put into operation almost immediately. Bullish as ever, the Curate asked "What will you promise to give between now and 1 September? – A little self-sacrifice all round should result in £100!"

Thursday, **1 June**, was Ascension Day, and the Church of England School was closed for the day. Holy Communion was celebrated in the Parish Church.

The Local Appeals Tribunal met this evening and the recruiting officer, Captain Wright, asked for cases in the boot trade to be adjourned; single men's for a week and married men's for a month, pending an arrangement between the military authorities and manufacturers being satisfactorily reached. A letter was read from the War Agricultural Committee pointing out that they viewed with alarm the number of indispensable men the Tribunal were taking from the land and urged them to be more lenient.

Six agricultural cases were then considered, three were given conditional exemption on them remaining in their present occupations; the other three were given either two or three months. The Thrapston Board of Guardians appealed for their 41 year old, married, superintendent of the Children's Home, who was given a similar conditional exemption. A builder/plumber/decorator appealed for his man who was given two months, although the military representative was of the opinion that there were a number of wounded soldiers who could do the work.

The Distributive Co-Operative Society appealed for their 36 year old, married, manager/buyer of the drapery and men's outfitting, and their 25 year old, married, slaughterman. Their argument was that out of 15 male employees of military age, eight had enlisted and two had been rejected, and they employed female labour where possible. As a result, both men were given three months exemption. Finally, a single man, but with a widowed, invalid mother, dependant on him, was also given three months.

Friday, 2 June, the Third Battle of Ypres begins.

At the County Appeals Tribunal, the co-proprietor of the Palace Theatre, Raunds, had his appeal, against the refusal of the Local Appeals Tribunal to grant him an exemption, dismissed. He was however, given leave to appeal to the Central Appeals Tribunal. In his defence, the appellant stated that if he was made to join the Army, he and his partner would go into bankruptcy.

It was announced that the Prince of Wales' War Relief Fund had reached a total of £5,899,809, and of this sum, £3,318,000 had been allocated to date for distribution for relief.

"For Sale – Quantity of Pea & Bean Sticks – Shaw, Basketmaker, Raunds"

The Distributive Co-Operative Society "Children's Holiday" was held on Saturday, **3 June**, and the event was favoured with good climatic conditions for, although clouds gathered in the forenoon and a shower of rain fell at midday, this was soon over, and the remainder of the day proved all that could be desired. The town itself looked festive by means of flags and streamers flying across the streets.

The procession, headed by the Temperance Silver Prize Band, left the Gas Works at one o'clock and marched by way of Grove Street, Brook Street, High Street, Midland Road and back to The Square. Under the conductorship of Mr W Hall, the children (of whom there were 1,022) sang hymns at various points en-route. Tea was served for the boys at the National School, and for the girls at the Wesleyan Schools. After tea, all processed to the "Home Close" at Thorpe House Farm, where sports had been arranged and dancing was also indulged in to music supplied by the Temperance Band.

Mr W Charter, manager of the Cambridge Co-Operative Society, gave an address urging the children to "play the game of life fairly", and speaking of the excellent work of the Raunds Society, claimed that "the members had the right to enjoy the beauties of life, as well as bear its responsibilities."

On Sunday, **4 June**, the Parish Church held its annual Sunday School festival, the preacher being the Rev A J Meakin, Vicar of St Albans, Leicester. In the afternoon Mr Meakin addressed the scholars and friends.

The Women's Adult School held an open meeting in the afternoon when the speaker was Mr Harry Lacon, of the Adult School Sub-Union, who gave a good address on "Rebuilding of the Nation".

Down the road at Irthlingborough, the Wesleyan Church Sunday School anniversary services also took place. Special anthems were sung by the choir at the afternoon service, Miss Grace Lawrence, of Raunds, being the soloist.

Monday, 5 June, Lord Kitchener drowns when HMS Hampshire in sunk.

On the day that the country mourned the loss of a national hero, the Raunds District Education Sub-Committee agreed the application for holidays from the managers of the Chelveston, Hargrave, Newton Bromswold, and Stanwick schools.

The Church of England School managers also met today and considered an application from Miss Gladys Essex to become a pupil teacher in the Mixed Department. They decided to recommend her appointment at a commencing salary of £42 per annum.

The flag of the Council School flew at half-mast on Tuesday, **6 June**, in memory of the late Lord Kitchener, whilst St Lawrence's Church at Stanwick suffered a setback this afternoon when the spire, which had only recently been repaired, was again struck by lightning.

Wednesday, 7 June, John William Victor Ashby (16), killed in action.

Today, Dr Mackenzie sent off 2,000 cigarettes to the men of the Northamptons, purchased with the balance of the proceeds of the draw he had recently organised for this purpose. The sum of £25 had already been expended in comforts, and the balance of nearly £3 had now been utilised for cigarettes.

Thursday, **8 June**, saw the news that Mr Ralph Pentelow, eldest son of the late Mr James Pentelow & Mrs Pentelow, of Raunds Mill, who had gone out to Australia some time ago, had joined the Australian contingent and was now at the front.

And this afternoon, the local boot manufacturers met and decided to close the factories on Monday of next week for the Whitsuntide holiday.

"Royal Edward Survivors – Local Ambulance Men at a Convalescent Hospital", proclaimed the local papers on Friday, **9 June**, and told of how Dr Mackenzie had recently received a photograph of some of the staff of the hospital at Port Said, Egypt. The men shown were from the Royal Army Medical Corps and most of them had been saved from the "Royal Edward" when it was sunk in the Aegean Sea by a submarine on 13 September, 1915. They included Raunds' Harry Hall, who was described as "only 20 years of age, but about 6 feet 4 inches in height!"

The death of Mr Harry (Sammy) Asberry, son of Mr and Mrs Wm Asberry, High Street, was announced today. He had had a severe attack of influenza three weeks previously, and during a fit of coughing, had burst a blood vessel in his brain requiring his removal to hospital. There the 41 year old had died.

And there was excitement for Raunds residents this afternoon when an aeroplane passed over the town at a considerable height. Local beekeepers, however, would have been more concerned with the considerable colony losses being suffered as "Isle of Wight Disease" swept through the county. Meanwhile, the district's shoe manufacturers revealed that a pair of the new Cossack boots would require 8 to 10 square feet of upper leather.

"A Bit Too Far" was the title of a story that on Saturday, **10 June**, three Raunds motorcyclists appeared at Huntingdon Police Court, charged with riding their machines without lights at Molesworth a few weeks previously. Pleading guilty, their leader explained that they had journeyed a bit too far and couldn't get home before dark. He was fined 5s-0d and his accomplices 3s-0d each.

The Temperance Band gave a concert on The Square on Whit Sunday, **11 June**, and amongst the items they played was "Great Britain", the test piece for tomorrow's Coalville Band Contest.

It was the Sunday School anniversary at the Baptist Church today, and both morning and evening services were conducted by Pastor Winch, of London, as was the afternoon's children's service.

At the close of the evening service at the Wesleyan Church, the organist, Mr A W Hazeldine, played the "Dead March" in memory of Lord Kitchener.

Whit Monday, **12 June**, saw the Baptist Church's annual treat for the scholars which commenced with tea at 3pm, followed by a public tea at 4pm. However, owing to the unfavourable weather conditions, the outdoor sports were abandoned and amusements were provided in the schoolroom.

The day also witnessed the wedding at the Wesleyan Church of Private Harold J Goodman, of the Royal Marine Light Infantry, fourth son of Mrs E Goodman, of St Neots, and Miss Helen Elizabeth Smith, eldest daughter of Mr David Smith, also of St Neots. The bride had for some years been an assistant at Raunds Post Office. Attired in a costume of khaki court coating, she was given away by her father. Her sisters, Misses Florrie and Alice Smith, were bridesmaids, and Lance-Corporal F Goodman attended his brother as best man. The Rev J Burrows officiated, and Mr A W Hazeldine, cousin of the bride, was at the organ.

Out of the county in Leicestershire, the Temperance Band took third prize at the band contest at Coalville.

And starting today at Blackpool, the annual general meeting of the National United Order of Free Gardeners included local delegates J T Pettitt, of Raunds, and T Robinson, of Ringstead.

Tuesday, **13 June** – "For Sale – 3 1/2hp Triumph Motorcycle, sound condition, fifty miles trial, £17-10s-0d – Tom Asbery, Spencer Street, Raunds"

Friday, 16 June, Alfred Bugby (28) and Percy Smith (105), die of wounds.

The quarterly meeting of the Raunds Wesleyan Methodists was held on Saturday, **17 June**, when it was confirmed that the former secretary, Mr J Bates, had joined HM Forces. Mr P Tanner was elected to take over as treasurer of the "Horse Hire Fund" due to the enlistment of Mr **Arthur Groom (55)**, and with Mr Arthur Tanner also having enlisted, the position of Temperance secretary had become vacant, and was filled by Mr Sam Smith. It was proposed by Mr Pendered that a letter of sympathy and help be composed by Rev Burrows, printed and sent to all men connected with the church and circuit now on active service.

The annual treat for scholars attending the Primitive Methodist Sunday School was held today. Commencing with tea at 3pm at which about 100 sat down, a public tea followed at 4pm. The assembly then proceeded to the "Manor House Field", kindly lent by Mr A Camozzi, who also gave adults permission to look around the Manor House grounds. Sports and games were entered into and as the scholars left, each was provided with a bun.

In the afternoon, the marriage took place at the Parish Church of Miss Sarah Hannah Kirk, daughter of Mr & Mrs George Kirk, Park Road, and Sergeant **Stanley Oswyn George (53)**, son of Mr & Mrs Owen George, The Square. The Rev W S Bethway officiated. The bride, who was given away by her brother, Mr E Kirk, of Denford, wore a gown of crepe-de-chine, with a tunic of lace and silver trimmings, and a hat of leghorn, trimmed with lace and white heather. She carried a shower bouquet of white malmaisons, sweet peas, and white heather. The bridesmaids, Miss Florence Kirk (sister) and Miss Kathleen Kirk (niece), were attired in dresses of white crepe-de-chine with hats of leghorn and tulle, and carried bouquets of mauve sweet peas. Mr Cecil Bailey was best man and the reception was held at the residence of the bride's parents.

A cricket match was played at Wellingborough today between the town's Wesleyans and those from Raunds. The result was a win for the home team by 60 runs, the scores being Wellingborough 121, Raunds 61. Wade, bowling for the homesters, took three wickets in one over. Batting at No.10 for Raunds, **H Rice (96)**, failed to trouble the scorers.

The Urban Council met on Monday, **19 June**, and the medical officer, Dr Mackenzie, reported that three deaths and five births were registered in the town during May, there was also one confirmed case of erysipelas.

The Waterworks Committee, in reply to a letter from the Midland Railway Co, recommended "That the Council do not undertake to extend the water main to Raunds Station under existing conditions" and the Cemetery Committee recommended "That the plans and specifications prepared by the Surveyor be approved for the proposed work in connection with the provision of a cemetery, and that tenders be invited for the work". Both were accepted.

The Highways Committee recommended the acceptance of various tenders for road materials and cartage, which were accepted, and plans were presented for a bathroom etc at "Meadow View" for Mr Ernest Gaunt, and conveniences at Messrs C W Stanley's factory. Both were passed.

The Local Government Board Auditor wrote that he had audited the accounts for the year ending 31 March last, "which were well prepared and kept with care". To this Mr Shelmerdine observed "That is a compliment to our Clerk".

Lasting just over 40 minutes, this was one of the shortest ever Council meetings.

At the Thrapston Police Court on Tuesday, **20 June**, a Raunds shoe laster, being a servant of Mr Walter Lawrence, shoe manufacturer, was charged with stealing 16 pairs of soles, value £3-8s-9d, between 1 June and 18 June. A Rushden hairdresser was charged with receiving the said soles knowing them to have been stolen. Superintendent Tebbey offered sufficient evidence such that both men were remanded in custody for a week. He said that some of the soles were Russian and were stamped in Russian, and the others were stamped with contractor's patent marks which they used instead of a name.

A nasty accident occurred today at the factory of Mr W Lawrence. A shoehand, Walter Litchfield, of Clare Street, was working at a machine called a "squasher" when it came down on his left hand, crushing his thumb and first finger and completely opening up the palm of his hand. Dr Mackenzie dressed the hand and sent him to Northampton General Hospital.

At the Thrapston Rural Appeals Tribunal held on Wednesday, **21 June**, a 40 year old Chelveston shoe laster, employed on Government work at Raunds, was granted an absolute exemption as he had nine children. However, a 38 year old Ringstead man, now employed on boot repairing at Raunds, was only granted a four week final extension as he was no longer doing hand sewn work for which his exemption badge had originally been given.

Members of the Women's Adult School had an outing today. The party left Raunds at about 9am in a charabanc for Woburn Sands, travelling via Olney and Newport Pagnell. After spending a few hours there they started on their return journey, coming back via Ampthill, where they called in to see some of the town's lads who were with the Bedfordshire Regiment in training; then on to Bedford, where tea was partaken of. Leaving Bedford early in the evening, they arrived home soon after 8 o'clock, having had a grand day out.

No doubt of interest to the town's womenfolk with men serving in the military would have been the Budget changes announced in the House of Commons today when significant concessions on income tax were granted to soldiers and sailors on active service. With immediate effect, their income up to £500 per year would be taxed at 1s-3d in the £ against the civilian rate of 2s-3d; for £501 to £1000, it would be 1s-9d (against 3s-0d); and for £1001 to £2000, 2s-9d (against 4s-4d). Though the number of local men being liable for anything other than the basic rate would surely have been minimal!

The latest Local Appeals Tribunal was held in the Council School on Thursday, **22 June**, when many varied cases were considered. Of the four agricultural workers appeals, three were each given three months exemption, the fourth, a keeper of 14 horses, was granted conditional exemption as long as he remained in that occupation. Two butchers were also given conditional exemption with the same stipulation; a third butcher received a three month extension. The Distributive Co-Operative Society appealed for four of its men. Three were given three month extensions, however, the fourth, a foreman-baker, was granted conditional exemption. Two cycle traders each received three month extensions, but the appeals of several single men from the boot trade were dismissed. The final case reviewed was that of a boot manufacturer's chauffeur and gardener who was granted just a two month extension "to enable the employer to make other arrangements".

On Friday, **23 June**, it was announced that to the list of reserved occupations had been added "boot and shoe repairing (married men over 35 years)".

Saturday, 24 June, the pre-Somme bombardment begins.

Even before the "Big Push" in France and Flanders had begun came the news, in lengthy articles in all of the local papers, of three Raunds men to have recently fallen. **John W V Ashby (16)**, had been killed in action on 7 June; whilst **Alfred Bugby (28)** and **Percy Smith (105)**, had both died of their wounds on 16 June.

And as the final build up to one of the most infamous battles of the Great War began, it was Hospital Week Demonstration Day in Raunds, with the President of the Board of Education, Mr Arthur Henderson, MP, the guest of honour. In his opening address he warned of the dangers of premature talk of peace: "What would humanity be if brute force took the place of moral force? The end is not yet in sight, we must go to the German people and say 'This worship of war must cease, and the sword you have forged must be broken'". Mr Henderson was a weekend guest at "The Hall", residence of Mrs Coggins. His visit to the town was largely brought about through the friendship of his daughter and the daughter of Mrs Coggins, the two young ladies having been at school together. *(Plate 15)*

As to the demonstration itself, visitors flocked in from the surrounding district, and the attendance was splendid. The procession formed in the grounds of "The Crossways", residence of Mr E A Milligan, JP, comprising of: the Temperance Band, the Raunds and competing Fire Brigades, members of the Urban Council, representatives of neighbouring Hospital Week Fund committees, local tradesmen, members of the Friendly Societies, the Rushden Girl Guides, the Church of England School Infants Department representing "The March of Time", entrants in the Fancy Dress competition, the Council School Infants Department representing "Nursery Rhymes", the Upper Department of the Church of England School representing "The Horn of Plenty" and "Peace & War", and the Upper Department of the Council School representing "Britannia and her children".

The band gave a selection on The Square and in the grounds of "The Hall", and the meeting was held on the tennis lawn. Two selections were given by the Wesleyan Prize Choir, Mr Corby apologised for Major Brassey, MP, who regretted that military duties kept him away, but sent £5 to the Fund. Mr Manfield, MP, said that in 41 years, the Fund had raised £49,000 for the County Hospital, and Raunds had played a magnificent part.

Of the various competitions staged in the field kindly lent by Mr Amos Lawrence, the winners were: *Fire Brigade Hose Drill*: Raunds; *Sports*: 100 yards Flat Handicap, Boys: S York; 120 yards Flat Handicap, Open: B Talbot; 220 yards Flat Handicap, Open: B Talbot; Half-Mile Flat Handicap, Open: H A Underwood. *Fancy Dress*: Individual Get-Up, Children: Ivy Martin, "Little Boy Blue"; Children's Group: Ethel Roberts, Elsie Rooksby & May Tidbury, "Witches"; Individual Get-Up, Adults: Mrs Martin, "Miss Hook of Holland"; Comic Group: Sophia Bettles' Party, "Till The Boys Come Home"; Artistic Group: Fred Bugby, "Indian's Revenge" ......

It was later announced that demonstration and parade was, as anticipated, a record, showing net proceeds of £101-8s-5d. This was £20-3s-5d higher than the previous record. Amongst the individual receipts that made up this total, were: Sale of Roses, £29-16-1d; Guessing Number Competition, £16-5s-0d; Collection by Two Dogs, £1-5s-0d; and £4-4s-0d raised by auction, from the sale of two decorative inkstands donated by the Belgian guests of the town, and made by a Belgian soldier relative at the front from pieces of German missiles found in the trenches.

Monday, **26 June** – "Wanted, Butcher (ineligible), to slaughter and deliver – Wingell, Butcher, Raunds"

The two defendants charged with stealing and receiving property of Mr Walter Lawrence, boot manufacturer, re-appeared at Thrapston Police Court on Tuesday, **27 June**. Pleading guilty, the Raunds shoehand received 3 months hard labour for the theft and the Rushden hairdresser was sentenced to 4 months hard labour for receiving the stolen goods. At the same session, a Raunds lift manufacturer was fined 10s-6d for failing to give notice of a change of ownership of a motor car, and a Raunds woman was fined 10s-0d for neglecting to send her child to school for the whole term, the Schools Attendance Officer, Mr Arthur Mantle, testifying that the girl had only attended 8 times out of a possible 112!

A Raunds publican appeared before Judge Wheeler at Thrapston County Court on Wednesday, **28 June**, sued by the entertainer "Prospero Benrino", for £20 and the return of a basket containing theatrical property worth £30, or £50 damages for detention. The plaintiff said that he had "starred" at Raunds, and was leaving for Manchester by train on 7 February, when on the platform, the defendant took away by force one of his baskets. As a result, he had been unable to give subsequent performances elsewhere, and had had to send away his troupe of four. He claimed that although he had paid the defendant 8s-6d for drinks, he did not owe the 17s-6d presented to him as a bill. The judge ruled that there was no case for substantial damages, but a case for trespass, fining the defendant £5 plus costs.

Also appearing today was a Raunds shoehand, sued by a poultry dealer from the town for £1-6s-0d, the value of the hens killed by the defendant's dog. Judgement was given in favour of the plaintiff, the defendant being ordered to pay £1, in monthly instalments of 5s-0d.

And today, the death took place of Mr Thomas E H Milligan, aged 20, the only son of Mr E A Milligan, JP, and Mrs Milligan, of "The Crossways". The deceased had always suffered from a weak heart, which was the cause of his demise.

Thursday, **29 June** – "For Sale, Broadwood piano, 27 guineas, Kirkman piano, 19 guineas – Archer, Park Road, Raunds"

The month closed with some cheerier news for the town's residents as local bakers announced a reduction in the price of a 4lb loaf from 8d to 7½d.

11 – July to September 1916

The Somme takes its toll as both tanks and a new minister arrive.

JULY – The Curate opened his Parish Notes with the news that there had been progress with the School Debt appeal, however, the response had been from the people who always do their share in supporting Church work, and he observed that "if a satisfactory result is to be obtained, we need the whole body of church people in Raunds to 'hang together' a bit more!"

Notice was given that the Sunday School Treat would be held during Feast Week on Saturday, 8 July. The children were to assemble at the school at 2pm, the service in the Church would take place at 2.45pm, followed by tea in the schools at 3.30pm. All would then proceed to the Vicarage Grounds and the sports would commence at 5pm. The public would be admitted to the Vicarage Grounds at 5pm at a charge of 3d. There would be sports and other attractions, and dancing on the lawn, with the Temperance Band providing the music. However, there would be no public tea as this received so little support from the congregation last year. It was felt that no risk with money could be taken in providing tea for people who did not turn up.

The National Mission of Repentance & Hope would be holding a meeting at Aldwincle on Friday, 7 July, and lastly, an appeal went out to "anyone who will offer to be responsible for the regular cleaning of the chancel gates".

Saturday, 1 July, the Battle of the Somme begins.

And local residents would soon be bombarded with such headlines as: "The Great Offensive – British Troops Hurled Against German Lines", "Fierce Battle Now Raging", "Terrific Onslaught on 20 Mile Front", and "German Front Lines All Occupied", some of which may have approximated towards the truth!

Although today marked the start of "Feast Week", the boot factories, being busy with orders for the Russian boots, had not closed early, and in a few cases were even at work during the afternoon until 4.30.

Sunday, **2 July**, was "Feast Sunday" in over fifty towns and villages throughout the county. A good number of visitors came into Raunds, and Messrs Thurstons, the amusement caterers, were in the Carter Hill Field as usual, opening their attractions the previous evening. The Temperance Band, as was their usual custom, gave a couple of concerts, the first being at 4.30pm on "The Hill", and the latter at 8 o'clock on The Square. Mr Owen Pentelow conducted and collections were taken in aid of band funds.

At the Wesleyan Church, Mr Milner Gray, of Luton, the Liberal candidate for Mid-Herts, was the preacher for the day, the collection for Trust funds amounting to £16. Meanwhile, at the Parish Church, the "Children's Service" was held in the afternoon when the scholars contributed about 300 eggs for the wounded soldiers.

Monday, 3 July, Arthur Horace Jervis (65), died of wounds.

The funeral took place in the Wesleyan burial ground today, of Mrs Sarah Ann Corby, aged 79, wife of Mr John Corby. She had died at her residence, "The Laurels", Grove Street, on Thursday, 29 June. A native of the town in which she had spent all her life, had she lived for just a few more days, she would have completed 58 years of married life.

Irthlingborough Church Institute entertained the Raunds Conservatives at bowls on the evening of Wednesday, **5 July**, and were victorious by 8 points, 64 to 56.

It was announced on Thursday, **6 July**, that Miss Burrows, daughter of the Rev J Burrows, superintendent minister of the Raunds Methodist Circuit, who had been working as a missionary in India, was at present home on sick furlough, and was staying in an old circuit on the south coast with her mother. She was said to be full of hope that the visit home and the quiet husbanding of her strength would completely restore her health and energy for the work she so much loved.

The Raunds Conservatives bowls team were in action again this evening, beating Thrapston Town at Manor Street by 62 points to 52.

Friday, 7 July, Thomas Henry Keeley (66), killed in action.

And three more Raunds men were reported today as being wounded in action. Private H Lawman, Northamptonshire Regiment, the third son of Mr & Mrs George Lawman, had been in a working party digging trenches behind the lines when the Germans opened fire on them. A bullet entered his body between the back bone and shoulder blade, just grazing his spine, and passed out through his neck, the fact that he was stooping when shot probably saved his life. Happily, the latest reports said he was making a good recovery. Private Hubert Clarke, another Northampton, who formerly worked for the St Crispin Productive Society Ltd, had been wounded in the knee whilst fighting near Armentieres. He was now at Dartford Hospital and was "going on well". Finally, Private A Andrews, also of the Northamptons, was on the latest wounded list, but no details were given.

Saturday, **8 July**, was a busy day in and around the town. The scholars attending the Church of England Sunday School had their annual treat in the afternoon. They assembled, with teachers and friends, at the school at 2 o'clock and, lead by the Temperance Band, processed to the Church via The Square, High Street, Rotton Row, and North Street. A short service was held and an address given by the Rev W S Bethway. The scholars then marched back to the schools where a substantial tea was provided for them, the 350 pupils being well looked after by the teachers and friends. After tea they proceeded to the Vicarage grounds where sports, games, houp-la, skittles, and other amusements were arranged. During the evening there was a race for the members of the vestry class, the starting point being the "Red House" on Station Road, and finishing at the Vicarage. This was won by Mr J Pound, Mr R Walker coming second. The Temperance Band played selections during the evening, and also for dancing.

Also that afternoon, the captain of the Fire Brigade, Mr Fred Adams, entertained members of the brigade to a splendid meat tea in the grounds of "Stanwick House", the residence of Mr & Mrs James Adams, to celebrate the winning of the cup at the Raunds Hospital Sports. After tea, a short business meeting was held and the members of the team were photographed with the cup. Bowls and other amusements were provided on the lawn, and during the evening the cup was filled, and the health of the host and hostess was drunk. Second Officer E Hazeldine moved a vote of thanks to Mr & Mrs Adams, Fireman B Bailey seconded, and it was heartily accorded. Mr Adams responded, and said that he as captain was pleased with their performance in winning the cup in so creditable manner.

The first draft of local stations from the Stationing Committee of the Wesleyan Conference was released today and revealed that the current superintendent minister of the Raunds Circuit, the Rev Joseph Burrows, would be leaving in the autumn for a new position at Walsall. His replacement would be the Rev E Percy Blackburn, currently enjoying the seaside ministry of Ramsgate. The Rev Harry Shaw would remain at Thrapston.

Of extreme significance to the boot factory owners in the district was the latest warning from the Government that in all probability it would be necessary for them to release at the end of August, all single men up to the age of 36 and all married men up to 25 years, "who are fit for service abroad".

On the sporting scene, Burton Latimer took on Raunds Town at cricket and emerged as victors by 61 runs, scoring 107 against the visitor's 46. Only O D Hall, with 13, managed to reach double figures for the visitors whilst the hometeam's E Capps, took a stunning 9 wickets for 21.

Meanwhile, on the bowls rink, Raunds Conservatives played their third match in four days, this time at home to Rushden Victoria Hotel, and after a "splendidly contested game", defeated the Vics by a margin of 4 points, 58 to 54.

Monday, **10 July** – "Wanted, At Once, good Clicker, on Army and Navy work, Apply: St Crispin's Ltd, Raunds"

"Raunds Feast – Thurston's Scenic Railway, and other Amusements, will remain at Raunds this week, and open: Monday, 10 July and Friday & Saturday, 14 & 15, from 6pm till 10.30pm."

Prices achieved at the Thrapston Market on Tuesday, **11 July**, were 1s-3d per pound for butter, eggs at 2s-6d per score, beef from 14s-0d to 15s-0d per stone, mutton from 1s-0d to 1s-3d per stone, lambs from 1s-2d to 1s-3d per stone, and pork at 12s-6d to 13s-0d per stone.

Coming shortly to the Palace Theatre, Rushden: "Dreamy Dud in King Koo Koo's Kingdom", and "On Dangerous Paths", a presentation of the dangers that beset the paths of girls ignorant of the lures of the big cities!

The quarterly meeting of the Hospital Week Committee was held in the Temperance Hall on Wednesday evening, **12 July**, and Mr Camozzi presided over a good attendance. The treasurer presented the accounts of the recent fete which showed a balance of £101-8s-5d, another record. The quarterly accounts showed receipts of £140-16-6d, expenditure nil, and on the motion of Mr W F Corby, seconded by Mr J Shelmerdine, JP, it was decided to forward a further sum of £140 to the county treasurer, making the total contributions for the half-year, £165.

"Wanted, A Man for Warehouse (ineligible), experience not necessary, Apply: Palmer's Stores, Raunds"

At the County Council quarterly meeting on Thursday, **13 July**, Mr J Adams represented Raunds and heard the chairman describe Irthlingborough as "the worst plague spot in the county!", because of its higher than average infant mortality rate and numerous deaths from tuberculosis.

That afternoon, the Rev J Burrows attended a meeting at Denford Wesleyan Chapel when Dr J Scott Lidgett, MA, of London, spoke on "England after the war". In his own address, refering to the object of the days' collection, the Rev Burrows said there had been a debt on the chapel of £100 for some time, which had now been raised. The friends were now extending the heating apparatus, putting radiators into the schoolroom, vestry, and infants' room, which would mean an additional cost of £30.

Readers would have been encouraged by the news from the Western Front on Friday, **14 July**, as the Allies were said to be making their "Second Push". "Strong Defensive Positions Captured", "Successful Advance", "German Ammunition & Howitzers Taken" "Villages Cleared & Enemy Driven from Thrones (sic) Wood", may have been true but the euphoria would be short-lived.

However, "Rushden Youth Killed" was another headline to remind those at home of the realities of warfare, for it told how Private **A H Jervis (65)**, of the Northamptons, had met his end earlier in the month. News of the 20 year old Raunds born man's death had arrived in a letter from Higham's Private J Mayes.

A success on the examination front was announced today when it was confirmed that a Raunds pupil, Edna Irene Pendered, had won a two year scholarship, renewable for a third year, to enable her to continue her studies at Wellingborough High School.

Saturday, 15 July, the Battle of Delville Wood.

The afternoon saw the members of the Thorpe House Tennis Club hold their tennis tournament on the court at "Thorpe House", when some very interesting games were played, the winners being Mr A Pettit and Miss Elsie Hardwick. During the afternoon, tea on the lawn was provided by the Raunds Distributive Co-Operative Society, and a very pleasant time was spent.

However, bad news came to those hiding in the attic or the cupboard under the stairs, trying to avoid military service, for there were now just nine days for unattested men to report to the recruiting stations.

Members of the Primitive Methodist Church held their annual camp meetings on Sunday, **16 July**, when they were assisted by their friends from Wellingborough and other places in the district.

At a busy Urban Council meeting on Monday evening, **17 July**, the medical officer, Dr Mackenzie, reported that six births but no deaths were registered in the town during June. However, three cases of erysipelas, one of measles, and one of diphtheria had been notified.

The surveyor reported that an employee had left without giving notice. It was agreed that he should be told to return to work for one week or pay one week's wages in lieu of notice. On the surveyor's recommendation, it was decided not to tar paint the road from "The Globe" to the middle of Brook Street until after the impending repairs. And a plan showing a proposed new coal shed for the Raunds Gas Company was reviewed and approved.

The Sanitary & Waterworks Committee made three recommendations: that a notice be served upon a householder in High Street requesting the abatement of a nuisance caused by overcrowding; that the trustees of the Temperance Hall be called upon to provide sanitary conveniences for both sexes, and also an additional exit; and that a veterinary inspector be appointed for the district – all were accepted. And at the recommendation of the Cemetery Committee, the tender of Mr W G Wilmott, of Rushden, was accepted for the proposed work at the cemetery for £310.

Mr John Adams was unanimously elected to be the town's representative on the Northamptonshire War Pensions Committee. This was in response to a request from Miss Wake, secretary of the committee, for the council to put forward a candidate. On the motion of Mr Adams, it was decided that the sub-committee appointed to consider the formation of a Volunteer Training Corps for the town, be again asked to meet on the matter.

Finally, on the proposal of Mr Asberry, it was decided to send a letter to the captain of the Fire Brigade congratulating him on the smart turn out of the men and the success achieved at the Hospital Fete on 24 June.

A property sale took place at the "The Globe" on Tuesday evening, **18 July**. Mr H H Bletsoe, auctioneer of Thrapston and Kettering, disposed of "a complete and valuable part freehold and part copyhold farm, with frontages to Grove Street and Chelveston Road, comprising of 36 acres,1 rod, 7 pole, with farmhouse, buildings and yards, currently in the occupation of Mr Wm Maddocks, at the yearly rental of £63-7s-6d". Bidding commenced at £800 and quickly ran up by fifties to £1,200, when the property was knocked down to Mr John Adams, JP, CC.

Raunds Conservatives entertained Irthlingborough Church Institute at bowls on Wednesday evening, **19 July**, and won a tightly contested match by 1 point, 62-61.

The Local Appeals Tribunal met at the Council Schools on Thursday evening, **20 July**, and reviewed a large number of cases including: a cartage contractor, 30, married, who was given three months exemption; a boot laster, 38, married, whose case was adjourned for a week; a coal carter's man, 35, married, given a final extension until 1 September; two men appealed on personal grounds, but as they had now been released by their employers, their appeals were dismissed.

The Urban Council appealed for their surveyor, sanitary inspector and waterworks engineer, however, the military representatives suggested that, as members of the Council were also on the Tribunal, these appeals should be considered by another Local Tribunal. This was agreed and the cases were referred to the Rushden LAT.

The Raunds Gas Light & Coke Co Ltd appealed for their gas stoker, 39, married, and he was granted conditional exemption subject to him remaining in his present occupation. Finally, Messrs Palmer's Stores appealed for their chauffeur-mechanic (who also assisted in the warehouse), and their grocer's assistant. In support of their cases, the company explained that they employed women in the stores and that several of their employees had already joined the forces. Two months and one month final were granted respectively.

There were some fine animals shown at the Thrapston & District Shire Horse Society's annual show today, and Mr W Denton, of Raunds, was successful in two classes when the results were announced at the public luncheon held at the "White Hart Hotel", Thrapston. In Class 5 (Mares & Fillies from 3 years upwards), his animal was said to be "far ahead of anything else for substance, was built all over like a brood mare, full of shire character, and a very good mover". In Class 7 (all entered), his winning steed was described as "an animal of size, weight, and quality, with good feet and pasterns".

Another town casualty was reported on Friday, **21 July**. Mrs Adams, of Chelveston Road, had received news from Lieutenant A W Holland that her son, Private Arthur Adams, Northamptonshire Regiment, had been wounded in a gas attack. He had been firing from the firestep when a trench mortar struck close by, wounding him in the back, legs and arm. The twenty-one year old, formerly employed by Messrs Tebbutt & Hall Ltd, had been on the Western Front since August 1915, having enlisted in the previous February. He was now recovering in a hospital in Nottingham with wounds that were more serious than first thought.

And trouble was brewing in the boot trade when local manufacturers discovered that the Army Contracts Department had agreed higher prices for the Russian boots with Northampton Borough manufacturers than those in this district.

The difference was 3d per pair on British Chrome tanned (21s-0d vs 20s-9d) and American Chrome tanned (20s-4d vs 20s-1d) and 1d on pairs of Kip boots (19s-6d vs 19s-5d).

The scholars of the Wesleyan Sunday School enjoyed their annual treat on Saturday, **22 July**, in glorious weather. A procession of pupils, teachers and friends, headed by the Temperance Band, paraded the town, halting at intervals to sing hymns, conducted by Mr W Hall. A scholars tea and one for the public followed and then all assembled in the Carter Hill field (kindly lent by Mr W Denton) where a programme of sports produced the following winners: half-mile, boys, A Coles; 120 yards, boys, H Webb; 90 yards, boys, B Bass; sack race, boys, A Coles; 90 yards, girls, A Webb; 70 yards, girls, E Coles; egg & spoon, girls, F Weekley. The band also played selections and for dancing during the evening.

A military wedding took place this afternoon at St George's Church, Hanover Square, London, when Captain Sydney Lawrence Wells, of the $2^{nd}/5^{th}$ Essex, youngest son of Mr & Mrs J B Wells, Wandsworth Common, married Miss Margaret Robina Milligan, only daughter of Mr & Mrs E A Milligan, JP, "The Crossways", Raunds. The wedding was of a quiet nature, owing to the recent bereavement in the bride's family, and no reception was held. The couple were the recipients of numerous presents and spent their honeymoon on the Isle of Wight.

In another bowls encounter at Manor Street, Raunds Conservatives took on Earls Barton Town and were again successful, by 11 points, 59-48, the quartette of H T Bailey, G Mason, A D Conyers, and A Lawrence, top scoring with 21.

A private from the Royal Defence Corps appeared at Thrapston Police Court on Tuesday, **25 July**, charged with stealing from a till, 5s-3d, the money of the landlady of the "Globe Inn", Raunds. The prisoner, who had a history of drunkeness for many years and had already been banned from the Woodbine Club, said he would give up drink altogether and sign the pledge! He was bound over in the sum of £10 for six months. To an additional charge of being drunk on the public highway at Raunds on 9 July, he pleaded guilty and was fined 2s-6d.

Also up before the Bench was a Raunds lift manufacturer, who was fined £5 for using a motor car without a licence. Police evidence stated that this situation had continued for nearly a year, to which the defendant replied "it was an oversight".

And a Raunds horse and cart owner was fined £10 for "driving a horse and vehicle at 10.25pm without a lighted lamp attached, on the public highway at Raunds on 9 July". To the defendant's claim that he was not driving, but was standing still, Sergeant Ellingham replied "that does not matter".

Meanwhile at the County Appeals Tribunal today, a conscientious objector claimed that if the Germans came and attacked his wife and family, he would run away!

"Wanted – good Golosh Machinist, also Outdoor Closers, on Russian Cossack boots etc, Apply: Adams Bros, Raunds"

On Wednesday, **26 July**, an inquest was held into the death of a 19 month old Raunds boy who had fallen into a tub of water and drowned. The boy's mother testified that he had earlier been playing with his father but had then gone missing. About 20 minutes later she had found him in the barrel of water. The tub had been placed to catch soft water from the old buildings in the yard opposite their house and up to that morning had been covered over. When questioned by the coroner, a Raunds pressman, from the Regulation Boot Company next door to the family, said that he removed the corrugated iron sheet from the tub to shade some cycles from the sun, but did not think of the dangers of his actions. The coroner replied "the iron sheet cover had been put there to stop people from falling in, if you had not taken it away then the child would not have fallen in. If I had done that I should think I was the cause of the child's death!" Dr McInnes told how he tried artificial respiration for over an hour, but without avail. The coroner recorded a verdict of "accidental death", but that was not the last to be heard of this sad affair.

The managers of the Church of England School met on Thursday, **27 July**, to reconsider the dates for the summer holiday. They decided by 4 votes to 1 in favour of closing on Friday, 18 August, until Monday, 25 September, to allow the children to work in the harvest fields. Also at the meeting, Mr A Camozzi was nominated to represent the managers on the District Education Sub-Committee in place of the late Mr J Bass.

In the afternoon, the Thrapston Habitation of the Young Helper's League (Dr Barnardo's Homes) held their annual garden fete in the grounds of "Nene House". As part of the entertainment, a concert was given in the schoolroom and included contributions from the Raunds trio of Madame Irene Lyne, Miss Lawrence, and Mr Oliver Hall, accompanied by Mr J D Hall.

"Wounded – 3 Raunds Brothers" read the headline on Friday, **28 July**, telling the story of the brothers Gates, sons of Mr & Mrs Thomas Gates, of Kingswood Place. Private Walter, Northants Regiment, was said to be seriously wounded in hospital at Rouen, and his parents had left for France to see him. Sergeant Fred, also of the Northamptons, was also wounded and now in hospital at Thorpe, Norwich. The two brothers were in the same company, receiving their injuries in the advance on 21 July. Fred was afraid that Walter had not got back as they didn't even see the enemy before being mown down by their machine gun fire. The third brother, Private Ernest, had recently been home wounded, and was now at Northampton.

The County Council Medical Officer of Health announced the 1915 death rate statistics today. The county average was 12.88 deaths per 1,000 of the population, compared to the national average of 14.8. Raunds, with 11.7, was the lowest of the county urban districts except for Brackley's 11. However, of the infant mortality rate, only Irthlingborough, with 157.8 deaths per 1,000 births, was worse than the 112.5 of Raunds.

The good folk of Denford held a fete on Saturday, **29 July**, in aid of the Soldiers Comforts Fund and the day brought success for two Raunds entrants in the Fancy Dress competition. Winners of the Fancy Dress — Group were the "Dodgers Ragtime Band" and in the Fancy Dress — Individual class, W Burton's costume as a "North American Indian Chief" earned him second place.

Miss Winnie Pentelow, of Clare Street, was involved in a nasty accident this evening while cycling home from Rushden with some companions. On coming down the hill from Chelveston School she got too much on the side, and caught a pedal of the cycle on the bank, with the result that she was thrown off, and received cuts to the nose and mouth, breaking some teeth and loosening others. On arriving home the doctor was called and she was later said to be "progressing".

Meanwhile at Stanwick, several ladies volunteered to canvass the village for the petition to prohibit the sale of drink during the war and for six months after. They were said to have been "courteously received, on the whole!"

No service was held at the Parish Church on Sunday morning, **30 July**, as the Curate, the Rev W S Bethway, was away on account of the death of his brother.

Monday, 31 July, Oliver John Barritt (21), died.

A "notice of correction" appeared in today's local press. It originated from Mr Harry Nicholls, owner of the Regulation Boot Company, and referred to certain comments made during the previous Wednesday's inquest into the death of the Raunds toddler, drowned in a tub of water. Mr Nicholls wished to point out that the tub was not the property of the boot company but the dead child's parents and that on the day of the accident, the corrugated iron sheet belonging to Mr Nicholls had been placed over the tub by the child's father, and it only covered half of the top. So even if it had not been removed by his pressman, it was no protection. Consequently, the jury had been misled and the comments made by the coroner to his pressman had been undeserved.

The 49th half-yearly meeting of the Raunds Distributive Co-Operative Society took place this evening, with Mr F W Miller in the chair. The sales for the half-year amounted to £20,485-18s-0d, an increase on last year of over £4,000. The available balance amounted to £1,725-16s-8d. The dividend set to members was: on grocery, butchery and coal, 1s-10d in the £, and non-members, 1s-0d in the £.

Also this evening, as Mr James Coles, of Clare Street, and employed at Messrs Owen Smith's factory, was putting in the light of one of the factory windows prior to leaving off work, somehow or another it slipped and fell on his head, cutting him rather badly at the back of the ear, and also on his forehead. He hastened to the doctor, who found it necessary to insert several stitches.

AUGUST – The Parish Magazine this month announced that Friday, 4 August, would be a "Day of Continuous Thanksgiving and Intercession" marking the anniversary of the declaration of war.

Two study circles had recently been formed to consider the teachings of the Prophets and their application to the present day. They would meet fortnightly, the men on the first and third Mondays in each month, the women on the following Thursdays. Wary participants were told not to be deterred by the word "study", as brains and scholarship were not necessary, just honesty and enthusiasm.

The Sunday School treat was hailed as an unqualified success, everything had gone off well, with everyone seemingly enjoying the afternoon in a quiet way. As a bonus, the financial result had given the organisers quite a shock – a balance in hand of £2-5s-8d! Thanks were expresssed to all who had worked so hard in the Vicarage grounds to extract money out of people's purses, and to those who kindly donated prizes. The children were congratulated for their good behaviour such that it was actually commented upon by several people. Total receipts were £16-6s-10d, including £1-14s-2d from the Houp-la, 13s-1d from Cake Guessing, and 3s-0d from Aunt Sally. The total expenditure of £14-1s-2d included £2-8s-0d for the band and 3s-0d for the hire of tables and forms.

With reference to the fabric of the Church, acknowledgement was made of Mrs W H Spicer's skilful and patient labour in producing new green frontal, frontlet, and orphreys, thus beautifying the altar.

Thanks had also been received from C M McRae, of the Kettering Home for Waifs & Strays, for the parcel of garments sent from the children of the St George's Guild. He said "It was a great help, especially as my family has increased from 25 to 34, needless to say, on account of the war".

The following brief note also appeared: "Killed in Action, June 16, **Alfred Bugby (28)**, aged 26 years".

On Wednesday, **2 August**, Mr & Mrs Camozzi, of "The Manor House", motored over to Duston Military Hospital with a consignment of cakes for the wounded soldiers. These had been baked "gratuitously" by a number of ladies in the town using ingredients bought with the proceeds, about £2, of a scheme devised by Mrs Camozzi in which she had had 400 recipes for a wartime cake printed, and then sold them for 1d each, the purchaser having the option of paying more if they liked!

"Wanted – Good Machinists for Closing Dept, R Coggins & Sons Ltd, Raunds"

Thursday, 3 August, the Battle of Romani, the Turks advance on the Suez Canal is halted.

Today, Mr Fred Agutter, foreman clicker for Messrs Horrell & Son, had the ends of two fingers cut off through the plate of a blocking machine falling on them. He was in the act of removing one of the plates when it came down on his hand.

In a happier vein, the results of the recent Trinity College Examinations in Pianoforte Playing were announced and Miss L Childs, of Harcourt Street, a pupil of Mr W Groom, ATCL, successfully passed at the Intermediate Grade.

At a meeting of the Joint Standing Committee in connection with the Government Boot & Shoe contractors, held in Raunds today, an increase was agreed to the War Bonus paid to day workers. The present bonus of 10% would be increased to 17½%, on weekly earnings of all male and female day workers aged 18 and above. The increased bonus would be likewise paid to all pieceworkers of the aforesaid ages, engaged on civil work. However, the increase would not be payable to the clickers until after the termination of the Russian Army Cossack Boot contract, when the current extra 5s-0d a week ceased. The following new piece rates were also agreed to come into effect immediately:

Italian Army Mountain Boot – Hand Sewn: tying tops over, rounding & feathering insoles, lasting (including seats), inserting puffs and cutting away waste material – 5½d per pair, sewing – 10½d per pair, filling bottoms, fixing middle sole, two shanks, sole & lift at end of welt, and making ready for stitching – 5½d per pair.

Field Service Boot: fixing toe tip – 9d per dozen pairs, fixing heel tip – 1s-0d per dozen pairs, jiggering seats – 3d per dozen pairs.

Russian Army Cossack Boot: closing complete (outdoor), operative to find machine and grinders – 9s-0d per dozen pairs.

The Raunds District Old Age Pensions Sub-Committee met this evening when ten new claims were considered, one each from Denford and Grafton Underwood, two from Burton Latimer and Ringstead, and four from Raunds. Nine were allowed at the full rate of 5s-0d per week, the tenth was disallowed on the grounds of excessive means. In addition, there were 38 dependancy claims (nearly all from Raunds) for consideration. Most of these were dealt with except in a few cases where the applicant's statement was considered unsatisfactory.

The second anniversary of the declaration of war was celebrated in the town on the evening of Friday, **4 August**, by a meeting held on The Square. Previous to the meeting the Temperance Band marched from Wellington Road to The Square, and a large brake, kindly lent by Mr W Gates, was utilised as a platform. Mr A Camozzi presided over the gathering supported by members of the Urban Council.

Mr George Lee moved the following resolution sent out by the Lord Lieutenant of the County: "That on this second annivesary of the declaration of the righteous war this meeting of the citizens of Raunds records its inflexible determination to continue to a victorious end the struggle in maintenance of the ideals of liberty and justice which are the common and sacred cause of the Allies". The resolution was unanimously carried and the meeting concluded with the band playing the National Anthems of the Allies and "God Save the King".

Today, in anticipation of an undoubted shortage of male labour, the County Council announced the introduction of "practical classes in clicking for female operatives". It stated that "in view of the fact that the 'certified occupation' protection is being withdrawn from all single men and married men under 25 employed on clicking and certain other processes in the shoe trade, the Council has decided to arrange short courses in practical clicking for girls and women at various centres, including Raunds. The course will last for six weeks, and each class will meet twice a week for two hours."

And the Raunds Urban Council appealed to the Rushden Local Tribunal for exemption from military service for its surveyor, a 26 year old and single man. The case had been refered to their neighbours by the Raunds Tribunal, who were also Urban Councillors and so were keen to avoid any perceived conflict of interest. Their Rushden counterparts duly granted the man 3 months exemption.

On Bank Holiday Monday, **7 August**, the Dean Horticultural Society held their 31st Annual Show of Horticultural Produce, Lace & Needlework. In one of the "other attractions", a Raunds XI defeated Dean at cricket. "The Raunds Dodgers Mixed (Very) Band" also attended the show and "operated" on the village's inhabitants with such success that they were able to hand 12s-0d to the committee to be used for the benefit of wounded Bedfordshire soldiers.

A Raunds shoehand, sensitively described as "a cripple", was summoned to appear before Thrapston Police Court on Tuesday, **8 August**, charged with breaking seven panes of glass and doing damage to the amount of 4s-8d at the "Barber's Arms" on 31 July. Evidence was given that during the evening in question, the man had been involved in scuffles whilst using bad language, as a result of which the landlord had taken away his crutch and stick and told the man to go away if he didn't moderate his language. On being given back his crutch, he broke the windows. Although the defendant pleaded guilty, he then addressed the Bench in a disrespectful manner, which drew a rebuke from Superintendant Tebbey. Then when a fine of 25s-0d including costs or 14 days imprisonment was imposed, he said "you might as well take me now as I shall not pay", he put on his cap, picked up his crutch and stick, and was escorted out of the court.

The boot factories, which had closed on Friday evening, reopened this morning, however, very few workers turned up and most of them closed again at lunchtime.

In the afternoon, an aeroplane passed over the town, flying quite low so that it could be seen distinctly. About 5pm, another one came over flying much higher, but the hum of the engine could be heard.

Mr & Mrs A Camozzi were back at the Duston Military Hospital on Wednesday, **9 August**, again delivering cakes for the wounded soldiers. The Raunds Red Cross Committee had asked for gateauic donations and parishioners responsed tremendously, with no fewer than 231 being given, as well as £6-6s-2d in cash.

The ladies responsible for collecting them were Miss Pulpher, Brook Street & The Square; Madames J Barringer & C Yorke, Hill Street, Gladstone Street, Spencer Street, Manor Street & Park Road; Madames W Agutter & J H Haynes, New Estate; Mrs J Hodson & Miss A Vorley, Marshall's Road; Mrs G E Smith, Thorpe Street & Newtown; Mrs J Bamford, Stanwick Road, Wellington Road & Grove Street; Madames T Adams & J Pentelow, Top End. Mrs Camozzi had carried out the secretarial duties.

The papers on Friday, **11 August**, presented Rance readers with several war related items involving men of the town: Private **Oliver John Barritt (21)**, of the Seaforth Highlanders, who prior to enlisting had lived with his brother in Beech Hill, was reported as having died of pneumonia on 31 July. This was the second Great War bereavement for his family, his brother Arthur having been killed at Aubers Ridge in May 1915; Drummer Albert Ernest Ward, of the Northamptons, son of Mr & Mrs J Ward, of Chelveston Road, was listed as suffering from shell shock and was now being treated in a hospital in Rouen; and the casualty lists published today also included: Wounded, Northants Regt, Tidbury, F S, Pte, 18606 and Bence, J, LCpl, 15452.

Prize Winners from the County Council Classes in Boot & Shoe Manufacture held recently at the Raunds Centre were announced as follows: *Honours Stage*: Second Class Certificate & Pass in practical machine finishing, Garner Matson; *Advanced Stage*: Second Class Certificate & Pass in practical machine finishing (with a County Council prize for practical machine finishing), Alfred York; County Council prize for well kept notebook, Sidney E Coles; *Elementary Stage*: County Council First Prize (books value £1), Arthur H Ward; County Council Third Prize (books value 5s-0d), George A Rollings; Pass, Alfred York.

Stanwick Feast was reported to have been very quiet this year, the highspot being the concert given on Sunday evening, 13 August, by the Raunds Temperance Band which attracted a fair number of visitors from the surrounding villages.

The sad tale of the death of the infant son of a Raunds boot finisher was recounted on Monday, **14 August**, when an inquest took place. Giving evidence, the father said that his son was born on the Saturday evening at about 8pm, and was apparently alright. However, on Sunday at about 10.45am, the women in attendance told him that the child was dead. Dr Mackenzie testified that he and his assitant conducted a post mortem examination finding that the infant's lungs had never been inflated, and also a defect in the heart causing cyanosis, but there were "no marks of violence". A verdict of "death from natural causes" was recorded.

And one wonders what intrigues prompted the Hospital Week Committee to issue the following statement today: "The warmest thanks of the town are due to the Raunds Temperance Silver Prize Band (conductor Mr O Pentelow) who helped so materially towards the success of the parade and fete. They very generously made no charge for their services and their splendid playing was greatly enjoyed"!

Thursday, 17 August, Roland Archer (15) and William Wrighting (136), killed in action.

On the day that the town lost two more men at the front, many more were appealing for exemption from military service to the Local Appeals Tribunal which met that evening.

A milk vendor, serving 320 customers, twice daily and also a poultry rearer, aged 28 and married with four children, appealed on grounds of serious hardship if called up, saying that if he had to go his business would stop. He was given exemption until 17 October. A farmer appealed for his man, 21 years old and single, as he only had an old age pensioner and casual labourer on his 150 acre farm. The man, who had been previously granted exemption, was given a final extension until 17 September. A smallholder, single, 27, with 17½ acres of arable land, pigs and poultry, previously given six months, received a final extension until 17 October.

A watchmaker, jeweller & optician, 35, married with two children, one of whom was described as "very delicate", was granted a further three months. A grocer & provision dealer with a country business, 29, married with two children, received three months. A fruiterer & confectioner, 30, and married with an infirm wife who was away, was granted another two months, as was a hairdresser & tobacconist, 31, married, with two shops. An organist, choirmaster, music teacher & "dealer in musical instruments", nearly 41, married with four children, the eldest of whom was serving with the Colours in Mesopotamia, was given exemption until 30 November. However, the case of the Gas Company fitter, who was "the only one who could do the work", was adjourned until the next meeting.

The Conservative Club concluded its bowling handicap this week. Thirty-two competitors took part and after some good play, Mr H Bamford secured the first prize, a pair of woods valued at 11s-6d. The second prize of 3s-6d was won by Mr J Sanders, with Messrs F T Bailey and V S Sykes being joint runners up.

Saturday, 19 August, Albert James Willmott (133), killed in action.

As the town suffered its 27th casualty of war, the Raunds Conservatives visited their Rushden counterparts for a bowls match. Our boys in blue ran out easy winners by 72 to 45. The victorious team trio's scores were: J Pentelow/G Kirk/W Patrick, 24; J Sanders/E W Chambers/V S Sykes, 21; H Bamford/J Chambers/R Harris, 27.

And today, a party of Primitive Methodist friends from Wellingborough had a drive round and called in at Raunds, where tea was served to them at the schoolroom. After tea, games and various amusements were provided, and were heartily entered into. Light refreshments were then handed round before the party left for home.

At the Wesleyan Church on Sunday, **20 August**, farewell sermons were preached by the Rev J Burrows, who was leaving shortly on the completion of his three years superintendency of the Raunds Circuit. There was an especially large congregation at the evening service.

On Monday, **21 August**, the funeral took place in the Wesleyan Churchyard of the late Mrs Eliza Turnhill, aged 71, widow of the late Mr Thomas Turnhill, pork butcher, who had passed away on the previous Friday.

A Raunds coal merchant appeared at Thrapston Police Court on Tuesday, **22 August**, summoned for a breach of the Defence of the Realm Regulations. He was accused of "making statements likely to prejudice the recruiting, training, discipline, or administration of His Majesty's Forces", at Raunds on 25 July. Evidence was given that the defendant had reacted badly to the decision of the Local Appeals Tribunal to only grant one month's final exemption to one of his employees. A witness stated that he had heard the defendant abuse the chairman of the Tribunal saying "he was a man who would rather see his own son shot than lose an order for a pair of Army boots!" *("the chairman" being a well known factory owner in the town)* and that the Tribunal were "nothing but a lot of dirty curs and murderers!" Although the accused had since expressed sincere regret as to his behaviour, the chairman of the Bench said he that he had had nearly a month to apologise but had failed to do so, and fined him £10.

The town hailed a hero on Wednesday, **23 August**, when it was announced in the London Gazette that "His Majesty the King has been graciously pleased to award the Military Medal for bravery in the field to Lance Corporal **Ernest Stringer (112)**, 9597, of the Northamptonshire Regiment".

An accident occurred at home that same day when a boy named Matthews, youngest son of Mr George Matthews, of High Street, was cycling when he met a man on a motorcycle. The boy lost his nerve, and ran into the motorist, and was knocked down. He was bruised about the head and body, his face was cut about, and also suffered concussion and bleeding from the left ear.

There was another nasty incident the following day, when a lad named Brayfield, from Grove Place, was getting onto the top of a spiked iron fence and he fell on one of the spikes, which penetrated the left side of his neck and cut clean through, reaching the roof of his mouth, cutting it severely. Witnesses described how they had had to lift him off the spike!

Town men listed as wounded on Friday, **25 August**, all from the Northamptons, were: Cuthbert, J, 8095; Gates, F, 16972; Gates, W C, 15817; & Heath, R, 17958.

On Saturday, **26 August**, the annual garden party of the Wesleyan Sunday School had been arranged to be held at "The Maples", by kind permission of Mr & Mrs John Horrell, but owing to the weather it was held instead in the schoolroom. About 100 sat down to tea, and a conference on Sunday School work followed.

The following day, the 104th anniversary of the Wesleyan Sunday School was celebrated when the Rev J Williams Butcher, Connexional Sunday School secretary, conducted the services for the day. In the morning, the choir rendered the anthem "I am Alpha and Omega", conducted by Mr Walter Hall, with Mr J W Hall at the organ. At the afternoon's young people's service, decorated with a splendid array of flowers, a collection of eggs was made on behalf of the wounded soldiers, 914 being given, in addition to fruit, sweets etc. These were sent to the Military Hospital at Duston and the VAD Hospital at Higham Ferrers. Bibles and hymn books were presented to the following scholars at the service, who had attained the age of 15 during the year: Ralph Harris, Herbert Miller, Edward Evans, Bernard Mayes, Horace Cuthbert, William Pettit, **Bertram Hall (152)**, Irene Sharp, Bertha Coles, Winnie Annies, Elsie Finding, Flossie Tebbutt, and Doris Pettitt. The collection totalled £29-6s-7d.

And in the grounds of "The Hall" that afternoon, by kind permission of Mrs Coggins, the Temperance Band gave a concert in aid of band funds.

"Wanted – Good Cowman, good wages paid, permanent, applications to be sent in not later than Tuesday next to the Raunds Distributive Co-Operative Society"

On Tuesday, **29 August**, Mr F W Dix was reported to having just received a postcard from his brother, Private Jack Dix, of the Northamptons, who had been a prisoner of war since soon after the start of the war. The POW said he was now in a working camp at Friedricksfeld and had received the parcel of cakes safely and had enjoyed them. He then went on to say that he had had a very hard time of it lately but that better days were in store, "then there will be no hell upon earth!"

Another industrial accident occurred on Wednesday, **30 August**. While working at the "lightning healer" at Messrs C E Nicholls' boot factory in Midland Road, an employee named Richardson got two fingers of his left hand completely smashed. He was taken to the doctor's surgery, to be attended by Doctors Mackenzie and McInnes and was later said to be "getting on as well as can be expected".

Details of Private R R Heath's injuries were reported on Thursday, **31 August**. Writing home from the VAD Hospital in Margate, he said "I got hit in both legs and twice in the back, but my haversack checked the shrapnel, so as to make only flesh wounds. My right leg is broken and there is a large wound in my left one". The 19 year old had earlier been in action at the Battle of Loos, when he was invalided back to a hospital in Scotland. Happily, his parents were later informed that his wounds were healing "splendidly".

And news of problems for Corporal **Arthur Burton (31)**, Northants Regiment, appeared when he was listed as "wounded". Although he would recover it would only be a temporary reprieve as he would be killed in action the following June.

Also this evening, the Local Appeals Tribunal gave judgement on another large number of requests for exemption. A letter was read from a smallholder, who had been given exemption to 1 October at the last meeting, asking for a further right of appeal if, owing to the weather, he had not cleared up at that time. His request was granted. A farmer appealed for his general labourer, 29, married, who received a one month extension to help get in the harvest. Another farmer appealed for his two sons, 18 & 22, both single. He had two farms and was giving one up at Michaelmas next, but currently his eldest son managed one and was also the horsekeeper, whilst the youngest was the stockman on the other farm. Both men were given exemptions until 11 October although the Tribunal suggested he might release one son to make the case for the other stronger.

A number of men from various trades were granted two month exemptions: a plumber, painter & decorator's son; a laundryman & smallholder, whose two brothers were already serving; a 39 year old carter, married with four children, who it was suggested might also help a farmer so as to free up a single man for military service; two Co-Operative Society employees, their 36 year old, married, manager/buyer of the drapery & outfitting department, and their 25 year old, married, slaughterman, of whom the advice was to find an alternative, older man; a builder's carpenter, joiner & machinist, 34 and married; and the 37 year old, married, chauffeur/gardener of a boot manufacturer.

* * * * * * * * * * * * * * * * * * * *

* * * * * * * * * * * * * * * * * * * *

SEPTEMBER – The Curate's notes this month were a series of "dates for the diary": The first Vestry Class meeting of the winter season would be on Sunday, 3 September, the Day Schools would re-open after the summer holidays on Monday, 25 September, and the collectors for the School Debt were to meet at 8pm on Thursday, 28 September, at the Vicarage to pay in outstanding contributions.

The annual Harvest Thanksgiving service would be held on Thursday, 5 October, and on the following Sunday. As the Vicar, the Rev C C Aldred, was expected back from France during that week, it was hoped that he would be able to conduct the Sunday service.

Finally, notice was given that beginning on Sunday, 1 October, and until further notice, Evensong would be at 5pm. As the clocks would be "put right again" during the night of Saturday, 30 September, this would be 5pm "ordinary time".

Friday, **1 September**, and a Raunds farmer appealed to the County Appeals Tribunal for a further exemption for his farm hand, he being his only man, except for an old age pensioner, "who did very little". The farm comprised of 180 acres, including several of corn, 42 head of cattle, 5 horses, and 171 sheep, and it was proving impossible to find any other labour. A final exemption until 30 September was granted.

Saturday, 2 September, the first German airship is shot down over Britain.

Today, in connection with the United Working Men's Clubs' Fund for Blind and Crippled Children, a Forget-Me-Not Day was arranged by the committee of the Woodbine Working Men's Club. The Temperance Band paraded the town and Mr Ashley, of Burton Latimer, came over with his goats, which proved a great attraction. The committee entertained the young ladies engaged in the sales to tea. The arrangements being carried out by Madames A Lawrence, W Richards, J Hodson, W L Lawrence, and Mr E Batchelor (secretary). The total amount collected was £13-9s-0d. *(Plate 17)*

The Primitive Methodists held a circuit rally this afternoon and were favoured with a visit by the Rev J Tolefree Parr, of Surrey Chapel, London, president-designate of the Primitive Methodist Conference. The reverend gentleman preached an excellent service in the afternoon at 3.15, basing his discourse on the text "I Know Him". A public tea followed at 4.30 when there was a good company present, the tables being presided over by Madames J Harrison, J Tanner, C Abbott, W Whitney, H Hazeldine, C York, W Payne, and Miss A Warner.

In the evening at 6.30, a lecture was given by the Rev Tolefree Parr entitled "Christianity vindicated", which was of a most interesting and inspiring character. And during the evening, Mr Frank Stringer, of Ruhsden, rendered a couple of solos in a creditable manner.

Miss Frances Wheatley, daughter of Mr & Mrs Thomas Wheatley, Hill Street, celebrated her 21st birthday today, when a number of relatives and friends were entertained to tea at the residence of her sister, Mrs E Evans, of Midland Road. After tea the proceedings were of a social character and Miss Wheatley was the recipient of a number of useful and handsome presents.

A men's service was held at the Parish Church on Sunday afternoon, **3 September**, at 2.30 when the Rev W S Bethway gave an interesting address on the subject "Has the War proved Christianity a failure?" A collection was taken to defray expenses.

At the Wesleyan Church, the newly appointed superintendent minister of the Raunds Circuit, the Rev E Percy Blackburn, occupied the pulpit for the day's services. At the evening service there was a large attendance when the reverend gentleman preached an excellent sermon taking his text from St John i 2. *(Plate 4)*

And another old inhabitant of the town died today in the person of Mrs Jane Harris, in her 80th year. She was buried in the Wesleyan Burial Ground the following Wednesday afternoon.

Tuesday, 5 September, George Benjamin Flavell (51), killed in action.

Wednesday, 6 September, the Battle of Guillemont.

A garden party was held in the grounds of "The Hollies", Thrapston, by kind permission of Mr & Mrs Geo Smith, on Thursday afternoon, **7 September**, in aid of Thrapston Wesleyan Church and as a public welcome to the new circuit minister, the Rev Blackburn. In his opening speech, Mr W F Corby warned the good reverend that "Raunds folk had been described as a 'queer lot', and yes, although they were a queer lot, and could be lead by a cord of silk, they could not be driven with a cat-o'-nine-tails!" A concert was held in the evening which included contributions from Raunds' Mr & Mrs Jethro Hall and Mr Oliver Hall

"To Manufacturers – Don't get behind with your contract. Rivetting, pegging, sewing, stitching, and screwing done for the trade – Inquiries to J Northern & Co, Trade Sewers, Raunds"

On Friday, **8 September**, it was reported that our old friend Sergeant Harold Lee, of the Meteorological Department of the BEF in France, had had a serious breakdown with sciatica and had for a time been in hospital at Rouen, and afterwards at Bristol. However, he was now said to be at the Red Cross Hospital at Minehead, Somerset, and was progressing favourably.

And there was, seemingly, better news of Second-Lieutenant **C A Vorley (117)**, of the Royal Sussex Regiment, who had been listed as "missing" a few days earlier. His father, Mr Joseph Vorley, of Marshall's Road, had just received a field card from his son saying that he was all right and quite well. Sadly, Joseph could not know that his son would succumb to his wounds just five days later!

The Raunds Conservatives bowls team were in action again on Saturday, **9 September**, when their Rushden counterparts were in town. The Rushdenites were victorious by 57 points to 51, but interestingly, the Rance quartette of G Kirby, E Pashler, A Bugby, and V S Sykes scored more than half of the home teams total with a creditable 27 points.

"Wanted – Companion-Help by lady in North London, one in family, young widow not objected to – Apply: Mrs Kirby, "The Hall", Raunds"

Sunday, 10 September, William John Bottoms Cross (24), died.

It was Harvest Festival Sunday at the two Methodist Churches today. At the "Prims", Mr T Glassby, of the South East London Mission, preached the sermons at both morning and evening services. At the evening service a solo was rendered by Mr T Hasseldine, accompanied by Mr J Tanner. On Monday, a public tea was held in the schoolroom when Madames E H Byrne, H H Twelftree, and G Tomlin presided over the tables. The sale of vegetables and fruit etc took place on the Tuesday evening.

Meanwhile, at the Wesleyan Church, a former minister of the town, the Rev J Williams, now of Pateley Bridge, returned to conduct the services. The previous afternoon, a welcome tea had been arranged, when about 120 sat down, in honour of the new circuit minister, the Rev E P Blackburn. At the Sunday evening service, the spacious building was well filled to hear the choir render the anthem "All Thy works praise Thee", with Mr J W Hall at the organ. The sale of vegetables & fruit etc took place on the Monday evening, and in all the net proceeds of the weekend amounted to £20.

Wednesday, 13 September, Charles Archibald Vorley (117), died of wounds.

A special sitting of the Thrapston Police Court, before Lieutenant-Colonel J S Benyon, took place on the morning of Thursday, **14 September**, when a private in the Northamptonshire Regiment, a native of Raunds, was charged with desertion from his regiment on 14 July 1915. The man pleaded guilty. PC Newberry stated that about 7.15 on Tuesday evening, 12 September, he visited the "Cock Inn" and saw the prisoner there. Knowing him to be a soldier, the witness asked him to produce his papers, which he could not do. The prisoner then admitted that he was a deserter, and that he had left his uniform in the trenches. On the application of Inspector Campion, the defendant was remanded to the cells to await a military escort. The inspector then stated that it was quite by accident that the constable came across the man, and asked that the PC be rewarded with 10s-0d, which the magistrate immediately granted.

"Wanted – Managing Butcher (not required to buy), must be smart, clean and a capable salesman – Applications, stating age and experience, with two references, not later than the 21st inst, to the Distributive Co-Operative Society, Raunds"

And it was another busy evening for the Local Appeals Tribunal. A farmer with over 500 acres, appealed for his horsekeeper, his only man, who had already received two exemptions. The man was given a final month to help complete the harvest operations. A heel manufacturer, 31, married, was granted a further two months. A boot manufacturer appealed for three young men who had reached the age of 19 since the agreement arrived at between the manufacturers and the military authorities – two were given until 7 October, the other until 1 October.

The Co-Operative Society appealed for five employees: their coal carter, 27, married (also a member of the Fire Brigade); the managers of two of their grocery & provisions stores, both married, 39 & 32; their baker & bread deliverer, married, nearly 41; and their slaughterman, who also delivered with the cart, single, 22. In support of their appeals, the secretary stated that they employed females where possible, and were also advertising for men in all their departments. They had recently lost the manager of the butchery department, and if this man had to go and they could not get another, they would have to close the department. The single man was granted one month and the married men two months. However, it was decided that in the case of the single man and the younger of the grocery managers, no further appeal would be allowed except to the County Tribunal.

The managers of a grocery & drapery store appealed for their chauffeur/mechanic, who also assisted in the warehouse and delivered goods. He was given a one month exemption but was also requested to be examined by the Army Medical Board in the meantime. Finally, the appeal from the Gas Company for their manager/secretary was withdrawn as he had now been given a war service badge.

Friday, 15 September, the first use of tanks by the Allies at Flers.

On the day that the folks at home were being thrilled to read the stories of the "new Allied weapon that walked", an article appeared in the "Shoe Trade Journal" conservatively estimating how many Army boots had been made in the UK since the war began. The figure was 30 million pairs, and one Northampton firm alone was said to have produced a million pairs!

Ringstead village held a fete on Saturday, **16 September**, entitled "On Parade for Our Protectors" and the Raunds Temperance Band lead the procession and provided music in the evening for dancing. Fancy dress winners from Raunds generously gave their prizes back to the fund and the town's Mr Hasseldine brought over the Red Cross Dog, which collected 14s-0d.

The Kettering, Thrapston & District Angling Association's "roving" competition concluded today. Competitors had been allowed to fish in any water rented by the Association between 1pm and 9pm over the past three days. The competition was won by Mr F Adams of Raunds, who caught 11 roach, totalling 6lb 9oz, caught in Denford and Woodford waters.

There was a full and varied agenda for the Urban Council at their meeting on Monday evening, **18 September**: Mr Camozzi was nominated as a member of the District Education Sub-Committee as a representative of the Church of England School, in place of the late Mr John Bass, and Mr Hodson became the Council School representative in place of the late Mr Joseph Gant; the Sanitary & Waterworks Committee recommended that Mr W Beal, of Thrapston, be appointed veterinary inspector to the Council at a salary of £10 per annum, this was unanimously agreed; and the tender of £6 from Mr E Farrington for grazing the "hospital field" until 31 December was accepted.

A letter was read from Mr A Potter resigning his position as agent of the Council under the National Regulation Act 1915, the resignation was accepted; plans for a bathroom etc for Mr A Pendered, and additions to the Temperance Hall for the Temperance trustees, were then presented and passed; and finally, the clerk was directed to convey the sympathy of the Council to Sergeant Lee, who had been invalided home from France and to express hopes for a speedy recovery.

News of two Raunds soldiers very much "in the wars" was reported on Wednesday, **20 September**: Mr William Cobley, of "Hargrave Lodge", had received news from the War Office that his son, Private William Cobley, of the Northamptons, was in hospital at St Pol, France, suffering from fever; and Mrs G Stock, The Square, had received a postcard from her son, Private Harry Stock, of the Seaforth Highlanders, postmarked Snow Hill Station, Birmingham. In it he said that he was passing through that station on an ambulance train on his way to hospital. Mrs Stock had previously heard from the War Office that her son had been admitted to the General Hospital, Rouen, suffering from a gunshot wound and the effects of gas.

Friday, **22 September** – "Notice of Sale, at Raunds on Friday, 29 September: Six acres of Mangold Wurtzel upon the Sewage Works Field, by instructions from the Urban Council, will be sold in convenient lots. Sale commences at 4.30pm. Arthur G Brown, Auctioneer, Thrapston, Wellingborough, Kettering & Raunds."

"For Sale – Four Freehold Cottages in Church Street, Stanwick – For price & particulars, apply: Fred A Corby, Raunds"

Saturday, 23 September, the Germans begin constructing the Hindenberg Line.

Enthusiastic praise was showered on the town's Wesleyan Sunday School scholars by the Rev J W Butcher in the latest edition of the "Methodist Times". Noting the school's illustrious past, stretching back over 104 years, he was eloquent in describing how the current children had recently brought 904 eggs to their "children's service", for the wounded soldiers, in addition to gifts of chocolates and flowers, and that over £100 had also been promised on the day towards the £1,000 lately spent on renovations.

The Rushden Working Men's Club held their 20th annual flower, fruit and vegetable show today, resulting in some moderate success for two Raunds growers. In the "Class A (Open) Eschalots" category, W Lack was awarded second place, whilst for "Fruit, Cooking Apples", J Eaton collected a similar prize.

And over this weekend, Saturday 'til Monday, harvest thanksgiving services and special meetings were held by the local Salvation Army.

Monday, 25 September, Harry Finding (50), killed in action.

At a meeting today in the Temperance Hall, called to consider the attitude of the town towards the various funds in existence for assisting the suffering consequent of the war, it was decided to form a War Charities Committee which would include members of the Urban Council and representatives from every factory and organisation in the town. The idea had originated at a recent meeting held at the Woodbine Working Men's Club whose members had expressed the very laudable desire to do something for the wounded soldiers or Red Cross Fund.

And the peculiarities of the current recruiting regulations were put to the test today at St Ives Police Court when a Raunds shoehand from the Regulation Boot Company, formerly a cinematograph proprietor at Huntingdon, was charged with being a deserter from the Army Service Corps. The prosecution alleged that the defendant had signed enlistment papers on 4 August. The defendant denied this and also claimed that his request to engage a solicitor to act on his behalf had been denied. The Bench were unsympathetic to the man's cause and handed him over to the military, who took him under escort to Grove Park, London. However, after further enquiries were made to the Northants military representative for recruiting, it was ruled that the man had indeed not enlisted and he was immediately released.

Tuesday, **26 September**, "Wanted – Slaughterman (ineligible), must also be capable of attending to cart round – Apply at once to the Distributive Co-Operative Society, Raunds"

The month ended with reports of more Great War casualties from the town. On Friday, **29 September**, the story of two brothers under the headline of "For the Old Country, Raunds Canadians Killed and Wounded" was published. The fatality was that of Private **George B Flavell (51)**, who had been living in Canada for nine years prior to enlisting. The 27 year old former R Coggins & Sons employee had joined up with his younger brother Ernest, and both had visited the town en route to France in June. The wounded soldier was Ernest. He had been hit on only his second day in the trenches but was now recovering in hospital. *(Plate 16)*

Another town transgressor appeared at Wellingborough Police Court this afternoon when a shoehand was fined 10s-0d for driving a horse and trap without a red rear light at 11pm at Finedon on 17 September. Giving evidence, Sergeant Avery said that the defendant, who pleaded guilty, only had an old cycle lamp with no glass in it at all.

"Wanted – Girl as Servant – for particulars apply to the Manager, Raunds Hotel & Coffee Tavern"

A long article appeared in the papers of Saturday, **30 September**, under the headline "Raunds Journalist Describes His First Charge". Private **Arthur March (75)**, of the London Regiment (Civil Service Rifles), wrote "Soon after we got into our position I had my first taste of 'going over the top'. We went for the German first line just as dawn was breaking, and I can assure you it was an experience to be remembered. And after going over the top a second and third time I could hardly credit that I came through with nothing more than a scratch made by a sniper's bullet on my arm!" Later, back at rest camp after being relieved, he enoyed "a fine dinner – the best since I have been in France, the rations of roast mutton and potatoes were augmented by tinned baked beans, spaghetti and fruit, and a bottle of pickles, gleaned from various food parcels."

On this Saturday afternoon, a pretty wedding was solemnised at the Parish Church, Wollaston, the contracting parties being Mr Albert Webb, of Ash Vale, Surrey, and Miss Grace Morris, of Raunds. The bride was neatly attired in white, with a wreath and veil of orange blossom, and carried a shower bouquet. She was attended by two bridesmaids, Misses Edith Woods and Ada Brown, of Raunds, who wore gold brooches, the gift of the bridegroom. After the ceremony, a large circle of friends were entertained at "Park Cottage" by Mr & Mrs T Woods. The presents included a silver teapot from Colonel & Mrs Champion de Crespigny.

Also this afternoon, Raunds Fire Brigade took part in a district competition at Burton Latimer when they challenged brigades from Burton, Higham Ferrers, Irthlingborough, and the Kettering Co-Operative Clothing Society. The panel of judges included Chief Officer F Adams, of Raunds, who witnessed his team's victory in the "Hose Cart Drill", as well as third places in the "Manual (4 man) Contest", and the "Dressing Race", when the town was represented by Fireman Dix. Afterwards, the teams partook of a capital meat tea at the Palace Restaurant, Burton, and Chief Officer Adams proposed a vote of thanks to the host brigade for entertaining them so well.

The "Shoe Trade Journal" happily reported that "the severe hardship predicted for Raunds caused by the stoppage of orders for hand sewn British Army ankle boots has now to a certain extent been met, for the Italian mountain pattern Army boot is now being made there in quantities. Never have the Italian Army had such boots, for the quality of both the material and the workmanship is superb". However, it also went on to say that "there is another pathetic side to the Army boot trade in the town, a great number of 'specials' for cripples are also being made and one does not have to seek far to know the reason for these orders!"

To close the month, an important notice entitled "Clocks Back!" announced the restoration of "Normal Time" at 3am tomorrow (Sunday, 1 October), when "Summer Time" would come to an end.

12 – October to December 1916

A sheep is lost in a barrel arch but Verdun is saved.

OCTOBER – In his final set of Parish Notes before the return of the Vicar, the Curate announced that the Harvest Service on Thursday, 5 October, would be held in the Institute as the Church could not be used in the evening owing to the lighting restrictions. Consequently, the Church would not be decorated until the following day when offerings of fruit and vegetables would be most acceptable and should be brought during that morning.

The efforts of the School Debt collectors was recognised with the news that to date £43-18s-4d had been raised meaning that £26-11s-4d and £17-7s-0d could be paid off the Building Fund account and Loan account respectively.

Lastly, he advised that, in connection with the National Missions, a "Quiet Day" would be held on Saturday, 14 October. The conductor would be the Rev A J Meakin, Vicar of St Alban's, Leicester and services would include War Intercessions and Addresses at 3pm and Tea (6d each) in the Upper School at 4pm. The Vicarage grounds would also be open for the use of those attending the Quiet Day. He explained that "a 'Quiet Day' is probably a new thing to many in this parish, 'The Rule of Silence' will be observed throughout the day and if you are able, spend the whole day forgetting everyday cares and distractions."

A "Men's Service" was held in the Parish Church on Sunday afternoon, **1 October**, when the Rev W S Bethway gave an address on the cheerful subject of "After death, what then?" Whilst up Marshall's Road at the Primitive Methodist Church, the annual distribution of prizes to Sunday School scholars took place, an address being given by the preacher for the day, the Rev J Phelps, of Dean.

Most of the factories were closed on Statute Monday, **2 October**. Unfortunately the weather turned out wet and upset the annual half day blackberrying. A number of folk made the journey to Potters Bar in motor cars and on motorcycles to see the remains of the Zeppelin that had been brought down in the early hours of the morning, and in spite of the wet had a very good time.

Some people were at work however, as the monthly meeting of the district Boot & Shoe Operatives Union was held in the Trades Union Club, Rushden today. The treasurer reported a quarterly balance showing a gain of £212 on the previous quarter. Contributions had amounted to £1,589, sick and funeral benefits had absorbed £477 and out of work benefit, £65. The chairman explained that during the past quarter, several Arbitration Board meetings had been held and the result had been that "further pecuniary advances had been attained", the greatest being the 7½% additional War Bonus, making 17½% in total. He added that this increase, owing to the ever increasing cost of living, had been much appreciated by all.

A recommendation of the executive to purchase a motorcycle for use in branch business was unanimously carried.

It was also announced that any member drawing on a sick fund would have to produce a certificate from a duly qualified medical practioner, stating the nature of the illness from which the member was suffering. A fresh certificate would also be needed every seven days so long as the drawing of the sick pay continued.

The Temperance Society held their annual tea today, generously provided by Mr & Mrs George Bass, when about 100 were present. At the meeting which followed, with Mr W H Lawrence presiding, the sum of £41 was promised for the renovation of the Temperance Hall, against the estimated cost of £250. Miss Pulpher recalled the hall before it was floored, and that it was built by working men some years ago, and added "we ought to do what we can to make the building up to date in memory of those temperance worthies who have gone before."

A meeting was held at the "White Hart Hotel", Thrapston, on the afternoon of Tuesday, **3 October**, of the Thrapston & District Farmers Association to discuss the details of their forthcoming sale in aid of the Red Cross Fund. The planning committee included Messrs W Denton, T C Jeeves, and T H Warth, of Raunds; the Ladies committee included Mrs Camozzi (of the "Manor House"), Mrs Denton, Mrs Lawrence (of "The Hall"), and Mrs Warth; with Mr Warth also sitting on the executive committee. And when promises were sought for the "butchers stall", Mr Denton offered 5 guineas or a good fat pig, Mr Jeeves, produce to the value of 5 guineas, and Mr Warth, a store bullock.

The Raunds War Charities Committee held its first meeting this evening, at the Temperance Hall, enjoying a large and representative attendance. The following officers were elected: Chairman, Mr A Camozzi; Secretary, Mr W F Corby; Assistant Secretary, Mr L W Sheffield; Treasurer, Mr H W Lawrence; Auditor, Mr J Shelmerdine, JP; and committee members, Messrs J C Horrell and E Batchelor.

Also discussed was the question of forming a War Savings Association in the town. Mr G E Abbott, of Islip, urged the need for saving in war time "to prepare for the slump in trade which always follows war", and also "in order to provide the money required for the carrying on of hostilities!" The proposal of Mr A Camozzi "that a War Savings Association be formed in Raunds" was carried unanimously, and the following were elected to form the first committee: Chairman, Mr John Adams, JP, CC; Treasurer, Mr A Camozzi; Secretary, Mr W F Corby; and committee members, Messrs B Green and F Abbott.

The Raunds Old Age Pensions Committee met in the Woodford Temperance Hall on the afternoon of Thursday, **5 October**, when there were five claims and four questions for consideration. Three of the claims were allowed at the full rate of 5s-0d per week, one at 2s-0d per week, and the other disallowed as there was no proof of age produced. Of the questions, two resulted in pension increases from 1s-0d to 5s-0d per week, one from 3s-0d to 5s-0d per week, and one from 4s-0d to 5s-0d per week. Twelve dependancy claims were also dealt with.

In the evening, as previously announced, the Rev W S Bethway presided over the Church of England Harvest Thanksgiving service, which was held in the Church Institute owing to the lighting restrictions preventing the use of the church, with its undarkened windows.

On Friday, **6 October**, the name of Richards A, 22456, Northamptonshire Regiment, of Raunds, appeared on the latest list of wounded.

The results of the recent examinations on the theory of shorthand were published today, and three town girls, Misses Winnie Abbott, Lizzie Billington, and Deborah Jackson, all pupils of Miss Foster, successfully gained their certificates.

"Wanted – Good Ground Labourer at new Cemetery, Raunds – Apply, Foreman on the Works, W G Wilmott, Contractor"

The town put on what was described as "a splendid effort" in aid of the funds of the Northamptonshire Red Cross Association on Saturday, **7 October**. In addition to the Flag Day, arrangements for which were made by Mrs Camozzi, there were fancy dress and comic sports, arranged by the committees of the Woodbine and Conservative Clubs, and a Khaki Concert, organised by Mrs A Lawrence. The good lady also managed cake guessing (cake donated by Mr G Rixon), sweet guessing (sweets donated by Mr A Camozzi), and coal guessing (coal donated by the Co-Operative Society) competitions, and gave a tree of walnuts to the person guessing the nearest amount of receipts taken by the sale of flags. This was won by Miss E Ball, of Hill Street, who guessed £21-3d-11d against the £21-4s-2d actually collected. Mr W Richards was in charge of the pork pie guessing competition which produced a tie between four gentlemen who were all within a quarter of an ounce of the actual 3lb-10oz weight. The good gents gave back the pie to be sold by auction for the funds.

The concert was held in the Wesleyan School, the performers being Councillor Harvey Reeves, of Northampton, Miss Gertie Smith, Mr T Swan, Private Walton, Lance-Corporal Burnaby, and Miss Hodges on the piano. Councillor Reeves, giving a brief address on the work of the local Red Cross, said that that afternoon they had received 100 stretcher cases from Dover by the 3 o'clock train, and such was the efficiency of the organisation, all were able to be at this evening's concert!

Selected placings in the sports were: 60 yards dash, 1st, L J H Edwards; comic race, 1st, W Higby; tug-of-war, 1st, Sergeant Ellingham's team; and 2nd in the band race, **H Bugby (29)**. Meanwhile in the fancy dress competition, the winners were: Ladies' fancy get-up, Rose Moules, "Red Indian Girl"; Gentlemen's comic get-up, G Hall, "Tired Tim"; Girls' fancy get-up, Olive Ferry, "The Reaper"; Boys' fancy get-up, R Sibley, "Little Boy Blue". *(Plate 19)*

The net result of the event was expected to be in excess of £90.

Harvest Festival Thanksgiving services continued at the Parish Church on Sunday, **8 October**, commencing at 7.30am, and including an "egg and fruit" service in the afternoon, the gifts being for the Military Hospital. In the evening there was a crowded congregation to hear the Vicar who had just returned home from France having been a chaplain to the Forces for some months past. The reverend gentleman based an appropriate sermon upon the words "What reward shall I give unto the Lord" (Psalm 116, v 11 & 12). The choir rendered the anthem "Honour the Lord with thy substance", and Mr J P Archer accompanied at the organ.

Monday, 9 October, the Battles of Ancre Heights and Transloy Ridge.

Today, a Raunds estate clerk appeared before Higham Ferrers Police Court, charged with "driving a motor cycle without a licence at Higham on 7 September". PC Powell said that the defendant nearly knocked over a perambulator, and when he stopped him and asked for his licence, the accused said that he had not got one as he was just trying out the bicycle, adding that he had been told by Lord Lilford that if he carried the application paper supplied by the County Council, he would be all right. The Bench disagreed and fined him 10s-0d inclusive of costs.

Tuesday, 10 October, Walter Ernest Lawman (71), killed in action.

The Raunds Liberal Literary Institute held its annual meeting on Wednesday evening, **11 October**, when a large attendance heard the secretary, Mr W F Corby, read the treasurers accounts for the past year, the 21st time they had done so. These showed a balance in hand of over £40, £12-7s-7d up on the previous year. The assembly decided to celebrate their 21st anniversary with a meat tea and social, and to have the billiards board recovered.

The latest Local Appeals Tribunal took place on Thursday evening, **12 October**, when Captain Wright confirmed the arrangements agreed with the Manufacturers Federation regarding the Army shoe trade. All men had been granted exemption until 1 October, and he would not oppose further exemptions to the end of the year to men considered necessary for Army work. However, he wanted the 10% of men as agreed with the federation, and the young men as they arrived at military age, who would automatically become soldiers. He would give them short exemptions, and if Army orders ran into next year they could appeal again.

The eligible lists were gone through, and were accepted with one or two alterations. In some cases the masters had sent in names of married men whom they were willing to release instead of single men, however, the Tribunal were unanimous that single men must go first, and the cases were accordingly refered back to the masters for single men to be substituted.

And whereas two years earlier, when everyone was clamouring to join up, now the list of men appealing for exemption from military service appeared longer each week, and the latest sitting of the Tribunal considered nearly 30 cases, from the agricultural, commercial, and boot & shoe trades .....

These included: a boot manufacturer who wished to retain his pressman, a 40 year old single man, and release a 25 year old married man "who would not put in the time at his work that he might", the request was granted; a farmer, who also had working for him an 81 year old pensioner and a one armed man, appealed for three married men and his 20 year old son who was single. One of the married men was given until 1 April 1917, the others until 1 January; a single man, a chemist/druggist/dispenser, who dispensed for two doctors, had his case adjourned awaiting a letter from the Insurance Committee; however, the appeal from a 33 year old single man, with a widowed and infirm mother to support, who had previously been exempt on personal grounds, was dismissed.

The papers printed a letter today from Sergeant Fred March, of the Northamptons, to his parents, Mr & Mrs H March, of Grove Street. He was stationed at Harrogate and had recently been busy with bombing competitions, his company having won and been presented with a silver cup. He had also won a silver mounted pipe for long distance throwing at the Northern Army competitions, by throwing a bomb 69 yards. Previous to enlisting, Sgt March had worked for Mr T Broker, grocer.

"Raunds Soldier's Death" and "Raunds Man Missing", were headlines on Friday, **13 October**. The former gave news that Private **Harry Finding (50)**, of the Bedfordshire Regiment, had fallen some days earlier. The sad tidings came in a letter from Private Cecil Clark, of Raunds, who was near him at the time, and said "he was shot through the head and died instantly!" The 20 year old had previously been employed in the Co-Operative Society office since leaving school, being home on leave just seven weeks earlier.

The latter concerned a request by the parents of Private **Roland Archer (15)**, who were very anxious to hear any news of their son who had been listed as "missing" since 17 August. News, when it eventually arrived, confirmed their worst fears.

"OFFICIAL NOTICE – Raunds Council School: Applications are invited for the post of Caretaker at the School at a Salary of £57 pa. List of duties may be seen at the school, and any other information obtained from the present caretaker. Applications to be received not later than Wednesday morning, 18 October, and addressed to: Mr A Mantle, Clerk to the Managers, District Education Office, College Street, Rushden"

On Saturday, **14 October**, the Rushden, Kettering, Finedon & Raunds Friendly Society Councils held a meeting at Raunds and Brother Cave, of Leicester, gave an address on "Friendly Society topics and the National Conference". Also discussed was the problem facing doctors who were expected to give adequate medical attention to 3,000, 4,000 or even 5,000 members.

The Primitive Methodist Church celebrated their Chapel anniversary over this weekend with a tea and meeting on the Saturday, and with services conducted by Mr Waller of Luton, on the Sunday.

Two concerts were held at the Woodbine Club on the evenings of the weekend, presided over by the secretary of the club, Mr E Batchelor. Mr George Litchfield, of Higham Ferrers, was the artiste, and Mr W Knighton accompanied.

Another full agenda was dealt with by the Urban Council on the evening of Monday, **16 October**: A sub-committee was formed to effect the purchase of a new horse; the new Veterinary Inspector, W Beal, had sent in a report, considered very satisfactory, of his visit to several cowkeepers; and a letter from Sergeant Lee was read out, in which he thanked the Council for their recent good wishes.

The medical officer, Dr Mackenzie, was unable to attend but advised that there had been nine births and four deaths registered, but no notifiable infectious diseases in the town during September.

Several procurements were agreed: to order a snow plough from Messrs T Newton & Co of Hargrave at a cost of £5-15s-0d; to accept the tender of Mr W H Spicer for painting a luminous band around the district's lamp posts for £3-10s-0d; to purchase 3 rainproof capes and sou'-westers for the street scavengers; and to repair the fence against the watercourse in Butts Road, and to extend it a further 15 feet with a rail fence.

The Finance Committee recommendations that the wages of W Bird be increased by 2s-0d per week, and G Cooper's by 1s-0d per week, and that G Tomlin be paid an extra 2s-0d per week for the five weeks he was engaged in the work of scavenging, were all accepted.

A letter was read from the captain of the Fire Brigade giving the names of Messrs G Cooch, J Munns, and J Sale as new members in place of those who had left the town or joined HM Forces. Mr J Shelmerdine proposed the sending of a letter to the captain congratulating the brigade on its success in recent competitions.

Finally, another letter was read out, this from Mr W Denton with respect to the loss of a sheep in the barrel arch of the culvert in Crow Spinney, and asking for £3 compensation. After discussion it was decided to inform him that the Council accepted no responsibility.

"Wanted – Raunds Hotel & Coffee House, Manageress or Man & Wife as Managers – For particulars, apply to F W Miller, "The Manse", Raunds. Applications to be in by Friday, 20 October."

"Thanks – Mr & Mrs Wm Finding and family, 11 Park Road, wish to thank all friends for their kind expressions of sympathy in the sad loss they have sustained by the death of their dear son **Harry (Finding) (50)**, 1st Beds, who was killed in action in France on 23 September 1916, age 20."

At the Thrapston Police Court on Tuesday, **17 October**, a Raunds labourer was fined 15s-0d including costs for "not subduing the lights at his house". He had been walking about the house with a lighted candle and no blinds at all. Only able to pay 10s-0d immediately, he was allowed a fortnight to find the balance.

At the same hearing, a clicker from the town was summoned to show cause why an order should not be made upon him to contribute towards the maintenance of his son, an inmate of Heswell Reformation School in Cheshire. The 15 year old had been convicted of larceny and sent to the Reformatory to be detained until the age of 19. The man, who did not appear, was ordered to pay 5s-0d per week plus 6s-0d costs.

Today's papers also contained a story likely to have caused much "chopsin in the jitties". Apparently, the Rector of Thrapston had resigned after being found guilty of false declarations under the Aliens Act. He had been staying at a Warrington hotel with a young Thrapston woman whom he had registered as his wife!

News of another military death greeted readers on Friday, **20 October**. Locally, the wife of Private **W E Lawman (71)**, of the Northamptons, had received a letter from Major F W Butley, Officer in Command of the regiment in France, notifying her that her husband had been "killed in action" a few days earlier. While working in No Man's Land, the 29 year old was felled by the bursting of a shell which also killed a comrade with him, leaving his widow and three small children.

Parochially, Raunds had welcomed back the Rev C C Aldred, just returned from his duties as Army Chaplain in France. The reverse was said of the Curate, Mr Bethway, as he was due to leave the parish next week to take up a military chaplaincy across the Channel.

The Hospital Week Fund committee held its quarterly meeting this evening in the Temperance Hall. A fair attendance heard a presentation of the accounts for the quarter which showed receipts to have been £33-3s-9d, making a total for the year of £198-6s-2d, of which £165 had been forwarded to the county treasurer. The accounts were accepted and another £30 ordered to be sent to Northampton.

In the Rushden & District Clubs' Billiards League on Saturday, **21 October**, Rushden Conservative Club entertained their Raunds counterparts and ran out winners by 60 points, 537 to 477.

The Bishop's Messenger to Raunds was in town on Sunday, **22 October**, when the Rev L P William Freeman conducted the day's Church of England services in connection with the National Mission of Repentance and Hope. Interestingly, the evening service was held in the Picture Palace owing to the lighting regulations.

Meanwhile at the Wesleyan Church, the first of the season's Brotherhood meetings took place and the speaker was the new superintendent minister for the circuit, the Rev E P Blackburn. As it was an "open" meeting, members of both sexes were present. A list of names of members serving with HM Forces was read out and a collection totalling £4-16s-9d was taken for sending them gifts at Christmas. The Wesleyan Prize Choir under Mr W Hall, was in attendance and rendered the "Hallelujah Chorus" and the anthem "O Rest in the Lord".

Tuesday, 24 October, the French recapture Fort Douaumont, Verdun is saved.

On Wednesday, **25 October**, the Thrapston Board of Guardians received the resignations of Mr & Mrs Rosser, the superintendent and matron of the Raunds Cottage Homes, who thanked the Board for the kind consideration they had always received during their fifteen month residence. The Cottage Homes committee recommended that: the resignations be accepted; advertisements be issued inviting applications; and, owing to the meetings of the Board being monthly, asked that they be delegated to make the new appointments.

Also at Thrapston today, the District Farmers Association, of which several Raunds agriculturalists were prominent members, announced that their second sale in aid of the Red Cross had raised about £900, this compared to £760 realised at their first sale in May of last year. The sale was opened by Lord Lilford and Mrs Wentworth Watson and the proceeds included £120 from the auction of the celebrated "Warboys cockerel", which had been brought over by its enthusiastic owner, Mr Frank Fyson.

At their monthly meeting on Thursday, **26 October**, the Church of England School managers were read a letter from the school caretaker, John Finding, asking them to recommend a 3s-0d per week pay increase for him owing to high prices due to the war. The managers named Monday, 13 November, as a half-holiday in place of Statute Monday and received a request from the headmaster that the opening time of the afternoon school session in both departments be 1.30pm, with the Infants closing at 3.30pm, and the Upper/Mixed at 3.50pm.

Over a year after her husband had been listed as "missing", Mrs W Whiteman, of Westbourne Grove, received an official communication from the Infantry Record Office saying "that as no further news has been received in relation to your husband, Private **W Whiteman (130)**, Northamptonshire Regiment, the Army Council have been constrained to conclude that he is dead!"

And the Somme offensive continued to show no respite for men from the town either, as the papers of Friday, **27 October**, brought news of three more casualties, all wounded. Private Arthur Kirk, Northamptonshire Regiment, had been wounded at the end of September when a piece of shrapnel entered his back. He was said to now be in hospital in Dorset, "getting on well"; Gunner H Moule, Royal Garrison Artillery, had gunshot wounds to the head, but said in a letter home that he wanted "to stay at the front until victory is ours!"; and Private W H March, Essex Regiment, had shrapnel wounds in his neck and left shoulder, and a compound fracture of the collar bone. He was now recovering in Taplow hospital.

Also today, the details of the will of the late Mr Joseph Gant, JP, chemist, who died on 1 March, were made public. He left an estate of £2,217-7s-3d gross, with net personalty of £1,255-17s-7d. His son, Mr A W Gant, of Cambridge, and Mr Walter Adams, of Stanwick, had been appointed executors.

The War Charities Committee met on Monday, **30 October**, and the secretary reported that Colonel Stopford-Sackville, chairman of the County Council, had consented to open the jumble sale. The collectors advised that between £490 and £500 had already been promised in cash, and in addition, numerous promises towards the jumble sale were made. It was hoped to raise at least £600 in total.

At the County Appeals Tribunal on Tuesday, **31 October**, a married confectioner and fruiterer from the town had his appeal dismissed. Captain Cook said that the appellant had first been exempted on account of his mother's business, then through being in a boot factory, and now he asked for exemption on domestic grounds.

This evening, another meeting was held to consider the formation of a Volunteer Training Corps in the town. With Mr John Adams, JP, CC in the chair, Captain Dulley explained that the Volunteers would be needed to make themselves efficient and to hold themselves ready in case of any emergency. He also said that Raunds ought to be able to raise a squad of at least 120 men. Captain Henfrey then added that the town was now the only place in the district in the boot trade without a corps. As he had done at a similar meeting one year earlier, Mr Shelmerdine, JP, then proposed "that a Volunteer Corps be formed at Raunds". This was carried and by the end of the meeting, about 40 men had signed up.

"Wanted, Horsekeeper (with boy prefered), good wages, cottage & garden found. Also Youth (to live in), good home & wages; Apply: V Woolley, Farmer, Brooks Road, Raunds"

Five cases of breaches of the Lighting Order by Raunds residents were considered by the Thrapston Bench today. Four defendants, a widow, shoehand, married woman, and butcher, were found guilty and each fined 2s-6d, the case against the fifth, a machinist, was dismissed.

The final market of the month at Thrapston saw butter making 1s-9d per pound, eggs selling at 4s-0d per score, beef at 13s-0d to 13s-2d per stone, mutton at 1s-0d to 1s-2d per stone, and pork from 13s-6d to 14s-0d per stone.

Topping the bill at the Palace Theatre, Rushden, this week, was the amazing "Mademoiselle Dalmere's Table Circus" – 50 performing rabbits, cats, dogs, doves, rats, and monkeys, ably supported by "Billie Hale" – Ye parody comedian.

* * * * * * * * * * * * * * * * * * * *

* * * * * * * * * * * * * * * * * * * *

NOVEMBER – In his first set of Parish Notes since his return from France, the Vicar thanked the Curate, Mr Bethway, and members of the congregation who had "so faithfully carried on the work in the parish" adding that "one never had any doubt of this being done". He said he was glad that Mr Bethway would now have the opportunity to go out and work as a chaplain amongst some of our men and asked everyone to remember him and his new work in their prayers.

He announced that, owing to the lighting restrictions now in force, there would now be Sunday services in the Church at 3pm and in the Picture Palace at 6pm, with these arrangements probably lasting during the winter months.

The Harvest Thanksgiving services were described as bright and well attended. Collections realised £15-13s-11d and thanks were extended to all who had given flowers, fruit, and vegetables and those who decorated the Church. The sale in the Institute on the following Monday resulted in £9-10s-2d being raised. And from the Children's Services, 216 eggs had been sent to the 1st/5th Northern General Hospital, Leicester and also fruit and eggs to the VAD Hospital, Higham Ferrers.

All were asked to note the sale taking place on Saturday, 4 November, for the town's War Charities Fund; that the Lord Bishop of Peterborough would be holding a confirmation at Higham Ferrers Church on Saturday, 9 December; and that as the Vicar would be away from the parish from 13 to 17 November and 27 November to 1 December, acting as Bishop's Messenger, no weekday services would be held during those weeks.

At Wednesday, **1 November**'s meeting of the Raunds District Education Sub-Committee, the Clerk & Attendance Officer presented the attendance report for the quarter ending 30 September. The total number of pupils on the books was 1,138 against 1,134 in the corresponding 1915 quarter, and the percentage attendance was 87% against 85%. However, an application for a permit for agricultural employment by a Hargrave parent was refused on the ground of the lad's previous very unsatisfactory attendance at school.

The Local Appeals Tribunal met again on Thursday, **2 November**, and was presented with another large number of appeals from employees and employers for exemption from military service. Before commencement of the evening's business, the chairman expressed the opinion that all exempted men should be urged to join the Volunteer Training Corps, and the other Tribunal members unanimously agreed.

Exemptions granted included: *three months*, a plumber & decorator's son, a Co-Operative store manager/buyer, a carting contractor & smallholder, a builder contractor's carpenter/joiner, a grocer's groom & warehouseman, and a boot manufacturer's chauffeur/mechanic/gardener; *until 31 December*, a milk vendor (his final exemption), a cartage contractor & cab proprietor, a laundryman, smallholder & member of the Fire Brigade.

The Old Age Pensions Sub-Committee was also in action this evening and allowed one dependancy claim at 6s-0d per week and one new pensions claim at the full rate. Of the 24 claims for an additional allowance considered, 22 were allowed at the full additional rate of 2s-6d, and two were adjurned to the next meeting. However, a question raised by the pension officer resulted in one pensioner's allowance being reduced from 5s-0d to 4s-0d per week.

Friday, 3 November, Phillip Ernest Stubbs (113), killed in action.

"For Sale – Second-Hand Baker's Truck, cheap – G Talbot, Grove Place, Raunds"

A jumble sale was held on Saturday, **4 November**, by the Raunds War Charities Committee in the Church of England Infants schoolyard, Sir Stopford-Sackville, chairman of the County Council, performing the opening ceremony. The proceeds were in aid of the Northamptonshire District Nursing Association, the Romanian Flag Day, Blind Soldiers & Sailors, the YMCA War Emergency Fund, the Army Christmas Pudding Fund, Kitchener's Memorial Fund, Sailors Day, the Armenian Red Cross & Refugee Fund, and the local Red Cross Fund. Over £500 had been collected prior to the day. Mrs Camozzi organised a Romanian Flag Day and the Temperance Band paraded the town.

At the opening ceremony, Mr W F Corby said that if they raised only £100 on the day, the total contributions to war charities during the last month would amount to 3s-6d per head from the population of the town. The actual proceeds of the sale exceeded £100, bringing the total up to nearly £610. A feature of the event was an auction of nearly 200 items, many of which were "sold" several times over. The lots, all of which were donated, included a Crimea War Medal, 1854, which fetched variously between 3s-6d and 7s-0d, a goose, fowls, ducks, a large doll's house, a rocking chair, and a tiny kitten. The winner of the coal guessing competition was Mr W H Lovell of Stanwick, who gave the 15cwt of coal to the town's Belgian refugees. The winner of the corresponding number competition was Mr James Adams, of "Stanwick House", who gave back the prize, a pig, for a further competition.

The day's successful proceedings closed with a dance in the Temperance Hall, the Temperance Band providing the music.

"Wanted – Hand Lasters for box call Marine boots, Apply: Adams Bros, Raunds"

While home on leave, Sergeant Harold Lee presided over the Brotherhood meeting on Sunday, **5 November**, when the speaker was the Rev E Woodward, from South India.

Two meetings took place on the evening of Thursday, **9 November**. The War Charities Committee met to review the previous Saturday's demonstration, jumble sale and Flag Day and to award grants from the proceeds. A net total raised of £607-12s-6d was announced, including £446-18s-0d in prior subscriptions and £51-10s-6½d from the house-to-house collection.

The following grants were then agreed: Northamptonshire District Nursing Association, £30; Romanian Flag Day, £25; Blind Soldiers & Sailors, £10; YMCA War Emergency Fund, £30, Army Christmas Pudding Fund, £30; Sailor's Day, £50; Armenian Red Cross & Refugees Fund, £25; Lord Lieutenant's County Red Cross Fund, £100; and Duston Hospital (for tobacco), £10. A sub-committee was also formed to carry out the sending of Christmas gifts to every Raunds soldier serving with the Forces, from the balance in hand.

And when the Old Age Pension's Sub-Committee met, they approved the four new claims presented at the full rate and the one dependancy claim submitted. Of the 35 claims for an additional allowance, 32 were allowed at 2s-6d per week, one at 2s-0d, one was adjourned awaiting further particulars, and one disallowed.

On Friday, **10 November**, a special illustrated number of the Northampton County "Shoe & Leather News" featured many local firms. A reviewer called it "a splendid compendium of the staple trade of East Northants", adding that there were "many interesting and reliable accounts of Raunds, Higham Ferrers and other towns in the district, with many beautifully reproduced photographs".

Saturday, 11 November, William Moules (80), killed in action.

Today, the 21st anniversary of the Raunds Liberal Literary Institute was celebrated and Mr W M Lawrence, treasurer since the commencement of the Institute, was presented with a gold mounted umbrella. Mr W F Corby, who likewise had been secretary since the start, made the presentation on behalf of the members.

At the Wesleyan Church on Sunday, **12 November**, the pulpit was occupied by the Rev E P Blackburn. It being "Temperance Sunday", the reverend gentleman delivered a stirring temperance sermon at the evening service. That afternoon at the Brotherhood meeting, he had also given an address on "The manliness of Jesus", and Miss Winnie Pentelow had nicely rendered the solos "The King of Love" and "Red Rose of England", accompanied by Miss Lily Robinson.

Monday, 13 November, the Battle of the Ancre begins.

The opening meeting for the season of the Wesley Guild took place today when a large number attended. The proceedings consisted of a coffee supper followed by a social in which vocal and instrumental music was provided, recitations were given, and games etc were indulged in.

On Wednesday, **15 November**, the Raunds Red Cross Committee announced that during its second year of operation, completed on 2 September, the following items had been forwarded to the Northampton headquarters: 178 pairs of mittens, 54 mufflers, 80 night shirts, 38 pairs of day socks, 66 handkerchieves, 17 vests, 23 pairs of pants, 131 pairs of slippers, 15 day shirts, 18 small bags, 36 pillow cases, 32 hand towels, 10 sheets, 8 dressing gowns, 33 bed jackets, 6 pairs of bed socks, 10 pairs of operation stockings, 3 body belts, and one pair of knee caps .....

In addition to these items, Raunds schoolchildren had also made 118 pairs of mittens and 24 mufflers during the past 14 months. In January 1916, the committee had been formally recognised by the War Office as a branch of the Northamptonshire County Association for the Administration of Voluntary Work.

Another meeting of the Local Appeals Tribunal took place on the evening of Thursday, **16 November**, when the needs of local businesses were again the prime concern. Cases reviewed and exemptions granted included: *until 31 December*, a motor & cycle agent, the Co-Op coal carter and a clicker; *until 31 January*, a boot heel manufacturer, the Co-Op's managing butcher, grocery manager, and baker & bread deliverer; and *until 1 April*, a blacksmith's man (in a certified occupation), a master tailor, a farmer & baker, a watchmaker & jeweller, the Gas Company stoker (in a certified occupation), and the overseer & collector of taxes' assistant. However, one appeal was rejected, that of an architect and partner in a building business, who had now been passed for general military service.

The agenda for the Raunds Old Age Pensions Sub-Committee this evening was brief, with only one new pension claim, granted at 5s-0d per week, and 4 dependancy allowance and a few additional allowance claims presented.

Two military stories published on Friday, **17 November** would have interested town residents: "Raunds Soldier Killed – Victim to a Shell" announced the death of Private **Phillip Ernest Stubbs (113)**, of the Kings Royal Rifle Corps. The parents of the eighteen year old had received the news of their only son's death in a letter from his chum in the same platoon. The Kimbolton School old boy was killed, with five comrades, by a large shell bursting in the middle of them. He had left school at Christmas 1915 and was described as "a strong, well built fellow for his age, and was a great favourite with the other scholars when at school".

The more cheery news was that of Sergeant Fred Gates, of the Northamptons. It was announced that this son of Thomas Gates had just been awarded the Military Medal. Sergeant Gates had been wounded in the "big push" in July. *(Plate 24)*

Also today, it was reported that three aged and respected residents of the town had recently died: Mrs Charles Smart, 89, widow of the late Mr Charles Smart, died after being confined to her bed for nearly two years; Mr George Harrison, 76, of Rotton Row, passed away after a painful illness; and Mr William Hills, 86, of "The Poplars", a staunch Churchman and Conservative, and a former member of both the old Parish Council and the Urban Council.

Saturday, 18 November, the end of the Battle of the Somme, 420,000 BEF and 200,000 French losses in total. Arthur Clark (35), killed in action.

At home, as one of the most infamous battles in history ground to an inconclusive halt and another town man fell, Raunds Conservatives travelled to meet their Rushden namesakes in the Rushden & District Clubs' Billiards League and once again were defeated, this time by 587 to 448.

And during this evening, a heavy snowstorm upset the district's motor bus service.

"Official Notice – Raunds Urban District Council: Wanted, reliable man to take charge of Waterworks undertaking. Applicants must be capable of reading the Water Meters, and will be required to do all the work of a practical plumber. Permanent position for suitable man.

Further particulars on application to the undersigned, to whom applications, and starting wages required, are to be sent not later than Monday, 27 November. W F Corby, Clerk to the Council, Raunds."

The Brotherhood meeting on Sunday afternoon, **19 November**, was well attended and heard an excellent address given by Mrs E P Blackburn, her subject being "Memories". Miss Grace Lawrence rendered the solos "There is a green hill far away" and "How lovely are Thy dwellings", accompanied by Mr W Cyril Groom.

Coming to the Palace Theatre, Rushden this week was "The Greatest Attraction of the Age" – "The Official War Pictures of 'The Battle of the Somme'" – "A night with the Boys at the Front".

On Monday, **20 November**, the Urban Council met and their ranks were swelled by the appearance of Sgt L G H Lee, home on leave, for the evening's business.

The medical officer, Dr Mackenzie, making a welcome return after illness, reported two cases of erysipelas and one case of tubercular meningitis in the town during October. He also called attention to a case of scarlet fever reported to the Irthlingborough Council as it was said that it might be traced to Raunds. He wished this to be contradicted, as there had been no cases of the disease in the town for seven months!

Attention was called by one worried councillor to one of the Council cheques drawn recently in favour of a firm with a German name, as he hoped that they were not dealing with Germans. Reassurance was given that they were not!

The Highway Committee recommended that two crossings in Grove Street, opposite Mr Jeeves', be improved at an estimated cost of £9-15s-0d. This was adopted subject to the owners putting in a surface water gulley on their property. It was also decided to approach the police authorities with a view to obtaining permission to have seven street lamps to be lighted at night.

Brought forward was the question of the delay in the telegraph service due to the Post Office only receiving telegrams hourly from the telephone office. To this matter, it was resolved to call the attention of the postal authorities and also request that the Raunds Sub-Office be opened at 8am.

Finally, the surveyor and inspector had written that an opportunity had arisen for him to serve his country in his own line of work, and he felt it his duty to go. His request was for the Council to pay him his salary, less the rate of pay he received from the Army, while he was away. However, the twelve good men decided not to entertain the application.

Elsewhere, Mrs E P Blackburn was in action again this evening, when she gave an address on "Spiders" to the Wesley Guild.

On Tuesday, **21 November**, the Cottage Homes committee reported to the Board of Guardians, the appointment of Mr & Mrs H B Clarke, of Huckfield, as master and matron at Raunds, in place of Mr & Mrs Rosser. Also requested and agreed was the purchase of the usual extra Christmas fare for the children.

Another war casualty from the town featured in the newpapers of Friday, **24 November**. Private **William Moules (80)**, eldest son of Mr James Moules, of High Street, serving with the Durham Light Infantry, had a few days earlier been hit by a shell and died instantaneously. A letter from Second Lieutenant C West had described Private Moules as "a most upright and courageous fellow who I could always trust to do the right thing under all conditions."

On the home front, Messrs John Adams, JP, CC, and W F Corby attended a meeting held in the Hargrave schoolroom this evening, to explain the workings of the War Savings Association and the necessity for saving at the present time.

And a nasty accident befell Miss Roughton whilst cycling home to Raunds from Earls Barton, where she was a teacher at the Council School. Just after passing under the Rushden turn railway bridge, she ran into a man with a bundle of straw on a fork on his back, falling heavily to the ground and fracturing her left elbow.

Dr Mackenzie announced on Saturday, **25 November**, that he had just received sufficient dollars to purchase about 1,000 "Woodbines" for Raunds men at the front. The funds had come from Mr & Mrs Fred Gilbert and son, 1617 South Burdick Street, Kalamazoo, Michigan, late of Raunds. This was the third instalment received by the doctor from the USA for Raunds men serving with the Northamptons, and the "smokes" would be forwarded within the next few days.

The Rev Peter Welsch, of Northampton, was the guest preacher at the Wesleyan Church on Sunday, **26 November**, when he delivered two powerful sermons. He also addressed the Brotherhood meeting in the afternoon, his subject being "An antidote for the dumps". Miss Louie Smith rendered in a splendid manner the solo "Praise the Lord", the lesson was given by Mr King Turner, of Folkstone, and the collection, for Christmas gifts for soldier members, amounted to £4-17s-9d.

Mr T Richardson, MP for Whitehaven, was the principle speaker at a meeting held at the Temperance Hall on Monday evening, **27 November**, to protest against the increasing food prices. The meeting was arranged by the educational department of the Raunds Distributive Co-Operative Society and there was a large attendance. The MP informed the audience that, according to Government figures, the average increase in the price of foodstuffs between August 1914 and August 1916 was "not less than 72%", and the average increase of household commodities was 55% .....

Adding his weight to the argument, Mr G Underwood, representing the town's Boot & Shoe Operatives Union, said it seemed "very strange that the food of the people should be the last thing that the Government should attempt to deal with on behalf of the people", and that "the exploitation of the people by some persons for their own advantage was one of the greatest evils this country had ever known."

An appropriately worded resolution was put to the assembly and carried unanimously and the mood of the meeting was then lightened somewhat by pleasing vocal solos from Mr W Gibbs ("Storm King" and "Son of Mine") and Miss Louie Smith ("The March" and "Smile of Spring"), accompanied by Mrs W Gibbs and Mr A W Hazeldine.

At Tuesday, **28 November's** Thrapston Police Court, a Stanwick farmer was fined 15s-0d for allowing 13 beasts to stray on the public highway at Raunds on 14 November, and a Raunds grocer was fined 10s-0d for a breach of the Lighting Order at his shop. Although the defendant did not appear, he sent a letter of regret.

The Council School managers met on Wednesday evening, **29 November**, and they decided to ask for the schools to be closed for a clear fortnight for the Christmas holidays. A letter was read from the head teacher of the Infants Department drawing attention to the fact there was a crippled scholar who was now so helpless that it could only get to school when brought. As the attendance was, therefore, getting to be very irregular, the managers were asked for any suggestions. Mr Camozzi remarked that he could probably find a carriage for that purpose and Mr Shelmerdine suggested that some of the older boys be asked to undertake the duty of bringing the child to school. This was agreed and laid before the head and subsequently put into operation.

Following on from the manager's meeting, the District Education Sub-Committee reviewed the attendances for November. Those of Raunds and Newton Bromswold schools showed satisfactory percentage of attendances, but Hargrave, Stanwick, and Chelveston schools showed a considerable decrease due in the former case to an outbreak of chicken pox and in the latter cases to special permits for agricultural purposes.

The Local Appeals Tribunal met again on Thursday, **30 November**, although Mr T C Jeeves, the agricultural representative, was unable to attend as he was confined to his house with a bad cold. Nearly twenty appeals were considered and all were granted temporary exemption. These included: *until 31 December 1916*, a previously rejected boot manufacturer, the Co-Op Society's slaughterman, and a boot manufacturer's consol laster; *until 1 February 1917*, a farmer's horsekeeper, waggoner/stockman, and yardman/stockman, an organist & music teacher (passed for sedentary work), the Urban Council's engine driver from the waterworks pumping station, and a chemist/druggist; *until 1 April 1917*, a boot manufacturer's managing director & secretary, a currier's man (in a certified occupation), and a 38 year old widower with four little girls, one of whom was partially crippled.

DECEMBER – The Vicar began his Parish Notes expressing the view that "When we heard the statement of accounts for the past year at the recent All Saints meeting, no one could have been surprised to find that the Church Expenses Fund showed a large deficit after watching the month by month collections total". He added that "Although so many of our men are away, who used to give so much, considering the times here have not been so bad, it is disquieting to find how much less the collections are now". And closed with the plea that: "We have a collection for Northampton Hospital on Sunday, 31 December, let us do our best for such a work as is very dear to our hearts!"

Other news was that Mr Bethway had written to say that he had settled down in France working amongst the troops, and that part of his work was looking after a recreation hut built by the Church of England Men's Society, and that after a long and wearying illness, William Hills had been laid to rest on 15 November in the churchyard of the Church he loved so much. A former churchwarden and sidesman, it had been during his office that the spire was last repaired.

Finally, two more men were listed under the heading "Died in the Service of Their Country": **William Moules (80)** and **Phillip Stubbs (113)**.

Friday, **1 December** – "Messrs Pendered & Sons Ltd will sell by auction at the "George & Dragon" early January next, valuable freehold agricultural land and other properties, full particulars in due course."

In the evening, the Liberal Literary Institute held a whist drive in the billiard room in aid of the town's War Charities Fund for Christmas parcels for the soldiers. Over 40 competed for the prizes which had been donated by Messrs A Hazeldine and G E Smith. The first prize, a pair of boot uppers, was won by Mr Harrison, and the second prize, value 2s-6d, was secured by Mr S Twelftree.

The funeral of Mr William Wagstaff, aged 50, took place at the Wesleyan Burial Ground on Saturday, **2 December**, the Rev E P Blackburn officiating. At the close, the "Dead March" was played by the organist, Mr J W Hall. The deceased, of Hill Street, had been a partner in the firm of Messrs Parker & Wagstaff, of Finedon.

A public tea and concert, arranged by the Town War Charities Committee, was held today in the Wesleyan Schoolroom. About 300 sat down to the feast, the catering for which was admirably carried out by the Distributive Co-Operative Society under the able supervision of Mrs A Camozzi, of the "Manor House", and by whose efforts the trays for the tea were given. This was followed by the capital concert, arranged by the capable hands of Mr O D Hall, and in which the following took part: Mrs Humphreys, Thrapston, Mr F D Brazier, Higham Ferrers, Mrs Fenton, Yeldon, Mrs J W Hall, Miss Grace Lawrence, and Mr A Tebbutt (elocutionist). Mr W F Corby, occupying the chair, complemented Mrs Camozzi on the success of her effort and Mr Hall and all who took part in the entertainment.

In the Rushden & District Clubs' Billiards League, Rushden Athletic Club entertained the Raunds Conservatives, and after some good play and close contests, the home team won by just 4 points, 554 to 550. Both A B Conyers and W Mason scored maximum 100's for the team from Manor Street. However, after four matches, they remained bottom of the league, having suffered four defeats!

At Sunday, **3 December**'s Brotherhood meeting, the Rev W H Jarman, of Northampton, gave an address entitled "An old agreement", Miss L Spicer rendered the solos "Wait" and "Come unto me, ye weary", accompanied by Miss G Reynolds at the piano, and Mr W Roberts, of Denford, presided.

The local Boot & Shoe Operatives Union branch's monthly meeting took place on Monday, **4 December**, at the Rushden Trade Union's Club and a long discussion ensued regarding the question of recruiting for the Colours in the shoe trade. As a result, Labour members of the Advisory Committee and Local Appeals Tribunals were asked to carefully watch the interests of the boot industry.

In the evening, a concert was held in the large room of the Woodbine Club, arranged by members of the Town Fire Brigade, in aid of the National Fire Brigade Union Widows & Orphan's Fund. The room was well filled with an appreciative audience entertained by: Madame Irene Lyne, Madame Ella Barlow, Mrs & Miss Baker, Messrs Gibbs, Coles & Coles, our elocutionist friend, Mr A Tebbutt, and the Temperance Band Quartette Party. A large number of tickets had been sold and the net proceeds amounted to the splendid sum of £14-10s-0d.

Tuesday, 5 December, the Coalition Government falls, Mr Asquith resigns as Prime Minister.

At a meeting today of the Boot & Shoe Operatives Union at Raunds, it was resolved to write to the Lord Lieutenant of the county asking for the appointment of a magistrate, representing Labour interests at Raunds, on the Thrapston Bench, and for Irthlingborough and Rushden, on the Wellingborough Bench.

The Church of England School managers met this evening and heard that the Local Education Authority had replied to the request from the caretaker, John Finding, for a pay increase. The recommendation was £5 per annum which would take his annual salary to £62-4s-0d.

The managers received the resignation of Miss Marie Yorke, an uncertifed teacher in the Upper Department, with effect from 31 December. It was accepted and thanks would be sent to her for her past services. As a result of her impending departure, it was recommended that Miss Florence Hall be placed on the staff to replace Miss Yorke. Miss Hall was already working at the school "on supply". It was also agreed that as Mr Edge, a certified teacher in the Upper Department, had now returned from military service, it was unnecessary to request another teacher.

Wednesday, 6 December, Stanley Frederick Nunley (84), died.

Thursday, 7 December, Mr Lloyd George becomes Prime Minister.

"Wanted – Good Lasters on Army and Navy work; also Women and Girls to be taught the following machines: Slugging, rivetting, studding; patching & stitching – Adams Bros, Raunds"

The local papers of Friday, **8 December**, carried a short article on Private Horace Finding, of the Northamptonshire Regiment, who was reported to be in hospital with wounds in the leg.

"Wanted – a Caretaker for the Raunds Wesleyan Church and Schools – For particulars apply to the Secretary, A Hazeldine, Midland Works, Raunds"

Under the headline entitled "Threatened Destruction of Local Trade", the president of the National Union of Boot & Shoe Operatives warned that Raunds should urgently aquaint itself with the position of the hand sewn men as some War Office officials had described the hand sewn Army boot as no good!

The Rushden & District Working Mens Clubs' Blind & Crippled Children's Association held a tea on Saturday, **9 December**, at the the Rushden WMC, when there was a good number present. The accounts for the year ending 6 December 1916 included receipts of £13-9s-1d from Raunds for the sale of Forget-Me-Nots, and a 10s-0d donation from the Woodbine Club. Expenditure included a grant of £1-5s-0d to blind persons, and £7-4s-9d for surgical appliances and treatment of crippled children in the town. The secretary also read a letter of gratitude from the father of a Raunds girl who had been assisted by the Association.

A "Thanksgiving" meeting took place today at the the Wesleyan Church in aid of circuit funds. The tea was well patronised. A Christmas tree had been decorated by Mrs Blackburn, Mrs G E Smith and others, and the children brought their silk bags with silver enclosed, which were hung on the tree. Each child then received a cracker. Competitions were provided, including hat-trimming for the men, whistling for the ladies, and lighting candles etc, arranged by the Wesley Guild. Musical items were given by Mrs J W Hall, Misses G Lawrence, M Sanders and W Pentelow. Mrs A Tebbutt contributed with sleight of hand tricks and a musical monologue. The proceeds were £43-1s-1d, of which the children gave £2-7s-7d.

Today also saw the annual show of the Fanciers Society when the Rushden Athletic Club hosted a fine display of poultry, pigeons, rabbits and cage birds. As the concert room was in the occupation of the military, it was a less ambitious show than in previous years. G Bolton, of Raunds, secured two first prizes, in the "British Birds – Goldfinch & Bullfinch" and "Other Varieties" classes.

"Wanted – at once, a practical Clicker for Army & Navy work – apply: St Crispins Ltd, Raunds"

Tuesday, 12 December, the Germans publish a "peace note" stating that they were not responsible for the war!

At the Thrapston Fat Stock Show today, there was much success for Raunds farmers. First prize in each of the three classes for sheep was taken by Mr W Denton, Mr J Webster secured firsts for his three lambhogs and his ox, and a second for his two steers, whilst Mr Bellamy collected a third prize for his single steer. The prize offered by Mr T C Jeeves of Raunds, for "the most roots taken from not less than 5 acres", was won by Mr W H Lovell, of Stanwick, who also took second prize for his kohlrabi. At the evening's annual dinner, held at the "White Hart Hotel", Thrapston, Mr Denton commented that he had "experienced the hardest time in his career in rearing his sheep".

The Thrapston Police Court imposed fines on four Raunds citizens for breaches of the Lighting Order: a boot manufacturer was ordered to pay 7s-6d, two shoehands received 5s-0d fines, and a baker, a 2s-6d penalty.

And a concert was given this evening at the VAD Hospital, Higham Ferrers, which included songs by Misses Lily Denton and Spicer of Raunds.

News of the death in September of Lieutenant **C A Vorley (117)**, finally reached Raunds when his father, Mr Joseph Vorley, of Marshall's Road, was reported to have received a communication from the German authorities via His Majesty's Minister at Berne. The message was brief: "Vorley, Charles A, Lieut, 11ᵗʰ Royal Sussex, Died Sept 13ᵗʰ 1916, Buried in cemetery at Caudry, Effects forthcoming." He had in fact died just six days after sending his father a postcard which contained the classic trench humour message: "I am alive and kicking, unfortunately with only one leg, the other was amputated yesterday!"

Wednesday, **13 December** – "Wanted, good Hand Welt Sewers on boots – Horrell & Son, Raunds"

At the annual meeting of the British & Foreign Bible Society held in the Wesleyan Schoolroom on Thursday evening, **14 December**, the Rev Elias George, district secretary, of Bedford, gave a very interesting account of the work of the society, especially amongst the soldiers at the present time.

The clerk of Rushden Urban District Council reported on Friday, **15 December**, that he had received an approach from the clerk of their Raunds counterparts with a view to the Rushden Inspector of Nuisances being allowed to act in the Raunds district for the Council in any case of emergency. The request, being made in consequence of the Raunds inspector being about to leave for military service, was agreed.

At the quarterly meeting of the Raunds Wesleyan Methodist Circuit on Saturday, **16 December**, members were informed that no accounts had been forthcoming for the "Horse Hire Fund" as Mr P Tanner was joining the H M Forces. Mr Tanner expressed his regret at having to resign, and Mr Walter Smith was elected to fill the position. The Rev E P Blackburn reported that the numerical returns showed an increase in membership of 39 .....

Of the quarterly accounts: receipts were £134-18s-2d, expenditure £101-17s-8d, leaving a balance of £33-0s-6d, which was considered "highly satisfactory". The question of the possibility of local preachers being taken to their "long appointments" by motor was discussed and referred to a sub-committee comprising of Messrs John Adams, JP CC, W F Corby, and A Hazeldine. After the meeting the members were entertained to a substantial tea by Mr & Mrs J C Horrell, who were heartily thanked for their hospitality.

The Rev Harry Shaw gave an address on "The Greater Sin" at the Brotherhood meeting on Sunday, **17 December**. Mrs Shaw was the soloist, rendering "Crossing the Bar" and "Lead, Kindly Light", accompanied by Mr A Hazeldine, whilst Mr L W Sheffield took the chair.

Monday, 18 December, the end of the Battle of Verdun.

As the French and German Armies licked their considerable wounds, a meeting of the Northamptonshire Federation of Boot Manufacturers was held at Kettering, and it was unanimously agreed to accept the suggested scheme of local option for the control of the boot & shoe industry. A committee to administer was selected which included Mr John Adams, representing Raunds.

And at this evening's Urban Council meeting, the medical officer, Dr Mackenzie, reported seven births and six deaths registered in the town in November, and the town free from notifiable infectious diseases. The surveyor reported a nuisance in the back road leading from Harcourt Street to Sackville Street, and was instructed to remove the same and warn the parties concerned. Finally, the members were advised of Mr H Thurston's offer of £3 for the use of The Square during Feast Week 1917, this was accepted.

At Tuesday, **19 December**'s meeting of the Thrapston Board of Guardians, it was revealed that the recently arrived superintendent and matron at their Cottage Home in Marshalls Road, Mr & Mrs H F Clark, had tendered their resignations. The Board immediately decided to offer the posts to Mr & Mrs A R Beaumand, of Derby, at the respective salaries of £35 and £25 per annum, with rations, apartments, and washing provided. It was also learned that the only tender received to supply bakery products to the Children's Home was from Mr Rixon. As a result, his quotation of bread at 8¾d per 4lb loaf, flour at 3s-0d per stone, seed cake at 6d per pound, and currant cake at 6d per pound, was duly accepted.

The Town War Charity Committee met in the evening in the Temperance Hall and several letters of thanks were read out from the secretaries to the funds that had benefited from grants from the committee. Mr L W Sheffield presented a report of the Christmas Parcels Sub-Committee which showed that the following parcels had been sent out: Salonika & other distant parts, 47; Germany (prisoners of war), 3; France, 113; UK, 140; total 303. The cost of these was £96-17s-6d .....

A hearty vote of thanks was accorded to Mrs Camozzi for arranging the tea and social which produced £17-8s-0d, and to the band whose social evenings had yielded £8-15s-0d. A question was raised of a Christmas gift to the six soldiers on duty in Raunds itself, and it was decided to treat them to the same value as had been sent to the town's soldiers away on service.

On Friday, **22 December**, the death occurred of Mr William Litchfield, aged 86, of Marshall's Road, after an illness lasting over twelve months.

It was also learned today that a number of special envelopes had recently been received by the request of the head teachers of the Church of England schools from Mr A Shirley Benn, MP, honorary treasurer of the National Committee for Relief in Belgium. The envelopes had been distributed among the children last week and had since been brought back to school. The total amount collected was £2-15s-3d, of which 14s-0d came from the infants department and £2-1s-3d from the mixed department. This compared to the £2-17s-0d collected last July.

Christmas Eve, and the annual musical service arranged by the Brotherhood was held in the Wesleyan Church, with Mr John Adams presiding. Letters of thanks from the soldier recipients of the Christmas parcels sent out by the Brotherhood were read by Mr W F Corby, and an address was given by the Rev E P Blackburn. Musical items were contributed by the Temperance Band Quartette Party, and Messrs David Francis, a prize winner at the Welsh National Eisteddford, E Vickers, who gave a euphonium solo and Fred W Adams, founder of the Brotherhood String Band, home on leave, whose violin solo was very well received. Mr A W Hazeldine was at the organ, and a collection for the County Hospital realised £6-14s-2½d.

In the evening, the Primitive Methodist Carol Singers went round the town, and repeated the journey on Christmas morning, as did the Temperance and Salvation Army Bands.

The death of Mrs Elizabeth Miller occured on **Christmas Day**, the deceased, aged 79, had resided with her brothers, Messrs J & W Ekins.

On **Boxing Day**, the Wesley Guild arranged a young people's party at which nearly 100 young folk attended. The programme consisted of seasonal games and musical items followed by a coffee supper.

News of another wounded Raunds soldier was received on Thursday, **28 December**. Private Reg Farrar, of the Coldstream Guards, the eldest son of Mr & Mrs A Farrar, of Hill Street, was reported as being in a Cardiff hospital suffering from a head wound affected by a sniper. The 22 year old was said to have celebrated three birthdays in France, having enlisted immediately on the outbreak of war. Another of the Farrar's sons, Private William, had initially been sent to the Western Front at the age of 16 years 4 months. He had subsequently been returned to England before being drafted to Egypt ten months ago.

That evening, the members of the Temperance Band arranged a dance in the Temperance Hall, the proceeds being for New Year gifts to the bandsmen serving in HM Forces, and the local War Charities Fund. Music for dancing was supplied by band members and the duties of MC were admirably carried out by Miss Ivy Adams. The 120 plus present enjoyed dancing from 7pm until midnight.

A reduction in train services on the Kettering to Cambridge line was reported on Friday, **29 December**, when the Midland Railway Company announced that from Monday, 1 January 1917, only three trains daily in each direction would stop at Raunds.

It was also announced today that from next Monday, white bread would disappear from every baker's shop in the country, to be replaced by "Government bread". Housewives were advised that the bread would be creamy yellow in colour, and assured that, according to experts, it would be more satisfying and nourishing, and if properly made, should also keep better.

And most factories closed this evening for a week, to reopen on New Year's Day.

A whist drive was arranged by the Stanwick Reading Room on Saturday, **30 December**, and held in the Church rooms. There were ten tables of participants and the winning lady was Mrs Knighton of Raunds. A total of about 30s-0d was raised.

Thus ended 1916, the town had lost twenty-one more men to the war, however, even after the carnage of the Somme, the end was no nearer in sight.

At home, the ever climbing price of food was the daunting battle the housewife had to endure, and although in the factories the order books were full, the struggle to maintain a sufficient workforce, in the face of ever increasing demands from the military, was a constant spectre haunting the employers.

Like the rest of the country, the big question in the minds of Rance folk must have been: "Can it really get any worse?" – Sadly, the answer was "Yes!"

* * * * * * * * * * * * * * * * * * *

*You are missing one of the pleasures of life if you are not having puddings made from
"Brown's Barley Kernels"
One Box for 4½d will make 10 Puddings!*

* * * * * * * * * * * * * * * * * * *

MANNING THE BRITISH ARMY IN WW1

In the years between the end of the Boer War and the period leading up to the start of the First World War, the British Army was used as a police force for the Empire, with the Royal Navy commanding the seas and projecting British power. Until the build up of tension prior to the start of the war, a confrontation between European nations had not been considered. The Army responded to this tension by preparing an expeditionary force, the British Expeditionary Force (BEF), comprising six Infantry Divisions. The so called "Old Contemptibles", who were the first British troops to go out to France in 1914. They took their name from the Kaiser's "Order of the Day" on the 19th August 1914, when he called upon his armies to exterminate first the treacherous English and "walk over General French's contemptible little army".

The army could also call upon the reserves, men who had served in and left the Army and Navy. They were formed in various groups, but in 1914 the total strength was around 350,000.

There was also the Territorial Force (TF), which was the predecessor of today's Territorial Army. This force was only expected to serve in the United Kingdom, but if the individuals chose to do so they could volunteer for service overseas, which most of the men did. After the outbreak of war some TF Battalions were sent out to the colonies to release regular battalions for service in France.

Once the war started in August 1914 and the BEF and reserves were mobilised, Lord Kitchener called for 100,000 volunteers for the new army or K1 as it became known. Response was so high that in less than three months they were up to K5 and enough men had volunteered to form 30 new Divisions.

By the end of 1914 the small professional British Army had been all but wiped out.

As the number of volunteers began to slow down, the Government passed the National Registration Act on the 15th July 1915. This called for all men between the ages of 16 and 65 to register and allowed the Government to work out the numbers of able bodied men and the trades in which they were involved.

In an effort to stimulate the recruitment of volunteers, Lord Derby, the Director General of Recruiting, brought out a scheme in October 1915 whereby men between the ages of 18 and 40 could enlist voluntarily with an obligation to join up if they were called for. The men were then able to carry on working until the call came and to make sure that people did not think they were avoiding military service, they were issued with arm bands. These men were divided into various groups and their call up began in January 1916.

The Derby Scheme did not bring in the numbers that had been hoped for, so, on the 27th January 1916 the Military Service Act was passed and voluntary enlistment stopped, apart from in Ireland. All British males were now conscripted if they were between the ages of 18 and 41, were residing in Great Britain and were unmarried or a widower on the 2nd November 1915. This is when the regiments of the British Army began to fill with men from out of their traditional recruitment areas, because conscripts were not given any choice over which service, regiment or corps they joined. You could, however, volunteer for the Royal Navy and if they wanted you, you could instead join the senior service. On the 25th May 1916 the act was extended to include married men.

This did not mean that every man was immediately called up as there were various reasons for which a man might be precluded from enlistment. Tribunals heard the appeals of men who felt that they should not be called up on the grounds of employment, health or reasons on conscience. Certain trades, called "starred occupations", were vital to the war effort and men employed within these were exempt from being called up.

Surprisingly conscription still did not bring in the numbers required to fulfil the requirements of the forces. Some 43,000 went into general service in the army, nearly 1,500,000 men were in "starred occupations", whilst around 750,000 claimed exemption of one kind or another, meaning a great deal of work for the tribunals. Some tribunals, including Raunds, deferred the call up for a few months depending on the circumstances of the petitioner or sometimes they found a solution to a problem that might have been put forward at the tribunal, thus releasing the petitioner.

However, despite the numbers of men that volunteered or were called up, the British Army never reached its planned establishment.

* *

The Sensible Gift for your Soldier Friends
"Hitchman's Chest and Lung Tablets"
At 6½d per quarter pound, no Xmas period will be complete without some,
Read what the men write home about them:
"The Best Gift of All", "Absolutely Top-Hole", "Worth a shilling each",
"Don't forget to send me some more!"

* *

INDEX

RANCE FOLK